YOUR PERSONAL
HOROSCOPE
2016

JOSEPH
POLANSKY

YOUR PERSONAL HOROSCOPE 2016

Month-by-month forecast for every sign

The only one-volume horoscope you'll ever need

Thorsons

Thorsons
An imprint of HarperCollins*Publishers*
1 London Bridge Street
London SE1 9GF

www.harpercollins.co.uk

First published by Thorsons 2015

1 3 5 7 9 10 8 6 4 2

© Star ★ Data, Inc. 2015

Star ★ Data assert the moral right to
be identified as the authors of this work

A catalogue record of this book is
available from the British Library

ISBN 978-0-00-759403-0

Printed and bound in Great Britain by
Clays Ltd, St Ives plc

MIX
Paper from
responsible sources
www.fsc.org **FSC C007454**

FSC™ is a non-profit international organisation established to promote
the responsible management of the world's forests. Products carrying the
FSC label are independently certified to assure consumers that they come
from forests that are managed to meet the social, economic and
ecological needs of present and future generations,
and other controlled sources.

Find out more about HarperCollins and the environment at
www.harpercollins.co.uk/green

The author is grateful to the people of STAR ★ DATA, who truly fathered this book and without whom it could not have been written.

Contents

Introduction

Welcome to the fascinating and intricate world of astrology!

For thousands of years the movements of the planets and other heavenly bodies have intrigued the best minds of every generation. Life holds no greater challenge or joy than this: knowledge of ourselves and the universe we live in. Astrology is one of the keys to this knowledge.

Your Personal Horoscope 2016 gives you the fruits of astrological wisdom. In addition to general guidance on your character and the basic trends of your life, it shows you how to take advantage of planetary influences so you can make the most of the year ahead.

The section on each sign includes a Personality Profile, a look at general trends for 2016, and in-depth month-by-month forecasts. The Glossary (*page 5*) explains some of the astrological terms you may be unfamiliar with.

One of the many helpful features of this book is the 'Best' and 'Most Stressful' days listed at the beginning of each monthly forecast. Read these sections to learn which days in each month will be good overall, good for money, and good for love. Mark them on your calendar – these will be your best days. Similarly, make a note of the days that will be most stressful for you. It is best to avoid booking important meetings or taking major decisions on these days, as well as on those days when important planets in your Horoscope are retrograde (moving backwards through the zodiac).

The Major Trends section for your sign lists those days when your vitality is strong or weak, or when relationships with your co-workers or loved ones may need a bit more effort on your part. If you are going through a difficult time, take a look at the colour, metal, gem and scent listed in the 'At a Glance' section of your Personality Profile. Wearing a piece of jewellery that contains your metal and/or gem will strengthen your vitality, just as wearing clothes or decorating your room or office in the colour ruled by your sign, drinking teas made from the herbs ruled by your sign or wearing the scents associated with your sign will sustain you.

Another important virtue of this book is that it will help you to know not only yourself but those around you: your friends, co-workers, partners and/or children. Reading the Personality Profile and forecasts for their signs will provide you with an insight into their behaviour that you won't get anywhere else. You will know when to be more tolerant of them and when they are liable to be difficult or irritable.

In this edition we have included foot reflexology charts as part of the health section. So many health problems could perhaps be avoided or alleviated if we understood which organs were most vulnerable and what we could do to protect them. Though there are many natural and drug-free ways to strengthen vulnerable organs, these charts show a valid way to proceed. The vulnerable organs for the year ahead are clearly marked in the charts. It's very good to massage the whole foot on a regular basis, as the feet contain reflexes to the entire body. Try to pay special attention to the specific areas marked in the charts. If this is done diligently, health problems can be avoided. And even if they can't be completely avoided, their impact can be softened considerably.

I consider you – the reader – my personal client. By studying your Solar Horoscope I gain an awareness of what is going on in your life – what you are feeling and striving for and the challenges you face. I then do my best to address these concerns. Consider this book the next best thing to having your own personal astrologer!

It is my sincere hope that *Your Personal Horoscope 2016* will enhance the quality of your life, make things easier, illuminate the way forward, banish obscurities and make you more aware of your personal connection to the universe. Understood properly and used wisely, astrology is a great guide to knowing yourself, the people around you and the events in your life – but remember that what you do with these insights – the final result – is up to you.

A Note on the 'New Zodiac'

Recently an article was published that postulated two things: the discovery of a new constellation – Ophiuchus – making a thirteenth constellation in the heavens and thus a thirteenth sign, and the statement that because the Earth has shifted relative to the constellations in the past few thousand years, all the signs have shifted backwards by one sign. This has caused much consternation, and I have received a stream of letters, emails and phone calls from people saying things like: 'I don't want to be a Taurus, I'm happy being a Gemini', 'What's my real sign?' or 'Now that I finally understand myself, I'm not who I think I am!'

All of this is 'much ado about nothing'. The article has some partial truth to it. Yes, in two thousand years the planets have shifted relative to the constellations in the heavens. This is old news. We know this and Hindu astrologers take this into account when casting charts. This shift doesn't affect Western astrologers in North America and Europe. We use what is called a 'tropical' zodiac. This zodiac has nothing to do with the constellations in the heavens. They have the same names, but that's about it. The tropical zodiac is based on the Earth's revolution around the Sun. Imagine the circle that this orbit makes, then divide this circle by twelve and you have our zodiac. The Spring Equinox is always 0 degrees (Aries), and the Autumn Equinox is always 0 degrees (Libra). At one time a few thousand years ago, these tropical signs coincided with the actual constellations; they were pretty much interchangeable, and it didn't matter what zodiac you used. But in the course of thousands of years the planets have shifted relative to these constellations. Here in the West it doesn't affect our practice one iota. You are still the sign you always were.

In North America and Europe there is a clear distinction between an astrological sign and a constellation in the heavens. This issue is more of a problem for Hindu astrologers. Their zodiac is based on the actual constellations – this is called the 'sidereal' zodiac. And Hindu astrologers have been accounting for this shift all the time. They keep close tabs on it. In two thousand years there is a shift of 23 degrees, and they subtract this from the Western calculations. So in their system many a Gemini would be a Taurus and this is true for all the signs. This is nothing new – it is all known and accounted for, so there is no bombshell here.

The so-called thirteenth constellation, Ophiuchus, is also not a problem for the Western astrologer. As we mentioned, our zodiac has nothing to do with the constellations. It could be more of a problem for the Hindus, but my feeling is that it's not a problem for them either. What these astronomers are calling a new constellation was probably considered a part of one of the existing constellations. I don't know this as a fact, but I presume it is so intuitively. I'm sure we will soon be getting articles by Hindu astrologers explaining this.

Glossary of Astrological Terms

Ascendant

We experience day and night because the Earth rotates on its axis once every 24 hours. It is because of this rotation that the Sun, Moon and planets seem to rise and set. The zodiac is a fixed belt (imaginary, but very real in spiritual terms) around the Earth. As the Earth rotates, the different signs of the zodiac seem to the observer to rise on the horizon. During a 24-hour period every sign of the zodiac will pass this horizon point at some time or another. The sign that is at the horizon point at any given time is called the Ascendant, or rising sign. The Ascendant is the sign denoting a person's self-image, body and self-concept – the personal ego, as opposed to the spiritual ego indicated by a person's Sun sign.

Aspects

Aspects are the angular relationships between planets, the way in which one planet stimulates or influences another. If a planet makes a harmonious aspect (connection) to another, it tends to stimulate that planet in a positive and helpful way. If, however, it makes a stressful aspect to another planet, this disrupts that planet's normal influence.

Astrological Qualities

There are three astrological qualities: *cardinal, fixed* and *mutable*. Each of the 12 signs of the zodiac falls into one of these three categories.

Cardinal Signs
Aries, Cancer, Libra and Capricorn
The cardinal quality is the active, initiating principle. Those born under these four signs are good at starting new projects.

Fixed Signs
Taurus, Leo, Scorpio and Aquarius
Fixed qualities include stability, persistence, endurance and perfectionism. People born under these four signs are good at seeing things through.

Mutable Signs
Gemini, Virgo, Sagittarius and Pisces
Mutable qualities are adaptability, changeability and balance. Those born under these four signs are creative, if not always practical.

Direct Motion

When the planets move forward through the zodiac – as they normally do – they are said to be going 'direct'.

Grand Square

A Grand Square differs from a normal Square (usually two planets separated by 90 degrees) in that four or more planets are involved. When you look at the pattern in a chart you will see a whole and complete square. This, though stressful, usually denotes a new manifestation in the life. There is much work and balancing involved in the manifestation.

Grand Trine

A Grand Trine differs from a normal Trine (where two planets are 120 degrees apart) in that three or more planets are involved. When you look at this pattern in a chart, it takes the form of a complete triangle – a Grand Trine. Usually (but not always) it occurs in one of the four elements: Fire, Earth, Air or Water. Thus the particular element in which it occurs will be highlighted. A Grand Trine in Water is not the same as a Grand Trine in Air or Fire, etc. This is a very fortunate and happy aspect, and quite rare.

Houses

There are 12 signs of the zodiac and 12 houses of experience. The 12 signs are personality types and ways in which a given planet expresses itself; the 12 houses show 'where' in your life this expression takes place. Each house has a different area of interest. A house can become potent and important – a house of power – in different ways: if it contains the Sun, the Moon or the 'ruler' of your chart; if it contains more than one planet; or if the ruler of that house is receiving unusual stimulation from other planets.

1st House
Personal Image and Sensual Delights

2nd House
Money/Finance

3rd House
Communication and Intellectual Interests

4th House
Home and Family

5th House
Children, Fun, Games, Creativity, Speculations and Love Affairs

6th House
Health and Work

7th House
Love, Marriage and Social Activities

8th House
Transformation and Regeneration

9th House
Religion, Foreign Travel, Higher Education and Philosophy

10th House
Career

11th House
Friends, Group Activities and Fondest Wishes

12th House
Spirituality

Karma

Karma is the law of cause and effect which governs all phenomena. We are all where we find ourselves because of karma - because of actions we have performed in the past. The universe is such a balanced instrument that any act immediately sets corrective forces into motion - karma.

Long-term Planets

The planets that take a long time to move through a sign show the long-term trends in a given area of life. They are important for forecasting the prolonged view of things. Because these planets stay in one sign for so long, there are periods in the year when the faster-moving (short-term) planets will join them, further activating and enhancing the importance of a given house.

Jupiter
stays in a sign for about 1 year

Saturn
2½ years

Uranus
7 years

Neptune
14 years

Pluto
15 to 30 years

Lunar

Relating to the Moon. See also 'Phases of the Moon', below.

Natal

Literally means 'birth'. In astrology this term is used to distinguish between planetary positions that occurred at the time of a person's birth (natal) and those that are current (transiting). For example, Natal Sun refers to where the Sun was when you were born; transiting Sun refers to where the Sun's position is currently at any given moment – which usually doesn't coincide with your birth, or Natal, Sun.

Out of Bounds

The planets move through the zodiac at various angles relative to the celestial equator (if you were to draw an imaginary extension of the Earth's equator out into the universe, you would have an illustration of this celestial equator). The Sun – being the most dominant and powerful influence in the Solar system – is the measure astrologers use as a standard. The Sun never goes more than approximately 23 degrees north or south of the celestial equator. At the winter solstice the Sun reaches its maximum southern angle of orbit (declination); at the summer solstice it reaches its maximum northern angle. Any time a planet exceeds this Solar boundary – and occasionally planets do – it is said to be 'out of bounds'. This means that the planet exceeds or trespasses into strange territory – beyond the limits allowed by the Sun, the ruler of the Solar system. The planet in this condition becomes more emphasized and exceeds its authority, becoming an important influence in the forecast.

Phases of the Moon

After the full Moon, the Moon seems to shrink in size (as perceived from the Earth), gradually growing smaller until it is virtually invisible to the naked eye – at the time of the next new Moon. This is called the waning Moon phase, or the waning Moon.

After the new Moon, the Moon gradually gets bigger in size (as perceived from the Earth) until it reaches its maximum size at the time of the full Moon. This period is called the waxing Moon phase, or the waxing Moon.

Retrogrades

The planets move around the Sun at different speeds. Mercury and Venus move much faster than the Earth, while Mars, Jupiter, Saturn, Uranus, Neptune and Pluto move more slowly. Thus there are times when, relative to the Earth, the planets appear to be going backwards. In reality they are always going forward, but relative to our vantage point on Earth they seem to go backwards through the zodiac for a period of time. This is called 'retrograde' motion and tends to weaken the normal influence of a given planet.

Short-term Planets

The fast-moving planets move so quickly through a sign that their effects are generally of a short-term nature. They reflect the immediate, day-to-day trends in a Horoscope.

Moon
stays in a sign for only 2½ days

Mercury
20 to 30 days

Sun
30 days

Venus
approximately 1 month

Mars
approximately 2 months

T-square

A T-square differs from a Grand Square (see above) in that it is not a complete square. If you look at the pattern in a chart it appears as 'half a complete square', resembling the T-square tools used by architects and designers. If you cut a complete square in half, diagonally, you have a T-square. Many astrologers consider this more stressful than a Grand Square, as it creates tension that is difficult to resolve. T-squares bring learning experiences.

Transits

This term refers to the movements or motions of the planets at any given time. Astrologers use the word 'transit' to make the distinction between a birth, or Natal, planet (see 'Natal', above) and the planet's current movement in the heavens. For example, if at your birth Saturn was in the sign of Cancer in your 8th house, but is now moving through your 3rd house, it is said to be 'transiting' your 3rd house. Transits are one of the main tools with which astrologers forecast trends.

Aries

THE RAM

Birthdays from
21st March to
20th April

Personality Profile

ARIES AT A GLANCE

Element – Fire

Ruling Planet – Mars
   Career Planet – Saturn
   Love Planet – Venus
   Money Planet – Venus
   Planet of Fun, Entertainment, Creativity and Speculations – Sun
   Planet of Health and Work – Mercury
   Planet of Home and Family Life – Moon
   Planet of Spirituality – Neptune
   Planet of Travel, Education, Religion and Philosophy – Jupiter

Colours – carmine, red, scarlet

Colours that promote love, romance and social harmony – green, jade green

Colour that promotes earning power – green

Gem – amethyst

Metals – iron, steel

Scent – honeysuckle

Quality – cardinal (= activity)

Quality most needed for balance – caution

Strongest virtues – abundant physical energy, courage, honesty, independence, self-reliance

Deepest need – action

Characteristics to avoid – haste, impetuousness, over-aggression, rashness

Signs of greatest overall compatibility – Leo, Sagittarius

Signs of greatest overall incompatibility – Cancer, Libra, Capricorn

Sign most helpful to career – Capricorn

Sign most helpful for emotional support – Cancer

Sign most helpful financially – Taurus

Sign best for marriage and/or partnerships – Libra

Sign most helpful for creative projects – Leo

Best Sign to have fun with – Leo

Signs most helpful in spiritual matters – Sagittarius, Pisces

Best day of the week – Tuesday

Understanding an Aries

Aries is the activist *par excellence* of the zodiac. The Aries need for action is almost an addiction, and those who do not really understand the Aries personality would probably use this hard word to describe it. In reality 'action' is the essence of the Aries psychology – the more direct, blunt and to-the-point the action, the better. When you think about it, this is the ideal psychological make-up for the warrior, the pioneer, the athlete or the manager.

Aries likes to get things done, and in their passion and zeal often lose sight of the consequences for themselves and others. Yes, they often try to be diplomatic and tactful, but it is hard for them. When they do so they feel that they are being dishonest and phoney. It is hard for them even to understand the mindset of the diplomat, the consensus builder, the front office executive. These people are involved in endless meetings, discussions, talks and negotiations – all of which seem a great waste of time when there is so much work to be done, so many real achievements to be gained. An Aries can understand, once it is explained, that talk and negotiations – the social graces – lead ultimately to better, more effective actions. The interesting thing is that an Aries is rarely malicious or spiteful – even when waging war. Aries people fight without hate for their opponents. To them it is all good-natured fun, a grand adventure, a game.

When confronted with a problem many people will say, 'Well, let's think about it, let's analyse the situation.' But not an Aries. An Aries will think, 'Something must be done. Let's get on with it.' Of course neither response is the total answer. Sometimes action is called for, sometimes cool thought. But an Aries tends to err on the side of action.

Action and thought are radically different principles. Physical activity is the use of brute force. Thinking and deliberating require one not to use force – to be still. It is not good for the athlete to be deliberating the next move; this will only slow down his or her reaction time. The athlete must act instinctively and instantly. This is how Aries people tend to behave in life. They are quick, instinctive decision-makers and their decisions tend to be translated into action almost immediately. When their intuition is sharp and well tuned, their actions are powerful and successful. When their intuition is off, their actions can be disastrous.

Do not think this will scare an Aries. Just as a good warrior knows that in the course of combat he or she might acquire a few wounds, so too does an Aries realize – somewhere deep down – that in the course of being true to yourself you might get embroiled in a disaster or two. It is all part of the game. An Aries feels strong enough to weather any storm.

There are many Aries people who are intellectual. They make powerful and creative thinkers. But even in this realm they tend to be pioneers – outspoken and blunt. These types of Aries tend to elevate (or sublimate) their desire for physical combat in favour of intellectual, mental combat. And they are indeed powerful.

In general, Aries people have a faith in themselves that others could learn from. This basic, rock-solid faith carries them through the most tumultuous situations of life. Their courage and self-confidence make them natural leaders. Their leadership is more by way of example than by actually controlling others.

Finance

Aries people often excel as builders or estate agents. Money in and of itself is not as important as are other things – action, adventure, sport, etc. They are motivated by the need to support and be well thought of by their partners. Money as a way of attaining pleasure is another important motivation. Aries function best in their own businesses or as managers of their own departments within a large business or corporation. The fewer orders they have to take from higher up, the better. They also function better out in the field rather than behind a desk.

Aries people are hard workers with a lot of endurance; they can earn large sums of money due to the strength of their sheer physical energy.

Venus is their money planet, which means that Aries need to develop more of the social graces in order to realize their full earning potential. Just getting the job done – which is what an Aries excels at – is not enough to create financial success. The co-operation of others needs to be attained. Customers, clients and co-workers need to be made to feel comfortable; many people need to be treated properly in order for success to happen. When Aries people develop these abilities – or hire someone to do this for them – their financial potential is unlimited.

Career and Public Image

One would think that a pioneering type would want to break with the social and political conventions of society. But this is not so with the Aries-born. They are pioneers within conventional limits, in the sense that they like to start their own businesses within an established industry.

Capricorn is on the 10th house of career cusp of Aries' solar Horoscope. Saturn is the planet that rules their life's work and professional aspirations. This tells us some interesting things about the Aries character. First, it shows that, in order for Aries people to reach their full career potential, they need to develop some qualities that are a bit alien to their basic nature: they need to become better administrators and organizers; they need to be able to handle details better and to take a long-range view of their projects and their careers in general. No one can beat an Aries when it comes to achieving short-range objectives, but a career is long term, built over time. You cannot take a 'quickie' approach to it.

Some Aries people find it difficult to stick with a project until the end. Since they get bored quickly and are in constant pursuit of new adventures, they prefer to pass an old project or task on to somebody else in order to start something new. Those Aries who learn how to put off the search for something new until the old is completed will achieve great success in their careers and professional lives.

In general, Aries people like society to judge them on their own merits, on their real and actual achievements. A reputation acquired by 'hype' feels false to them.

Love and Relationships

In marriage and partnerships Aries like those who are more passive, gentle, tactful and diplomatic – people who have the social grace and skills they sometimes lack. Our partners always represent a hidden part of ourselves – a self that we cannot express personally.

An Aries tends to go after what he or she likes aggressively. The tendency is to jump into relationships and marriages. This is especially true if Venus is in Aries as well as the Sun. If an Aries likes you, he or she will have a hard time taking no for an answer; many attempts will be made to sweep you off your feet.

Though Aries can be exasperating in relationships – especially if they are not understood by their partners – they are never consciously or wilfully cruel or malicious. It is just that they are so independent and sure of themselves that they find it almost impossible to see somebody else's viewpoint or position. This is why an Aries needs as a partner someone with lots of social graces.

On the plus side, an Aries is honest, someone you can lean on, someone with whom you will always know where you stand. What he or she lacks in diplomacy is made up for in integrity.

Home and Domestic Life

An Aries is of course the ruler at home – the Boss. The male will tend to delegate domestic matters to the female. The female Aries will want to rule the roost. Both tend to be handy round the house. Both like large families and both believe in the sanctity and importance of the family. An Aries is a good family person, although he or she does not especially like being at home a lot, preferring instead to be roaming about.

Considering that they are by nature so combative and wilful, Aries people can be surprisingly soft, gentle and even vulnerable with their children and partners. The sign of Cancer, ruled by the Moon, is on the cusp of their solar 4th house of home and family. When the Moon is well aspected – under favourable influences – in the birth chart, an Aries will be tender towards the family and will want a family life that is nurturing and supportive. Aries likes to come home after a hard day on the battlefield of life to the understanding arms of their partner and the unconditional love and support of their family. An Aries feels that there is enough 'war' out in the world – and he or she enjoys participating in that. But when Aries comes home, comfort and nurturing are what's needed.

Horoscope for 2016

Major Trends

Many of the trends that we've written about in previous years are still very much in effect in 2016. Uranus has been in your sign for over five years now and those of you born before April 9 have been feeling its influence the strongest. Uranus brings sudden and dramatic change, and there is no question that most of you Aries people are in dramatically different conditions and circumstances than you were five years ago. And the change is not finished. Those of you born after April 9 are feeling this especially strongly this year. You are redefining yourself – your image and personality. You are exploring your personal freedom. Many old ties and obligations have gone by the board over the past five years. Many seemingly 'bed rock' structures in your life are no longer there. You have been learning to deal with major change – to find stability as the changes happen around you.

Pluto has been in your 10th house of career since 2008 and will be there for many years to come. This shows career changes, both personal and in your industry. It also shows that you've been dealing with issues around death and perhaps surgeries. Many Aries have had near-death type experiences.

Neptune has been in your spiritual 12th house since February 2012 (he flirted with this house in 2011, but entered permanently in 2012). Thus the spiritual life is very active these days and many are seeing the spiritual agenda behind all the changes and dramas that are going on. Neptune will remain in your 12th house for many years to come.

Saturn has been in your 9th house since late 2014 and will be there for the year ahead. This is basically a happy transit that boosts your career. You're travelling this year, but it's more related to business, not so much for pleasure. Students at college level have to work harder on their studies.

The main headline this year is Jupiter's move from your 6th to your 7th house on September 10. This will make the year ahead a banner love and social year – one of the best in your life. For some of you, it will be the best you've ever known. Much depends on your age. Love is in the air and marriages or serious committed relationships are likely. More on this later.

Your areas of greatest interest this year are: the body and image; health and work (until September 10); love, romance and social activities (from September 10 onwards); foreign travel, higher education, religion and philosophy; career; and spirituality.

Your paths of greatest fulfilment this year are health and work; and love and romance (after September 10).

Health

(Please note that this is an astrological perspective on health and not a medical one. In days of yore there was no difference, these perspectives were identical. But now there could be quite a difference. For a medical perspective, please consult your doctor or health practitioner.)

Health needs watching this year, especially from September 10th onwards. Three long-term planets are stressing you out. The good news is that you are paying attention here and you are not ignoring things. And this is a positive health indicator.

It should be mentioned that if you got through the first half of 2014 with your health and sanity intact, this year will be a breeze.

Our regular readers know that there is much that can be done to enhance the health and prevent problems from developing. The first step is to maximize your energy level. This is always the first line of defence against disease. With a high energy level the body naturally resists disease. But when energy drops, it becomes more vulnerable. In many cases people are frittering away their energy on inessential things and frivolities. In other cases, their low energy is astrological in nature. When many planets are in stressful alignment, more energy is burned just doing the normal things. It is like driving a car uphill: it takes more gas to drive uphill than to drive a similar distance on level ground. Thus there is greater vulnerability to disease.

The second line of defence is to give more attention to the vulnerable areas in the Horoscope. These are the areas where problems are most likely to begin. If we can keep them strong – healthy and fit – we can prevent (or assuage) future problems.

In your Horoscope these are the areas that need more attention (the reflexology points are shown in the chart below):

- The heart. You should pay attention to this area all year, but especially from September 10 onwards. Learn to relax more. Practise relaxation exercises. Avoid worry and anxiety, the two root causes of heart problems.
- The head, face and scalp. This area is always important for Aries. Regular scalp and face massage will do wonders for your health, and craniosacral therapy should be powerful this year too.
- The adrenals. Avoid anger and fear, the two emotions that stress the adrenals.
- The musculature. Good muscle tone is always important. A weak muscle can knock the spine or skeleton out of alignment and cause many other problems. Vigorous physical exercise - according to your age and stage in life - is good for you.

Important foot reflexology points for the year ahead
Try to massage all of the foot on a regular basis - the top of the foot as well as the bottom - but pay extra attention to the points highlighted on the chart. When you massage, be aware of 'sore spots' as these need special attention. It's also a good idea to massage the ankles and below them.

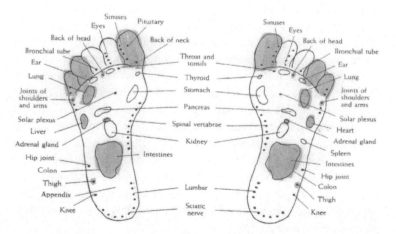

- The lungs, small intestine, arms, shoulders and respiratory system. These are also always important for Aries. Arms and shoulders should be regularly massaged.
- The liver and thighs (until September 10). Liver action seems more sluggish this year; a herbal liver cleanse or detox might be a good idea.

Pluto, the planet that rules surgery, is near your Mid-heaven (and has been that way for many years now), and so you have a tendency towards surgery. Keep in mind though that detoxing will often achieve the same result, although it takes longer.

Mercury, your health planet, is a fast-moving planet. Month to month he will be in different places and receive different kinds of aspects. Thus there are many short-term trends in health that are best dealt with in the monthly reports.

Home and Family

Your 4th house of home and family is not particularly prominent this year. Generally this shows a year tending towards the status quo. You're relatively content with things as they are and have no need to make dramatic changes. There's nothing against change by the way – you have the freedom to make changes or move if you like – but there's just no driving need for it.

Pluto has been in your 10th house of career for many years now – since 2008. This aspect impacts on parents and parent figures in your life. If you are male, this impacts on the father figures; if you are female it has an impact on the mother figures. It indicates many dramas in their lives such as surgeries or near-death kinds of experiences – encounters with death. In most cases these are merely encounters, but in some cases there has been actual death. These parent figures are in dialogue with the dark angel (figuratively speaking). He is around them and teaching them what they need to learn. Life is eternal, but here on earth it is short and fragile and can end at any time. They need to focus on the essentials, on the reason they came here in the first place. They seem in a more spiritual kind of period – since late 2014 – and this is probably the reason for it.

Saturn, the planet that rules parent figures, is in harmonious aspect with you and so you seem on good terms with them. The challenges they face don't seem to involve you personally.

Uranus in your 1st house shows restlessness. This is not necessarily manifested as physical moves, but shows someone who lives in different places for long periods of time. There is a need for constant change.

If you are redecorating or beautifying the home, June 21 to July 23 is an excellent time for this. It is also a good time for buying art objects for the home.

Finance and Career

Your 2nd house of finance is not strong this year. Generally this indicates a stable kind of financial year and I read this as a good thing. You're basically satisfied with your earnings as they are and have no need to make dramatic changes.

However, if you are experiencing financial difficulties, the Horoscope is explaining why. Most probably you're not paying enough attention to them. You're distracted by other things and not focusing here as you should. With an empty money house it will be challenging to focus on this area – you might not be in the mood for it – but you need to force yourself.

Venus is your financial planet. Thus, your social skills, your ability to get on with others, are very important in financial matters. Aries people are not known for their social skills – they are independent types – but if you want to earn more and attain your financial goals, these skills need to be beefed up.

Venus as your financial planet shows other things too. Who you know is just as important as how much you actually have. Your friends tend to be rich and this is like money in the bank – though it will never appear on any financial statement. Wealth of friendship is a form of wealth.

With Venus as your financial planet you have a natural affinity for the beauty industry – for fashion, cosmetics, fragrances, art and jewellery. These are viable as investments, businesses or jobs.

Jupiter enters your 7th house in September, bringing opportunity for a lucrative kind of business partnership or joint venture. If you own a company a merger could happen too.

Jupiter has been in your 6th house of health and work since August 12, 2015 and remains there until September 9. This is an excellent aspect for job seekers and many of you have landed dream jobs in the past year. And, if you have not, it can still happen in the year ahead. You seem in demand. These opportunities can be in foreign lands or with foreign companies.

Those of you who employ others have been increasing the workforce of late and this trend continues in the year ahead. Generally this is a sign of success.

With Pluto in your 10th house since 2008, career has been a strong focus. As we mentioned, there are many changes going on here – changes in your industry, changes in the hierarchy of your company, changes in governmental regulations that affect you. The rules of the game have been changing for many years. Many of you have actually changed the career path in the past few years – and it could still happen this year or in future years (Pluto is a slow-moving planet). The symbolism depicts 'death and rebirth'. An old career, career path or career approach dies and is reborn in another form. Pluto in the 10th house tends to career success. It produces storms and crisis, but also a strong focus on the career. It is this intense, laser-like focus that brings success.

Your career planet, Saturn, is also making nice aspects to you. So, you're comfortable with your career and seem to be enjoying it. Bosses seems kindly disposed to you – another big plus. Later in the year, Jupiter will start making nice aspects to your career planet and this will bring promotion and elevation. This happens from September 10 onwards.

Your willingness to travel plays a role in your career success.

Love and Social Life

This is really the main headline for the year. Your 7th house has been more or less dormant for many years. This year, from September onwards, it becomes powerful and happy.

Serious love has been complicated for many years. Uranus in the 1st house is not the best aspect for love. It is good for serial relationships but not for marriage. Perhaps you blamed your partners, but really the problem was with you. You have been very independent, self-willed and rebellious. You wanted (and still want) a lot of personal freedom, and this is difficult in a serious relationship. By definition a serious relationship is a limitation of personal freedom. You've had five years of personal freedom and now maybe it is time to settle down. What I see happening is that you'll meet someone who makes you feel this way. Somehow you'll be able to combine your need for freedom with a committed kind of relationship.

Wealth is always a romantic turn-on for you, and this year more so than normal. The person who fits the psychological profile of your love is someone educated and refined. Perhaps religious. A minister or professor – a mentor type – fits the bill. You have the aspects of someone who falls in love with a professor, guru or religious leader. Foreigners are unusually appealing too. And it wouldn't surprise me if you met this person in a foreign country. Physical beauty is also a factor here.

However, there are other scenarios. You could meet this person at your church, synagogue, mosque or ashram – or through the introduction of fellow worshipers. You could also meet him or her at university or university functions. These venues are not only conducive for romance, but for social opportunities in general.

Jupiter is the planet of religion and philosophy – and in your chart he is even more like this, as he is the ruler of your 9th house. Thus aside from wealth, education and personal appearance, there is a need for philosophical compatibility with your lover. This doesn't mean that you have to agree on every point, but you should be on the same page about things like the meaning of life and what is important in that life. Philosophical differences have sunk more relationships than has ever been reported. And, in your case, it is unusually important.

If you are already married (and we give you credit for holding things together) you can work through problems in the marriage by taking trips to foreign lands, by taking courses as a couple and by worshipping together as a couple. These things tend to harmonize the upper mental body.

Those of you working towards your second marriage also have wonderful love opportunities this year – only there's no need to rush into anything. Let love develop slowly and naturally. Those working towards a third marriage have a static love year, but the social life in general will be active.

Whatever marriage you're in, the social life expands this year. New and important friends are coming into the picture.

Self-improvement

Many of the trends we've written about in previous years are still in effect now. Long-term planets indicate long-term projects. These things are not achieved overnight.

Saturn in your 9th house – like last year – is testing your religious and philosophical beliefs. They get 'reality checked'. This is not always a pleasant thing. We tend to be very attached to our beliefs, and when they are challenged we feel we are personally challenged. But the end result is good. Some beliefs might be right, but need some modification. Some could be wrong and need to be eliminated. The end result will be a more stable, more realistic belief system. And it will serve you well in years to come.

Your spiritual planet Neptune in your 12th house is also involved in the testing of your beliefs. Many of you are having actual spiritual experiences – supernatural kinds of experiences – and revelations through dreams and through teachers. These will challenge long-held beliefs about the nature of life and reality. Spiritual revelation and experiences could also cause career changes, or a change in the way you approach your career.

Neptune will spend a lot of time on an eclipse point this year, which indicates a lot of spiritual change in your life: change of practice, attitudes and perhaps even teachings and teachers. It shows much instability in a spiritual organization you're involved with.

Uranus, still in your 1st house, shows that you need to get comfortable with change and apparent instability. As in previous years, your challenge is to make change your friend. Don't resist it, flow with it. Change brings insecurity, but in the end it is good. Uranus is about breaking attachments – and we all have many. Attachment to a person, a job, a situation, a physical kind of appearance. These attachments hold us back. We should be happy when they're broken.

Pluto in your 10th house shows more involvement with death and death issues. The cosmos is educating you about these things and they do need to be understood better. They do not need to be feared, but understood. When this happens, life goes better. Fear of death is perhaps the main obstruction to freedom and to our heartfelt goals.

Jupiter in your 6th house at the beginning of the year will show you the power of prayer in health issues. You respond well to this. Prayer changes the vibration of the body. It changes the mental attitude.

Month-by-month Forecasts

January

Best Days Overall: 6, 7, 15, 16, 24, 25
Most Stressful Days Overall: 1, 2, 3, 9, 10, 21, 22, 23, 29, 30
Best Days for Love: 1, 2, 3, 6, 7, 8, 15, 16, 26, 29, 30
Best Days for Money: 6, 7, 8, 9, 10, 15, 16, 17, 18, 26, 27
Best Days for Career: 6, 7, 9, 10, 15, 16, 24, 25

You begin your year in a yearly career peak. The power of your 10th house of career is really the main headline of the month. Half of the planets are either in or moving through the 10th house this month. (At least 70 and often 80 per cent of the planets are above the horizon as well.) This is a month for career success. Much progress is being made; pay rises, promotions and more recognition for your professional abilities are happening. (Sometimes a pay rise is covert rather than official, but management does things that increase your income – often through perks or other moves.)

With the planetary momentum forward this month, you should see faster progress to your career and other goals. Normally, strong forward planetary motion would make this an excellent period for starting new projects or launching new products. But in your case it is best to wait until after your birthday.

Mars, the ruler of your Horoscope, has been in your 7th house since November 13 of last year. So you have been very active socially – and quite popular. You've been there for your friends and beloved. You've put their interests first. But this is starting to taper off this month. The planetary power started to shift to the Eastern sector last month and this month on the 24th the shift gets even stronger. On the 4th Mars leaves your 7th house and enters the 8th house of transformation and regeneration. Your social goals are more or less achieved. You have been 'people pleasing' for a quite a while and now it is time to think of number one. Self-interest is often confused with selfishness. It is considered something 'evil'. But sometimes the best way we can help others or be useful to others, is to achieve our personal goals – to be personally happy. Your interests are no less important than other people's. You're in a cycle where you need to focus more on yourself. You have great personal power (and it will grow in coming months). You have the power to create your own happiness – to create conditions in your life that please you. It's up to you to use it, and to use it properly. It is time to be more independent and self-reliant.

Though this social life is tapering off, the month ahead looks socially active. The Moon will spend five days in your 7th house this month (usually she spends only two there), indicating there is more socializing from home and with the family. On the 24th the love planet Venus enters your 10th house, showing more socializing with people of high status and prestige. Your social skills enhance your career.

Health needs watching until the 20th. Be sure to get enough rest.

February

  Best Days Overall: 2, 3, 4, 11, 12, 20, 21
  Most Stressful Days Overall: 5, 6, 18, 19, 25, 26
  Best Days for Love: 5, 6, 13, 14, 25, 26
  Best Days for Money: 5, 6, 13, 14, 22, 23, 24, 25
  Best Days for Career: 2, 3, 5, 6, 11, 12, 20, 21

Health and energy are much improved this month. You can enhance them further by giving more attention to the spine, knees, teeth and bones until the 14th. Back and knee massage and regular visits to a chiropractor or osteopath will be beneficial. After the 14th give more attention to the ankles and calves. Regular massage will do wonders. You will also benefit from new, cutting edge therapies after this date.

Career is still good, although not as active as the past two months. Pay rises are still likely (if they haven't happened yet). Bosses, elders and parent figures are sympathetic to your financial goals. Your financial judgement is sound as well. You get good value for your money and aren't likely to overpay for things. You have a good long-term, conservative perspective on wealth (something Aries needs desperately). The 5th to the 8th are good days for paying down debt. But if you need to borrow, this period is good for that too. Your financial planet makes beautiful aspects to Jupiter from the 9th to the 11th and this brings a nice payday. There is financial good luck.

Mars has been in your 8th house since January 4 and will remain there for the rest of the month ahead. This is a sexually active kind of month. Whatever your age or stage in life, the libido is stronger than usual. The important thing is not to overdo it. Mars in your 8th house is an excellent aspect for detox regimes and weight loss programmes – if you need them. You seem unusually active in the financial affairs of your spouse, partner or current love.

The love life seems happy this month too. From the 5th to the 8th there is great passion with the beloved. Singles have sexual opportunity. From the 9th to the 11th there are happy romantic and social opportunities and singles can meet someone special during that period. Those already in a relationship have more romance in their relationship. On the 17th Venus enters your 11th house of friends and group activities. Singles find love opportunities in the online world, on online dating or social media sites. This is a good time to get involved in group activities or organizations too.

Be more patient with children or children figures in your life from the 4th to the 6th. You don't seem in synch. Children and children figures have excellent romantic and social aspects this month.

March

Best Days Overall: 1, 2, 10, 11, 18, 19, 28, 29
Most Stressful Days Overall: 3, 4, 16, 17, 23, 24, 31
Best Days for Love: 6, 7, 16, 23, 24, 26, 27
Best Days for Money: 3, 4, 6, 7, 12, 13, 16, 21, 22, 26, 27, 31
Best Days for Career: 1, 2, 3, 4, 10, 11, 18, 19, 28, 29, 31

The planetary momentum is overwhelmingly forward this month. On the 20th the Sun moves into your sign, Aries, the best starting energy of the zodiac. Many of you, especially if your birthday is from March 20 to March 31, are in an excellent period for starting new projects or launching new products. After your birthday is best.

The month ahead will be eventful. Two eclipses ensure this. Of the two, the lunar eclipse of the 23rd affects you most strongly – especially those of you born between the 20th and the 25th. Take it nice and easy. Spend more quiet time at home. Read a good book or watch a nice movie. There is no need to be your Aries daredevil self during this period.

The solar eclipse of the 9th (in America it happens on the 8th) occurs in your 12th house. This indicates changes in spiritual practices and attitudes. Since you're in a very spiritual kind of month until the 20th, these changes most likely come from new revelations that happen. This eclipse also shows upheavals – disturbances – and life-changing kinds of events in spiritual or charitable organizations you're involved with. There are dramas in the lives of guru figures too. Every solar eclipse affects your children or the children figures in your life. They should stay out of harm's way during this period and take life more easy. Life-changing kinds of events are happening with them and although they will turn out well, while they happen things can be frenetic.

The lunar eclipse of the 23rd occurs in your 7th house of love. This will test your current relationship. Be more patient with the beloved during this period as he or she is apt to be more temperamental than usual. Sometimes this is because of personal dramas in their own lives, sometimes it is just the cosmic energy. Good relationships survive these things and get even better. But flawed ones can be in trouble. Every lunar eclipse affects the home and family and this one is no different. Be more patient with family members too. Often there are dramas in the home – sudden repairs, or changes that need to be made. If you've got mice or other 'underworld critters' in the home, this is when you usually find out about them. There can be dramas in the lives of family members.

Health is good this month. Until the 5th you can enhance it through calf and ankle massage. From the 5th to the 22nd give more attention to the feet – foot massage is especially powerful – and from the 22nd onwards, scalp and face massage is beneficial.

Job seekers have good fortune from the 22nd onwards.

April

Best Days Overall: 6, 7, 14, 15, 16, 24, 25, 26
Most Stressful Days Overall: 1, 12, 13, 19, 20, 21, 27, 28
Best Days for Love: 6, 14, 15, 19, 20, 21, 25, 26
Best Days for Money: 1, 6, 8, 9, 14, 15, 17, 18, 25, 26, 27, 28
Best Days for Career: 1, 6, 7, 14, 15, 16, 24, 25, 26, 27, 28

Last month on the 20th, the Sun entered your sign and you entered one of your yearly personal pleasure peaks. This is a wonderful time to get the body and image in shape and enjoy all the pleasures of the senses – as long as you don't overdo it. This is a happy kind of month.

The planets are now in their Easternmost position. Thus you are at the maximum extent of your personal power and independence. You can easily create the conditions of life that please you – and you should. There's no need to adapt to the world – the world will adapt to you. Following your bliss – though it seems selfish – will actually benefit all those around you. It will, in subtle ways, bless all of life.

Love is happy this month – especially now that the dust from last month's lunar eclipse is settling. The 7th and 8th could be stressful, but after that things look smooth. Venus moves into your sign on the 5th and stays there for the rest of the month. Like most things in your life, you're having your way in love. The current love puts you first and caters to you. Singles don't have to do much to attract love – love finds you. Just go about your daily business. The 11th and 12th look especially good for love. Children or children figures in your life are also having a good romantic month – the 9th and 10th are especially good for them. Young children are meeting new friends and having happy social experiences.

With your 1st house very powerful all month, you look good. You have star quality and charisma. The eyes sparkle, the gestures are graceful. You dress with style – and probably expensively. This is a great month to buy clothing or personal accessories. Your sense of style is excellent now.

April is also a prosperous month. Venus crossing your Ascendant on the 5th brings money and financial opportunity. There could be a temporary financial disturbance – perhaps an unexpected expense – on the 7th or 8th, but it doesn't affect overall prosperity. Financial opportunity is seeking you out this month. On the 19th the Sun enters your money house and you begin a yearly financial peak. The 22nd and 23rd bring sudden, unexpected money. You have the favour of the money people in your life these days.

Health and energy are very good this month. Until the 6th you can enhance them further through head and face massage. From the 6th onwards neck massage is good.

May

Best Days Overall: 4, 5, 12, 13, 22, 23, 31
Most Stressful Days Overall: 10, 11, 17, 18, 24, 25
Best Days for Love: 6, 14, 15, 17, 18, 26, 27
Best Days for Money: 6, 14, 15, 24, 25, 26, 27
Best Days for Career: 4, 5, 12, 13, 22, 23, 24, 25, 31

On April 5, as Venus moved into your 1st house, the planetary power shifted. Most of the planets are now below the horizon of your Horoscope. Your 10th house of career is still strong – so career is important, but it can be downplayed now. The next five or so months should be devoted to getting the home and emotional life in right order. These are the hidden foundations upon which one builds a career. These need tending now. So, handle what needs to be handled in your career, but your main thrust is to find and function from your emotional comfort zone. When this is found, the career will naturally prosper in due course.

You're still very much in a yearly financial peak, until the 20th. Your money house is very powerful – and chock-full of beneficent planets. This is a period for happy money – money that is earned in happy and enjoyable ways. Your personal creativity is more marketable now. You have the financial favour of the spouse or current love – and of friends. Your social connections are more important than how much money you have. You end the month wealthier than you began it. The 2nd to the 4th and the 10th and 11th are nice paydays. There is luck in speculations those days.

Health and energy are still very good. With energy all kinds of vistas open up to us – things that seemed impossible when energy was low. Like last month, you can enhance it further through neck massage and craniosacral therapy. Tension in the neck needs to be released.

Mars, the ruler of your chart, started to retrograde on April 17 and will be in retrograde motion for the whole month ahead. This is really the only major complication right now. You have energy, health, money and love – you just lack direction. This is a time for gaining mental clarity about who you are and where you want to go. From the 7th to the 14th – a whole week! – Mars has his solstice. Mars pauses in the heavens. This pause is in latitude not longitude. Mars will stay in the same latitude. This could make you feel that your life is on 'pause'. It might be a good idea to take a break from the usual routine. It is a good time for parties and festivities, and especially good for spiritual work.

Venus will be in your money house until the 24th. Singles are attracted to the wealthy – the good providers – the givers of material gifts. Love is practical during that period. You show love in material ways and this is how you feel loved. On the 24th Venus enters Gemini, your 3rd house of communications, and good communication starts to become important in love.

June

Best Days Overall: 1, 8, 9, 18, 19, 27, 28
Most Stressful Days Overall: 6, 7, 13, 14, 20, 21, 22
Best Days for Love: 4, 5, 13, 14, 25, 26
Best Days for Money: 2, 3, 10, 11, 20, 21, 29, 30
Best Days for Career: 1, 8, 9, 18, 19, 20, 21, 22, 27, 28

There's more to love than just physical chemistry and material baubles, and you are learning this now. Mental intimacy is very important in love, and if this is lacking even the richest person will not satisfy. This month – especially until the 18th – love is about communication. Sharing ideas. The thought process of the person must be alluring. You value intelligence over beauty and wealth. Thus you're attracted to intellectual types these days, to writers, journalists, teachers and mental workers. Love opportunities for singles happen in educational settings – at lectures, seminars, workshops or school functions, perhaps even at the library or bookshop. Your search for intelligence can lead you way outside your normal social sphere, especially from the 13th to the 29th. Love is close to home this month, but even in your own neighbourhood, you find people outside your normal sphere.

On the 18th the needs in love change again. Venus enters the sign of Cancer, your 4th house. Now you look for emotional intimacy. You gravitate to those with whom you can easily share your feelings. This too could lead you outside your normal sphere. There is more moodiness in love during this period. The kind of mood you're in defines whether love is happy or unhappy. This moodiness can be with you or with the partner – sometimes both. Don't be surprised if an old flame comes back into the picture. Sometimes it is the actual person, sometimes it is someone who reminds you of the old flame. Usually this goes nowhere (but not always), but the good thing is that old love issues get resolved.

The financial intuition needs more verification on the 2nd and 3rd. Be careful of overspending on the 3rd and 4th. A financial disturbance on the 8th and 9th is only short term and not the problem that it seems to be at first. Financial intuition is excellent on the 27th and 28th. In finance, as in love, you're going outside your normal sphere in search

of earnings – especially from the 13th to the 29th. Family and especially a parent or parent figure is more supportive from the 18th
onwards. Family connections are playing an important role too.

Overall health is good, but you should rest and relax more from the
21st onwards. The most important thing is to get enough rest and
maintain high energy levels. Health can be further enhanced by neck
massage until the 13th, and through arm and shoulder massage after
that date. Avoid too much talking and thinking during this period as it
just wastes sorely needed energy. If you do think and talk, keep it
positive.

July

Best Days Overall: 6, 7, 15, 16, 24, 25
Most Stressful Days Overall: 3, 4, 10, 11, 12, 18, 19, 31
Best Days for Love: 3, 4, 10, 11, 12, 15, 24, 25
Best Days for Money: 3, 4, 8, 9, 14, 15, 18, 19, 24, 25, 27, 28
Best Days for Career: 6, 7, 15, 16, 18, 19, 24, 25

Last month on the 21st the Sun moved into your 4th house and will
spend most of the month ahead in this house. This shows many
things. Career issues can be downplayed (your career planet, Saturn,
has been retrograde since late March). This is a time to focus on the
home and family and get this in right order. It is an excellent period –
especially until the 12th – to redecorate, paint and beautify the home.
It is a better time for cosmetic changes than for heavy repairs. It's also
a good period in which to buy objects of beauty for the home (if you
need them). Getting the family relations right will not only help you
later in your career, but it also improves the love life and finances.

But there's much more to power in the 4th house than these
mundane issues. Most people are held back in life because of old
emotional baggage. Old traumas that might still be active, or negative
memories – or more scientifically, destructive records in the memory
body. When these get activated they produce negative states of mind
– fear, worry, anger, grief, etc. Many so-called sicknesses (the symptoms of sickness) have their roots in the memory body. So, every year,
the cosmos, in its wisdom, arranges natural therapy. It arranges for old

memories to arise again so that they can be dealt with and resolved from the present state of mind. Opinions that were made, for example, at the age of three under some trauma or stress are not necessarily 'truth'. The three-year-old made opinions from a three-year-old state of mind. When these are looked at from the present they are seen to be false and thus can be discharged and rendered harmless. It is OK for the three-year-old to form three-year-old opinions, but it's not so good when a forty-year-old holds these opinions.

So your feelings of nostalgia, your dreams of the past, your encounters with people from your past are all part of a therapeutic agenda. Old issues will get resolved and you'll be ready to move forward to your next step. When you can think of a past trauma or past relationship and smile and be emotionally calm, you know you're healed.

Those of you undergoing therapy should make very good progress this month.

Health still needs watching this month until the 20th. As always, the most important thing is to get enough rest. If you have any pre-existing conditions, these can seem worse at this period, but more rest should clear the issue. You can enhance the health through better diet and psychological therapies, until the 14th. After that give more attention to the heart. Happiness itself is a great healing force, as you will learn after the 14th. A night out on the town might do you as much good as a visit to the doctor.

August

Best Days Overall: 2, 3, 12, 13, 21, 22, 29, 30
Most Stressful Days Overall: 1, 7, 8, 14, 15, 27, 28
Best Days for Love: 3, 7, 8, 14, 15, 23, 24
Best Days for Money: 3, 4, 5, 14, 15, 23, 24, 31
Best Days for Career: 2, 3, 12, 13, 14, 15, 21, 22, 29, 30

You have been in an independent state of mind since the beginning of the year. On June 21 the planetary power shifted from the independent East to the social West. Hopefully, by now, you've used your enhanced personal power to create pleasing conditions for yourself. But now it is time to let go of self-interest and focus on others. It's time to take a vacation from yourself. The planetary power is moving away from you and towards others. Your personal abilities are not the issue these days. Likeability, your ability to get on with others, is the most important thing. Your social skills will bring you what pure ability can't, so it is time to develop these skills. Your good is dependent on others and their goodwill. Put others first and your own good will come to you very naturally.

On July 20 the Sun entered your 5th house of fun and creativity and you began a yearly personal pleasure peak. This goes on until the 22nd of this month. It is time to enjoy life. Time to have some fun. Time to enjoy the money that you have and spend it on leisure activities (according to what you can afford). It is time to be more creative too. You have special abilities to handle children and children figures in your life these days too. There is much we can learn from them – especially on how to enjoy life. It is said that an adult can't really enjoy life to the fullest. The adult has too many cares, worries and plans. It is the child that is truly joyous. This is a good month to get more in touch with your inner child.

Love is happy this month. You have been more carefree about it since mid-July. Even children and children figures in your life are having a happy social life. If they are of appropriate age, romance is likely – especially on the 15th and 16th. For singles there are happy romantic opportunities from the 26th to the 28th. For those already in a relationship this period shows more romance within the relationship.

You've had wonderful job aspects all year, and this month they get even better. Job seekers have good fortune and even those already employed can have offers of better jobs.

Health is good this month. After the 20th you seem very focused here, which makes it a very good period to get your health regime in order. If you're making important changes make them before the 30th, when Mercury, your health planet, starts to retrograde.

Speculations have been favourable since July 12. However, after the 5th money comes the old-fashioned way through hard work – generally through your job. Extra money can be earned through 'side jobs' from the 5th onwards (and these opportunities will come).

September

Best Days Overall: 8, 9, 17, 18, 25, 26, 27
Most Stressful Days Overall: 3, 4, 10, 11, 12, 23, 24, 30
Best Days for Love: 3, 4, 13, 14, 23, 30
Best Days for Money: 1, 2, 3, 4, 12, 13, 14, 19, 20, 21, 23
Best Days for Career: 8, 9, 10, 11, 12, 17, 18, 25, 26, 27

This is an eventful and tumultuous kind of month. Active. Hectic. Filled with change.

First off, there will be two eclipses this month – these practically guarantee dramatic change. Aside from this, Jupiter makes a major move into your 7th house of love on the 10th. Both the month and year ahead are strongly romantic. Then, on the 22nd, the planetary power shifts from the lower half of the chart to the upper half. This signals a psychological shift in you. Hopefully, by now, you've found your point of emotional harmony. You've brought the home and family into order. Now it is time to focus on the career and your outer objectives. Your career planet Saturn started to move forward on the 18th of last month, so there is now mental clarity and good forward momentum. Mars, the ruler of your Horoscope, spends the month 'out of bounds' and will 'pause' in the heavens from the 19th to the 28th. This pause is a good thing. With all the excitement going on this is a pause that refreshes. You need to get your bearings.

The solar eclipse of the 1st is a strong one, so make sure you have a nice easy schedule. Avoid risky, high stress kinds of activities – reschedule them for a better time. The eclipse not only impacts on the Sun, but on Mars and Saturn as well. It occurs in your 6th house of health and work, indicating job changes and changes in the conditions of work. These changes can happen within your present company or with a new one. (The impact on Saturn reinforces this – it shows career changes too.) There will also be changes in the health regime – dramatic ones. Sometimes this kind of eclipse brings a health scare. However, your overall health is good (though you need to be more careful from the 22nd onwards) and so this will most likely be nothing more than a scare.

There are also dramas with parent figures in your life and shake-ups in your industry or company. There is a need now to rethink the career path, to revise your plans and strategies. Many of you are into travelling this month – Mars is in your 9th house. But unless it is essential it is probably better to reschedule these visits, especially long trips or foreign trips.

The lunar eclipse of the 16th occurs in your 12th house, indicating important spiritual changes – changes in practice, teachings and perhaps teachers. There is much instability in charitable or spiritual organizations you're involved with, and life-changing dramas in the lives of gurus or spiritual figures in your life. Every lunar eclipse brings family dramas for you, and this one is no different. Thus it is good to be more patient with family members (and especially a parent or parent figure), as they are likely to be more temperamental than normal. If there are flaws in your home, now is when you find out about them so that corrections can be made.

October

Best Days Overall: 5, 6, 7, 15, 23, 24
Most Stressful Days Overall: 1, 2, 8, 9, 21, 22, 27,
   28, 29
Best Days for Love: 1, 2, 3, 4, 12, 13, 23, 24, 27, 28, 29
Best Days for Money: 1, 3, 4, 10, 12, 13, 16, 17, 18, 19, 23, 24,
   27, 28
Best Days for Career: 5, 6, 7, 8, 9, 15, 23, 24

Jupiter entered your 7th house of love on September 10. On September 22 the Sun also entered your 7th house and you began a yearly love and social peak. For many of you (depending on your age) you are at a lifetime love and social peak, which continues until the 23rd of this month. Many a marriage (or relationships that are 'like' marriage) will be happening in the year ahead. But as was mentioned earlier, don't be too quick to jump into marriage. This is only advisable if you're willing to put some limits on your freedom.

Neptune, your spiritual planet, spends the month very near the point of the solar eclipse of September 1. This shows continuing instability in spiritual or charitable organizations and in the lives of guru figures you're involved with. Your intuition and dreams need verification;

don't be so quick to make judgements or act on them. Take the time to ensure that you got the message properly.

Health needs attention until the 23rd. Make sure you get enough sleep and don't waste time or energy on frivolities. Focus on the important things in your life. You can enhance your health in the ways mentioned in the yearly report, and in addition you can give more attention to the diet and small intestine until the 7th. From the 7th to the 25th give more attention to the kidneys and hips. Massage the hips regularly. A kidney detox might be a good idea too. After the 25th pay more attention to the colon, bladder and sexual organs. This is a sexually active kind of month, but there is no need to overdo it. Listen to your body.

Mars, the ruler of your chart, has been 'out of bounds' since August 9, so you're venturing into faraway places – places outside your normal sphere. Travelling is much better this month than last. Avoid high stress activities or confrontations from the 18th to the 20th and from the 27th to the 29th. The 18th to the 20th brings intense sexual encounters; libido is higher than usual.

The month ahead seems prosperous. Until the 18th there is good financial support (and opportunity) from the current love or partner and there is good financial cooperation between you. This is a very good time to borrow or to pay down debt, according to your need. It is also a good time to get rid of old possessions that you no longer use or need. Clear the decks so that the new and better can come in. It's good to eliminate waste too, redundant bank or brokerage accounts or needless expenses. Until the 18th you prosper by cutting back – getting rid of the useless. After the 18th, you prosper by growth: earnings start to increase.

November

Best Days Overall: 2, 3, 11, 12, 19, 20, 29, 30
Most Stressful Days Overall: 4, 5, 17, 18, 24, 25
Best Days for Love: 2, 3, 13, 21, 22, 24, 25
Best Days for Money: 2, 3, 6, 7, 13, 14, 15, 16, 21, 22, 24, 25
Best Days for Career: 2, 3, 4, 5, 11, 12, 19, 20, 29, 30

Neptune is still very near the solar eclipse point of September 1. The spiritual instability that we've discussed in the previous months continues. Take your time in interpreting dreams, intuitions and psychic readings. The real meaning could be different from what you think it is. On a worldly level this aspect can show flooding and upheavals in the oil, natural gas and water industries.

Your 8th house of transformation became powerful on October 23 and remains so until November 22. This favours detox and weight loss regimes. Those of you involved in personal transformation and reinvention should have a more successful month. These projects go well.

Health and energy are good all month. You can enhance them further through detox regimes, as we have mentioned, and also by giving more attention to the colon, bladder and sexual organs. Like last month November is a sexually active kind of month and the tendency is to overdo it. After the 12th give more attention to the liver and thighs. Thigh massage and liver cleansing will be beneficial.

Your 9th house becomes powerful from the 22nd onwards, and there is travel or happy travel opportunities. College or post-graduate students are working hard, but there is success this month. Foreigners, foreign travel and foreign companies are important financially and from a job perspective.

Foreigners are appealing in love too. With Venus 'out of bounds' all month you're moving outside your usual social circle, and perhaps even to foreign countries. The same is true in finance. There's a need to think 'outside the box' – to try things you normally wouldn't try.

On the 12th Venus moves into your 10th house of career, and this transit boosts the career. It indicates social (and perhaps romantic) interactions with bosses, superiors and authority figures. You have both their social and financial favour. Pay rises – overt or covert – can happen. A parent or parent figure is financially supportive.

You seem very successful these days. Mars, the ruler of your Horoscope, has been in your 10th house since September 27 and remains there until the 9th of this month. You're working hard, but you're at the top of your game. And, you haven't really hit your career peak yet. This will happen next month.

December

   Best Days Overall: 8, 9, 16, 17, 26, 27
   Most Stressful Days Overall: 1, 2, 3, 14, 15, 21, 22, 29, 30
   Best Days for Love: 2, 3, 12, 13, 21, 22
   Best Days for Money: 2, 3, 4, 5, 10, 11, 12, 13, 21, 22, 31
   Best Days for Career: 1, 2, 3, 8, 9, 16, 17, 26, 27, 29, 30

Career is the main headline this month. Your 10th house is very strong – 50 per cent of the planets are either there or moving through there. This shows a lot of power – a lot of cosmic support – and a lot of focus. There is no obstacle that you can't overcome. Your yearly career peak technically begins on the 21st as the Sun crosses your Mid-heaven and enters your career house. But you will feel it even before that date, especially from the 8th to the 12th as the Sun moves over your career planet, giving it positive stimulation. This is also a nice career aspect for your children or the children figures in your life.

   Children or children figures should stay out of harm's way on the 1st, 7th, 8th, 11th and 12th. There is no need for them to indulge in daredevil-type stunts or to tempt the fates.

   You're working hard and succeeding this month, but after the 21st be more health conscious. This is a short-term issue, however. Next month, after the 20th, health and energy will improve. In the mean-time rest more and make sure you get enough sleep. Pay attention to the spine, knees, teeth, bones, skin and overall skeletal alignment. Regular back and knee massage will be powerful. If you feel under the weather, a visit to a chiropractor or osteopath might be just the ticket.

   Students at the college or post-graduate level have some educational surprises from the 19th onwards. There could be important changes to educational plans. Travel plans seem unstable during that period too.

   Mercury goes retrograde on the 19th, which means that job seekers need to do more research before accepting job offers. Be more careful how you communicate with bosses and superiors too. Make sure you say what you mean and that you heard what they're saying. Don't be afraid to ask questions and get clarity. Changes in the health regime also need more consideration.

Your financial planet has been in Capricorn since November 12 and is there until the 7th. This is good for finance. It indicates a sound and conservative financial judgement and a long-term perspective on wealth. It favours setting up savings and investment plans. On the 7th Venus will move into Aquarius, your 11th house. Friends seems financially supportive. Online activities boost earnings. It will be good to be involved with groups and organizations. Good to invest in high tech equipment.

Online activities boost the love life from the 7th onwards. Singles find good fortune on the online dating and social media sites. Love has been good for many months now, but becomes especially so from the 7th onwards.

Taurus

THE BULL

Birthdays from
21st April to
20th May

Personality Profile

TAURUS AT A GLANCE

Element – Earth

Ruling Planet – Venus
   Career Planet – Uranus
   Love Planet – Pluto
   Money Planet – Mercury
   Planet of Health and Work – Venus
   Planet of Home and Family Life – Sun
   Planet of Spirituality – Mars
   Planet of Travel, Education, Religion and Philosophy – Saturn

Colours – earth tones, green, orange, yellow

Colours that promote love, romance and social harmony – red-violet, violet

Colours that promote earning power – yellow, yellow-orange

Gems – coral, emerald

Metal – copper

Scents – bitter almond, rose, vanilla, violet

Quality – fixed (= stability)

Quality most needed for balance – flexibility

Strongest virtues – endurance, loyalty, patience, stability,
   a harmonious disposition

Deepest needs – comfort, material ease, wealth

Characteristics to avoid – rigidity, stubbornness, tendency to be overly
   possessive and materialistic

Signs of greatest overall compatibility – Virgo, Capricorn

Signs of greatest overall incompatibility – Leo, Scorpio, Aquarius

Sign most helpful to career – Aquarius

Sign most helpful for emotional support – Leo

Sign most helpful financially – Gemini

Sign best for marriage and/or partnerships – Scorpio

Sign most helpful for creative projects – Virgo

Best Sign to have fun with – Virgo

Signs most helpful in spiritual matters – Aries, Capricorn

Best day of the week – Friday

Understanding a Taurus

Taurus is the most earthy of all the Earth signs. If you understand that Earth is more than just a physical element, that it is a psychological attitude as well, you will get a better understanding of the Taurus personality.

A Taurus has all the power of action that an Aries has. But Taurus is not satisfied with action for its own sake. Their actions must be productive, practical and wealth-producing. If Taurus cannot see a practical value in an action they will not bother taking it.

Taurus's forte lies in their power to make real their own or other people's ideas. They are generally not very inventive but they can take another's invention and perfect it, making it more practical and useful. The same is true for all projects. Taurus is not especially keen on starting new projects, but once they get involved they bring things to completion. Taurus carries everything through. They are finishers and will go the distance, so long as no unavoidable calamity intervenes.

Many people find Taurus too stubborn, conservative, fixed and immovable. This is understandable, because Taurus dislikes change – in the environment or in their routine. They even dislike changing their minds! On the other hand, this is their virtue. It is not good for a wheel's axle to waver. The axle must be fixed, stable and unmovable. Taurus is the axle of society and the heavens. Without their stability and so-called stubbornness, the wheels of the world (and especially the wheels of commerce) would not turn.

Taurus loves routine. A routine, if it is good, has many virtues. It is a fixed – and, ideally, perfect – way of taking care of things. Mistakes can happen when spontaneity comes into the equation, and mistakes cause discomfort and uneasiness – something almost unacceptable to a Taurus. Meddling with Taurus's comfort and security is a sure way to irritate and anger them.

While an Aries loves speed, a Taurus likes things slow. They are slow thinkers – but do not make the mistake of assuming they lack intelligence. On the contrary, Taurus people are very intelligent. It is just that they like to chew on ideas, to deliberate and weigh them up.

Only after due deliberation is an idea accepted or a decision taken. Taurus is slow to anger – but once aroused, take care!

Finance

Taurus is very money-conscious. Wealth is more important to them than to many other signs. Wealth to a Taurus means comfort and security. Wealth means stability. Where some zodiac signs feel that they are spiritually rich if they have ideas, talents or skills, Taurus only feels wealth when they can see and touch it. Taurus's way of thinking is, 'What good is a talent if it has not been translated into a home, furniture, car and holidays?'

These are all reasons why Taurus excels in estate agency and agricultural industries. Usually a Taurus will end up owning land. They love to feel their connection to the Earth. Material wealth began with agriculture, the tilling of the soil. Owning a piece of land was humanity's earliest form of wealth: Taurus still feels that primeval connection.

It is in the pursuit of wealth that Taurus develops intellectual and communication ability. Also, in this pursuit Taurus is forced to develop some flexibility. It is in the quest for wealth that they learn the practical value of the intellect and come to admire it. If it were not for the search for wealth and material things, Taurus people might not try to reach a higher intellect.

Some Taurus people are 'born lucky' – the type who win any gamble or speculation. This luck is due to other factors in their Horoscope; it is not part of their essential nature. By nature they are not gamblers. They are hard workers and like to earn what they get. Taurus's innate conservatism makes them abhor unnecessary risks in finance and in other areas of their lives.

Career and Public Image

Being essentially down-to-earth people, simple and uncomplicated, Taurus tends to look up to those who are original, unconventional and inventive. Taurus people like their bosses to be creative and original – since they themselves are content to perfect their superiors' brainwaves. They admire people who have a wider social or political consciousness and they feel that someday (when they have all the comfort and security they need) they too would like to be involved in these big issues.

In business affairs Taurus can be very shrewd – and that makes them valuable to their employers. They are never lazy; they enjoy working and getting good results. Taurus does not like taking unnecessary risks and they do well in positions of authority, which makes them good managers and supervisors. Their managerial skills are reinforced by their natural talents for organization and handling details, their patience and thoroughness. As mentioned, through their connection with the earth, Taurus people also do well in farming and agriculture.

In general a Taurus will choose money and earning power over public esteem and prestige. A position that pays more – though it has less prestige – is preferred to a position with a lot of prestige but lower earnings. Many other signs do not feel this way, but a Taurus does, especially if there is nothing in his or her personal birth chart that modifies this. Taurus will pursue glory and prestige only if it can be shown that these things have a direct and immediate impact on their wallet.

Love and Relationships

In love, the Taurus-born likes to have and to hold. They are the marrying kind. They like commitment and they like the terms of a relationship to be clearly defined. More importantly, Taurus likes to be faithful to one lover, and they expect that lover to reciprocate this fidelity. When this doesn't happen, their whole world comes crashing down. When they are in love Taurus people are loyal, but they are also very possessive. They are capable of great fits of jealousy if they are hurt in love.

Taurus is satisfied with the simple things in a relationship. If you are involved romantically with a Taurus there is no need for lavish entertainments and constant courtship. Give them enough love, food and comfortable shelter and they will be quite content to stay home and enjoy your company. They will be loyal to you for life. Make a Taurus feel comfortable and – above all – secure in the relationship, and you will rarely have a problem.

In love, Taurus can sometimes make the mistake of trying to control their partners, which can cause great pain on both sides. The reasoning behind their actions is basically simple: Taurus people feel a sense of ownership over their partners and will want to make changes that will increase their own general comfort and security. This attitude is OK when it comes to inanimate, material things – but is dangerous when applied to people. Taurus needs to be careful and attentive to this possible trait within themselves.

Home and Domestic Life

Home and family are vitally important to Taurus. They like children. They also like a comfortable and perhaps glamorous home – something they can show off. They tend to buy heavy, ponderous furniture – usually of the best quality. This is because Taurus likes a feeling of substance in their environment. Their house is not only their home but their place of creativity and entertainment. The Taurus's home tends to be truly their castle. If they could choose, Taurus people would prefer living in the countryside to being city-dwellers. If they cannot do so during their working lives, many Taurus individuals like to holiday in or even retire to the country, away from the city and closer to the land.

At home a Taurus is like a country squire – lord (or lady) of the manor. They love to entertain lavishly, to make others feel secure in their home and to encourage others to derive the same sense of satisfaction as they do from it. If you are invited for dinner at the home of a Taurus you can expect the best food and the best entertainment. Be prepared for a tour of the house and expect to see your Taurus friend exhibit a lot of pride and satisfaction in his or her possessions.

Taurus people like children but they are usually strict with them. The reason for this is they tend to treat their children – as they do most things in life – as their possessions. The positive side to this is that their children will be well cared for and well supervised. They will get every material thing they need to grow up properly. On the down side, Taurus can get too repressive with their children. If a child dares to upset the daily routine – which Taurus loves to follow – he or she will have a problem with a Taurus parent.

Horoscope for 2016

Major Trends

Last year, as Saturn left your 7th house, the love and social life turned around. For some years – especially in 2013 and 2014 – it was severely tested. Many a Taurus got divorced – a traumatic experience for anyone, but especially for a Taurus. Good relationships survived, but it wasn't easy. Happily things are much better now. Last year, on August 12, Jupiter moved into Virgo and started to make harmonious aspects to your love planet, Pluto. This aspect is still in effect until September 9. More on this later.

Uranus has been in your 12th house for many years now. Thus spirituality has become very important in your life. In many cases, Taurus, you are opting for a spiritual career. Others are making it a priority in their lives. This trend continues in the year ahead.

Pluto has been in your 9th house for many years. This shows a death and rebirth of your philosophical and religious beliefs. Many are dying and many are being reborn in a new form. The belief system is an ultra-important part of life, too often ignored by the psychological community. But it influences every area of life. Changes here change the life.

Jupiter spends most of the year in your 5th house. This makes Taureans of childbearing age much more fertile than usual. This aspect also tends to involvement with children in general – your own or other people's. It's a fun kind of period. A party period.

Jupiter moves into your 6th house on September 10. This is an excellent aspect for job seekers and for those who employ others. Even if you're currently employed, many happy job opportunities will start to happen.

Saturn moved into your 8th house of transformation late in 2014 and will be there for all of the year ahead. This suggests a need to tone down the sexual expression. A need to focus on quality rather than quantity.

Your most important interests in the year ahead are: children, fun and creativity (until September 9); health and work (from September 10 onwards); personal transformation and reinvention, sex, occult studies, taxes and estates; religion, philosophy, higher education and foreign travel; friends, groups and group activities; and spirituality.

Your paths of greatest fulfilment this year are children, fun and creativity; and health and work (from September 10 onwards).

Health

(Please note that this is an astrological perspective on health and not a medical one. In days of yore there was no difference, these perspectives were identical. But now there could be quite a difference. For a medical perspective, please consult your doctor or health practitioner.)

Now that Saturn has left his stressful aspect with you (which he did late in 2014) your overall health and energy are super. All the long-term planets are either in harmonious aspect with you or leaving you alone. Health should be wonderful this year. If you have pre-existing conditions, you should see improvement with them.

Of course, as our regular readers know, there will be periods in the year where health is less easy than usual, perhaps even stressful, but these are temporary things caused by the planetary transits and not trends for the year. When the difficult transits pass, normal good health and energy return.

Health doesn't even seem a major concern until September 10. The 6th house of health and work is empty for the most part and you sort of take good health for granted. After that date, Jupiter moves into your 6th house and gives greater focus here. But it seems to me that the focus will be more on work than on health. Perhaps you're getting involved in a healthier lifestyle, but not much more than that.

Good though your health is you can make it even better. Give more attention to the following – the vulnerable areas of your Horoscope (the reflexology points for these areas are shown in the following chart):

- The neck and throat. These are always important for Taurus. Regular neck massage will do wonders for you, and craniosacral therapy is also good for the neck.
- The kidneys and hips. These areas are also always important for Taurus. The hips should be regularly massaged. Regular herbal kidney cleanses are also beneficial.

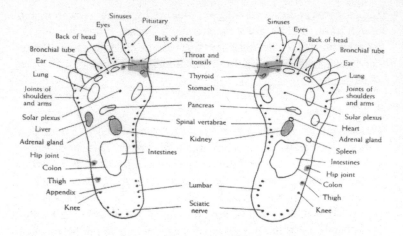

Important foot reflexology points for the year ahead

Try to massage all of the foot on a regular basis – the top of the foot as well as the bottom – but pay extra attention to the points highlighted on the chart. When you massage, be aware of 'sore spots' as these need special attention. It's also a good idea to massage the ankles and below them.

- The liver and thighs. These only become important from September 10 onwards. Thighs should be regularly massaged and a herbal liver cleanse or detox might also be a good idea.

Jupiter rules your 8th house of transformation, and his presence in your house of health from September 10 onwards suggests that detox regimes will be helpful after that date. It also indicates the importance of safe sex and sexual moderation.

Venus is your health planet. She is a fast-moving planet and every month she will be in a different sign and will receive different aspects. Thus there are many short-term trends in health, depending on her condition. These trends are best dealt with in the monthly reports.

Home and Family

Your 4th house of home and family has been strong for the past two years, but not this year. Many of you have moved or made any renovations that needed to be made. This year you can coast. You seem satisfied with the status quo and have no need to make major changes. There's nothing in the cosmos against it, by the way – just no compelling urge.

Jupiter has been in your 5th house since August 2015, and will remain there for the first half of this year. This indicates enhanced fertility for Taureans of childbearing age. Pregnancy wouldn't be a surprise.

We have two solar eclipses this year. One on March 9 and the other on September 1. Since the Sun is your family planet, these eclipses will affect the home and family situation. Generally, these are the times when we discover any hidden flaws in the home. Often repairs are needed. Family members will tend to be more temperamental during those periods too – so more patience is needed with them.

A parent or parent figure in your life is prospering this year. He or she is likely to be more generous with you. This same parent figure could be having a surgical procedure this year.

Children and children figures are prospering, and siblings or sibling figures in your life are likely to move or renovate their homes in the coming year – mostly likely from September 10 onwards. (It could happen in the first half of 2017 as well.) If they are of childbearing age, the women are more fertile. The family circle will get enlarged through birth or marriage.

Children and children figures in your life may want to move – they feel cramped where they are – but it is not advisable this year. They are better off making better use of the space that they already have. Grandchildren have a stable, static domestic year.

Siblings and sibling figures seem burdened by health issues. They can improve their health by paying more attention to the liver, thighs, spine, knees, teeth and bones. They need a daily disciplined health regime. Children and children figures can benefit from head and face massage.

If you are repainting, decorating or beautifying the home, July 12 to August 22 is a good time. This is also a good time if you're buying art objects for the home.

Though there doesn't seem to be a need for major renovations this year, if you choose to do these things (this is free will on your part) March 1–6, April 21–May 20 and July 22–August 22 are good times to do them.

Finance and Career

Taureans are always interested in money – it is basic to their nature – but this year less so than usual. It's merely a question of intensity. Some years are like that.

I read this as a very good signal. You are basically prosperous and content with things as they are. You have no need to pay too much attention here. However, should financial difficulties arise (and this is not likely until after September 10) the solution is to start paying more attention to this area of your life.

This is a prosperous year. Jupiter in the sign of Virgo is making fabulous aspects to your Sun, which is a classic indicator of prosperity and overall success. This aspect gives optimism and the feeling of good fortune. You catch the lucky breaks in life.

Jupiter in your 5th house for the first half of the year gives luck in speculations. If guided by intuition it might be a good idea to invest harmless sums on the lottery or some other kind of speculation. Prosperity need not happen this way – a person needs the right natal chart for this – but it is one of the avenues the cosmos can use.

A parent figure prospers and is more generous with you. There is good family support.

Jupiter is the ruler of your 8th house of transformation, and this gives many messages. There is good fortune with estates, taxes and insurance claims. There is good spousal support. It is easier to borrow and your line of credit is probably increased. Outside investors are easier to attract if you need them.

As we mentioned earlier, Jupiter will enter your 6th house on September 10, bringing very happy job opportunities to you. You're a hot commodity from September 10 onwards.

Career doesn't seem much of a focus this year, not the way it usually is. Your 10th house of career is empty with only short-term planets transiting through there. This is more of a party year than a career year.

I read this too as a good sign. You're basically content with the status quo and have no need for dramatic change. It will be a stable kind of year.

Your career planet, Uranus, has been in your spiritual 12th house for many years now. A strictly worldly kind of career is not appealing these days. You need something that is meaningful, something that benefits all of humanity, something idealistic. This aspect is excellent for careers in the non-profit world, with organizations dedicated to causes or charities. It also shows that even if you are in a worldly kind of career, being involved with charities and causes would advance your status. Bosses and superiors would make note of this. Important connections can be made in these kinds of activities.

With Uranus as the career planet, you need a career that offers much change and variety. It favours a freelance type of career. Also, your technological expertise is very important here. You need to stay up to date.

Love and Social Life

When Saturn left your 7th house late in 2014 a dark cloud lifted off you. The love life had not been happy. Marriages and serious relationships were tested, and many dissolved. The first half of 2014 was very serious in this regard.

Jupiter's move into Virgo last year was also a big help as he started making nice aspects to your love planet, Pluto. Right now – especially until September 9 – you are in a great love and social period. After a few years of stress and testing, you're a better person and more able to handle relationships.

The good thing about stress is that it reveals inherent flaws – both personal and in a relationship. Thus, it is easier to correct these flaws. Relationships that survived the past few years are good and will probably last for ever.

Love is happening now, but there's no need to rush into marriage. Take your time. Next year is much better for marriage than now.

Your love planet, Pluto, rules sex, among other things. Thus the sexual magnetism is the primary turn-on in love. There's nothing wrong with this, but sometimes people make too much of it. By itself, sex is not enough to hold a relationship together. (Many of you learned this over the past few years.)

Pluto rules your love life from the sign of Capricorn. This shows a practical approach to love. You like the good provider, the person of status, the person who can help your career. Also it shows more caution in love. You are slower to fall in love now than before 2008, when Pluto was in Sagittarius. You've become more careful.

Pluto will remain in your 9th house for many years to come. This is good. It shows that besides the sexual magnetism you like someone educated and refined. You like people you can learn from – mentor types. You like people who share your philosophical and religious beliefs. Philosophical differences will eventually sink even the best of sexual chemistries. Good sexual chemistry has a lifespan of about a year. But if there is also philosophical harmony, the relationship can last much longer – even for ever.

Love opportunities happen in religious or educational-type settings these days, at religious or university functions and through the introduction of people you worship with or attend school with. Foreign countries can also be the venue for romance these days. Foreigners are alluring – and the more exotic the better.

The love aspects are especially good for those working on the first or second marriage. For those working on the third marriage, this is a status quo kind of year. Next year will be a lot better.

Self-improvement

Your spiritual life has been important for some years now. Your career planet Uranus is in your spiritual 12th house and in many cases Taureans are opting for a spiritual-type career, working to balance that with the normal material concerns. In other cases, the spiritual life, the spiritual practice *is* the career. It *is* the most important thing these days, the mission in life.

Uranus in the 12th house shows much change, fermentation and experimentation in the spiritual life. Many are running from one teaching to the next, from one teacher to the next, from one practice to the next in search of the path that works for them. The danger here is 'faddishness'. It is great to be experimental and to try out different things, but more homework should be done. The fact that something is new and hot – popular – doesn't necessarily mean that it is good. This kind of attitude can set back your spiritual progress for years. On the other hand, experimentation often leads to new knowledge and insight. It's a mixed blessing.

Uranus in your 12th house suggests that you benefit most from a scientific approach to the spiritual practice. There is a deep and beautiful science behind all these strange and mysterious practices and teachings. It is good to understand this as it will enhance both your faith and your practice. Faith is very important in spiritual practice, and when it is bolstered by scientific understanding the practice will go better. Taureans are down-to-earth, practical people. So, letting go of evidence-before-your-eyes-based thinking and ideas is quite a challenge. This is another reason why the scientific approach will help you.

Uranus in the 12th house brings much ferment and change on its own. But this year, your spiritual planet, Mars, is more erratic in his motion than normal. He will be retrograde (which only happens once every two years) from April 17 to June 29. Then, for almost three months, from August 9 to October 30 he will be 'out of bounds'. The retrograde period of Mars will be good for reviewing your spiritual life and seeing where improvements can be made. Intuitions and dreams need more time to be deciphered and digested. Intuition needs more verification during this period. When Mars is 'out of bounds' it shows that you're going outside your normal sphere in search for spiritual truths. You're moving outside your 'box'.

With all this upheaval going on it is good that Neptune is in your 11th house of friends. This shows that you're attracting spiritual kinds of friends – and you need this now – to keep your practice stable.

All this spiritual activity and growth is challenging your personal religion and philosophy of life. This whole area is getting reformed. It is dying and will be reborn in a new and better form. It is wonderful when old and false beliefs die. These have been the cause of many of your problems. But, good though it is, it's not that pleasant while it's happening.

Month-by-month Forecasts

January

Best Days Overall: 9, 10, 17, 18, 26, 27
Most Stressful Days Overall: 4, 5, 11, 12, 24, 25, 31
Best Days for Love: 4, 5, 6, 7, 8, 9, 10, 15, 16, 17, 18, 26, 27, 31
Best Days for Money: 9, 10, 17, 18, 19, 20, 26, 27
Best Days for Career: 6, 7, 11, 12, 15, 16, 24, 25

You begin your year on a happy and successful note. Overall health looks excellent. The large number of Earth signs in your Horoscope sits well with you and plays into your comfort zone. It promotes prosperity too.

The planetary power is 80 per cent (and sometimes 90 per cent) above the horizon. The power is in the upper half of your chart. On the 20th, as the Sun crosses the Mid-heaven and enters your 10th house, you enter a yearly career peak. The focus is on the career – your outer world objectives – as it should be. Family is important, but they are supporting the career too. Your family could be more ambitious for you than you are for yourself. Both you and the family as a whole are successful this month. Your overall status is elevated. Happy career opportunities come and it looks like they are through family or family connections.

Finances are good, but they are more complicated this month than last. Your financial planet Mercury is retrograde from the 5th to the 25th. This will not affect the overall prosperity that you're having this year, but it slows things down a bit. Glitches and delays – some not your fault – are more likely to occur and your financial judgement might not be up to its usually high standard. Thus it is better to make important purchases or financial decisions before the 5th or after the 25th. During the retrograde period work to attain mental clarity on your finances. Resolve doubts and do more research. In addition, be more careful in how you communicate with superiors or authority figures (or the government) from the 5th to the 9th. Make sure you understand what's being said – sometimes they like to speak in jargon or vague generalities. Ask questions. Say what you mean and make sure as much as possible that your listener understood your message as you intended. Mis-communication is probably the greatest career danger right now. Be especially mindful how you communicate about finances.

The Western, social sector of your chart is still the most powerful for now, although this will change next month. But for this month you're still in a strong social cycle. Others come first. Your good happens through others and through their favour, so your social skills are more important than your innate abilities.

Mars moves into your 7th house of love on the 4th and spends the rest of the month there. This signals a socially active kind of month. You seem more aggressive in the pursuit of love. You're attracting spiritual-type people into your life. On the 5th and 6th there is a happy romantic or social opportunity through the family or family connections.

Make sure to get enough rest from the 20th onwards.

February

Best Days Overall: 5, 6, 13, 14, 22, 23, 24
Most Stressful Days Overall: 1, 7, 8, 20, 21, 27, 28, 29
Best Days for Love: 1, 5, 6, 13, 14, 22, 23, 25, 27, 28, 29
Best Days for Money: 5, 6, 13, 14, 15, 16, 17, 22, 23, 24, 25, 26
Best Days for Career: 2, 3, 7, 8, 11, 12, 20, 29

Health became more delicate on January 20 and needs some attention being paid to it this month – until the 19th. This, however, is a short-term problem and isn't the trend for the year ahead. The most important thing is to maintain high energy levels. You're busy and successful, but don't overwork. Enhance the health further by paying more attention to the spine, knees, teeth, bones, skin and overall skeletal alignment until the 17th. A back massage or a visit to the chiropractor or osteopath might be just what you need if you feel under the weather. When overall energy is not at its optimum, pre-existing conditions tend to flare up. There is no need to be overly concerned; more rest will most likely bring relief. Detox regimes are powerful from the 5th to the 8th. After the 17th give more attention to the ankles and calves. Massage them regularly.

Unnecessary foreign travel should be avoided from the 1st to the 5th. Students at college or post-graduate level can have dramas at school and perhaps make changes to educational plans.

Finances are much better this month than last. Mercury moves forward and there is more financial clarity and confidence. Until the 14th it is good to set up savings and investment plans – ways to achieve long-term financial goals. There is financial opportunity in foreign lands and with foreign companies. Foreigners in general can be important on the financial level. The 5th to the 7th brings a nice payday, as your financial planet makes wonderful aspects to Jupiter.

There is a sudden, unexpected romantic or social opportunity from the 5th to the 8th. The 9th to the 11th brings sexual opportunity. Your spiritual planet, Mars, is still in the 7th house of love this month. Again, you're attracting spiritual-type people into your life. Spiritual compatibility is perhaps just as important as physical chemistry these days.

Family members (and especially a parent or parent figure) are more idealistic on the 28th and 29th – and perhaps even before that. This is a good time to install high tech equipment in the home and to build team spirit in the family.

You're still in a period of career success this month – a yearly career peak. Venus, the ruler of your Horoscope, enters your 10th house on the 17th. You are personally elevated and seem above everyone in your world. Pay rises are likely from the 14th onwards, and you have the financial favour of bosses, elders and authority figures.

March

Best Days Overall: 3, 4, 12, 13, 21, 22, 31
Most Stressful Days Overall: 6, 7, 18, 19, 26, 27
Best Days for Love: 3, 4, 6, 7, 12, 13, 16, 21, 22, 26, 27, 31
Best Days for Money: 3, 4, 8, 12, 13, 14, 15, 16, 17, 21, 22, 28, 29, 31
Best Days for Career: 1, 2, 6, 7, 10, 11, 18, 19, 28, 29

Though two eclipses this month shake up the world and people around you, for you the month ahead looks happy and successful.

When Mars leaves his stressful aspect on the 6th there are no long-term planets in stressful alignment with you. Venus, a short-term planet, will move away from her stressful aspect on the 12th. The Moon will occasionally make stressful aspects – and we list them above – but that's about it. This shows good health and abundant energy. You have the energy to achieve whatever you set your mind to. Pre-existing conditions should be much improved too. You naturally have more energy and these conditions die back down. You can enhance the health even further by giving more attention to the ankles and calves until the 12th, and to the feet from the 12th onwards.

Career is still happy and you still seem on top of your world. But the focus this month is more on friends, groups and group activities. (This has been the case since February 19.) Though there is romance this month – especially from the 12th to the 20th – this is not the main focus. It is more about friendship, mixing with people of like mind and like interests. The month ahead is also very spiritual. The Sun is in spiritual Pisces until the 20th and then it enters your 12th house. Spiritual studies and spiritual practice go well.

The solar eclipse of the 9th (in America it is on the 8th) occurs in your 11th house. This tends to test friendships. Often it indicates important dramas in the lives of friends. Every solar eclipse affects the home and family. Family members tend to be more temperamental at this time so be more patient. It can bring dramas in their lives and the life of a parent or parent figure. Often flaws in the home are revealed and repairs have to be made.

The lunar eclipse of the 23rd occurs in your 6th house of health and work. Thus there can be job changes or changes in the job environment. If you employ others there is instability with them. Siblings and sibling figures in your life are having dramas – neighbours as well. Often under this aspect the neighbourhood gets renovated. Cars and communication equipment get tested too.

April

Best Days Overall: 1, 8, 9, 17, 18, 27, 28
Most Stressful Days Overall: 2, 3, 14, 15, 16, 22, 23, 29, 30
Best Days for Love: 6, 14, 15, 22, 23, 25, 26
Best Days for Money: 1, 8, 9, 10, 11, 17, 18, 27, 28
Best Days for Career: 2, 3, 6, 7, 14, 15, 16, 24, 25, 26, 29, 30

The planetary power is now moving towards you, to the Eastern sector of your chart. This shift began in February and is now much stronger. Though the Western social sector of your chart is still powerful – there will always be at least 40 per cent of the planets there – the Eastern sector has, for now, become slightly more dominant. You are in (and next month too) the height of your personal power for the year. Certainly there were years where personal power was stronger than now, but we're talking about the current year. It is easier now to create the conditions that please you. Though other people are very important in your life, you're less dependent on them than usual. Use the energy to create your personal happiness. A few months down the road it will be more difficult to do this.

The spiritual life is the main headline this month. Last month was spiritual and so is the month ahead, until the 19th. This is a period for internal growth. This type of growth is not seen by the senses but it is very real. Later this month – and next – it will reveal itself by your outward actions. Ever since Uranus moved into your 12th house, spirituality has been important, and these days even more so. This is a wonderful period for spiritual studies – the study of sacred literature – and practice. It is a period for transcending physical conditions, rising above physical limitations. A period for spiritual breakthroughs, enhanced extrasensory perception and a super-active dream life.

The interesting thing is that as you focus on your study and practice, very happy career opportunities come to you naturally and effortlessly. The month ahead is successful both spiritually and in a worldly kind of way.

Health and energy are good all month but especially after the 19th. The Sun crosses your Ascendant then and enters the 1st house. This is one of your yearly personal pleasure peaks. A time for getting the body and image in right shape and for enjoying all the physical delights.

There is prosperity this month too. On the 6th your financial planet Mercury crosses the Ascendant and enters your 1st house. This brings financial windfalls and opportunity. It is as if money is chasing you rather than vice versa. Personal appearance is a big factor in your earnings. It is a good month to spend on yourself, on clothing and accessories. Right now, you're the best investment there is.

The love life sparkles this month as well. Your love planet is part of a beautiful Grand Trine in Earth. Only keep in mind that Pluto starts to retrograde on the 18th – no need to rush into anything too serious just yet.

May

Best Days Overall: 6, 14, 15, 24, 25
Most Stressful Days Overall: 12, 13, 19, 20, 21, 27, 28
Best Days for Love: 6, 14, 15, 19, 20, 21, 24, 25, 26, 27
Best Days for Money: 6, 7, 8, 14, 15, 24, 25
Best Days for Career: 4, 5, 12, 13, 22, 23, 27, 28, 31

Another happy and successful month for Taurus. Enjoy!

Many of the trends that we wrote of last month are still in effect. You're still in a yearly personal pleasure peak, enjoying all the physical delights. And, with Mercury in your 1st house, you have the wherewithal to indulge yourself.

You look great. You have energy, charisma, sparkle and star quality. The opposite sex certainly takes notice. Venus is in your sign until the 24th. This gives beauty and style to the image. The personality is more graceful and pleasing. Last month was good for buying clothing and accessories, but this month – until the 24th – is even better. If you need to take or submit photographs of yourself for business or personal reasons, this is an excellent time to do so.

Like last month you're in a period of maximum personal power and independence. So, if conditions displease you, change them. Take the bull by the horns and create your own happiness. (Later on it will be more difficult to do.)

Like last month there is a beautiful Grand Trine in Earth – your own natural element – all month. This is comfortable for you and you feel very at home. This Grand Trine involves important planets: Venus, the ruler of your chart; Mercury, your financial planet; and Pluto, your love planet. This spells love and money. Romance is good all month. Singles have no problem attracting the opposite sex, and those already in a relationship are enjoying more harmony, more romance, within that relationship. The 13th and 14th are especially good for love. Singles are meeting significant people.

Prosperity – always important to a Taurus – is very strong all month. Mercury, as we mentioned, is part of a Grand Trine in Earth. Mercury spends the entire month in your sign. Thus windfalls and financial opportunities are seeking you out. You just have to show up. You're spending on yourself and giving the impression of wealth. People see you as prosperous. The only complication is Mercury's retrograde motion until May 22, which slows things down a bit. 'Gift horses' need more scrutiny and might not be all that they seem to be. Don't make important financial decisions until after the 22nd. On the 20th the Sun enters your money house and you enter a period of peak earnings.

June

Best Days Overall: 2, 3, 10, 11, 12, 20, 21, 22, 29, 30
Most Stressful Days Overall: 8, 9, 15, 16, 17, 23, 24
Best Days for Love: 2, 3, 4, 5, 10, 11, 14, 15, 16, 17, 20, 21, 25, 26, 29, 30
Best Days for Money: 2, 3, 4, 5, 10, 11, 12, 13, 20, 21, 23, 24, 29, 30
Best Days for Career: 1, 8, 9, 18, 19, 23, 24, 27, 28

Health was great last month and is still good in the month ahead. The Grand Trine in Earth is still in effect until the 13th. You can enhance your health even further by giving more attention to the lungs, arms and shoulders until the 18th. Tension in the shoulders should be released – massage, acupuncture or acupressure are very good for this. After the 18th make sure to eat right. Pay more attention to the stomach and breasts (for women). Mood control – good emotional health – is important after the 18th.

You're still in a strong prosperity period – a yearly financial peak. This will go on all month, even after the Sun leaves the money house, because your financial planet, Mercury, enters the money house on the 13th and stays there for the rest of the month. Good sales and marketing – good PR – is always important for you, but these days more so than usual. This is an excellent month for launching an ad or PR campaign. It is also a prosperous month for teachers, writers and journalists. Students, below college level, seem successful in their studies.

Finance is more of a priority than love this month and the love life could suffer because of it. Avoid power struggles in love, especially after the 18th – there is no need to make things worse. After the 18th you seem more distant from the beloved. You seem on opposite ends of the spectrum, seeing things in opposite ways. If you can overcome these differences romance can bloom.

Be more patient with family members on the 8th, 9th, 23rd and 24th – they seem more temperamental. It won't hurt to stay out of harm's way on the 8th and 9th either. There's no need for stressful kinds of activities; spend more quiet time at home instead.

A financial disturbance on the 23rd or 24th is short lived but it forces some needed changes. Avoid over-spending on those days.

On the 21st your 3rd house of communication and intellectual interests becomes strong. This is a good time to take courses in subjects that interest you, to read the books and magazines that you've wanted to read, and to catch up on the phone calls and emails you owe. Your financial goals are mostly achieved and you have the freedom to indulge your intellectual interests.

July

Best Days Overall: 8, 9, 18, 19, 27, 28
Most Stressful Days Overall: 6, 7, 13, 14, 20, 21
Best Days for Love: 3, 4, 8, 9, 13, 14, 15, 18, 19, 24, 25, 27, 28
Best Days for Money: 1, 2, 3, 4, 8, 9, 14, 15, 18, 19, 24, 25, 27, 28, 29, 30
Best Days for Career: 6, 7, 15, 16, 20, 21, 24, 25

The lower and upper half of your Horoscope has been basically in balance since May. Neither one half nor the other dominates. I read this as someone who is balancing the needs of the home and family with the demands of the career – someone who wants both a successful career and a good domestic life. This is not so easy to do, but this month, especially after the 22nd, you seem to manage it. There is happiness at home and happiness in the career. One supports the other.

Finances are good this month, but less of an interest than in the past two months. Your financial planet, Mercury, behaves strangely this month and this will reflect on your financial life. From the 1st to the 9th he is 'out of bounds' – thus you're going outside your normal sphere in search for earnings. There is a need to do unorthodox things. On the 1st and 2nd Mercury transits an eclipse point, provoking a short-term disturbance that perhaps causes you to do unorthodox things. On the 7th Mercury squares Pluto, your love planet. There is some financial disagreement with the beloved. On the 10th and 11th Mercury squares Uranus, causing more changes and perhaps an unexpected expense. So there's a lot of financial excitement this month. You'll get through it, though. There's good family support from the 14th onwards, and on the 26th and 27th there is good financial support from a parent, parent figure or boss.

Be more patient with the beloved on the 1st. Stay out of harm's way on the 6th and 7th and be more patient with bosses, parents and parent figures in your life.

Health needs watching from the 22nd onwards. However, any problems don't seem serious and appear to be of a short-term nature. Sometimes when people schedule scans or blood tests during these times they can test falsely positive. This is because the energy level is lower than normal and the body reflects this. Take the same test when your energy is high and the result is negative. As always, make sure you get enough rest and maintain high energy levels. If pre-existing conditions seem to act up, there is no need to be unduly alarmed. Low energy is most likely the cause and the solution is more rest. Health can be enhanced in the ways mentioned in the yearly report, but also by eating well and giving more attention to the stomach and breasts – until the 13th. After the 13th give more attention to the heart. Avoid worry and anxiety.

Neptune spends the month conjunct to the south node of the Moon. This indicates a lot of drama in the lives of friends. It could also make you feel 'deficiency' in friendships.

August

Best Days Overall: 4, 5, 14, 15, 23, 24, 31
Most Stressful Days Overall: 2, 3, 9, 10, 16, 17, 18, 29, 30
Best Days for Love: 3, 4, 5, 9, 10, 14, 15, 23, 24, 31
Best Days for Money: 4, 5, 14, 15, 23, 24, 25, 26, 31
Best Days for Career: 2, 3, 12, 13, 16, 17, 18, 21, 22, 29, 30

Your 4th house of home and family became powerful last month and is still strong until the 22nd of this month. So this is a time to get the home and family life in right order. Like last month you're doing a great job in balancing home and career and making a success of both.

This is a period for making psychological-type breakthroughs. Your understanding of your moods and feelings – and those of others – is increased. Those of you involved in psychological therapies make good progress. It is normal to feel nostalgic, to remember the 'good old' or 'bad old' days. It is normal to be more interested in history too. When the 4th house is strong, the past calls to us. It has lessons to teach us and this is a time to learn them.

Last month, on the 22nd, the planetary power shifted to the Western, social sector of your chart. The planetary power moves away from you and towards others. Personal power is lessened because less is needed. Your good comes through other people and their good graces now, not because of your innate abilities or through personal initiative. Your social graces are the important thing now. Let others have their way – so long as it isn't destructive – and your own good will follow naturally. It is now more difficult to create the conditions you desire. You can, of course, but it will take greater effort. Now, it is better to live with the conditions you created in the past few months and make the best of them. If you have built well, life is pleasant. If there are flaws in your creation, take note and when the planetary power shifts back to the Eastern sector next year, you'll be able to make the changes that need to be made.

On the 22nd the Sun enters your 5th house and you begin another of your yearly personal pleasure peaks. This is party time. A time to enjoy life, a time for more leisure and recreation. You've been having fun the whole year, but this month even more so. With your financial planet also in the 5th house all month, you have the wherewithal to enjoy yourself. In fact, happy financial opportunities will come as you enjoy your life. Perhaps you meet an important contact at the golf course or theatre, or at a resort.

Children and children figures in your life are prospering and seem supportive. If they are very young, they motivate you financially. Speculations are favourable until the 30th. Avoid them afterwards. There are nice paydays from the 20th to the 24th and from the 26th to the 28th.

Health is greatly improved after the 22nd. The Earth element is strong this month from the 22nd onwards and this is comfortable for you. Love is much happier than last month – especially from the 5th onwards.

September

Best Days Overall: 1, 2, 10, 11, 12, 19, 20, 28, 29
Most Stressful Days Overall: 5, 6, 7, 13, 14, 25, 26, 27
Best Days for Love: 1, 2, 3, 4, 5, 6, 7, 10, 11, 13, 14, 19, 20, 23, 28, 29
Best Days for Money: 1, 2, 10, 11, 12, 13, 19, 20, 21, 22, 28, 29
Best Days for Career: 8, 9, 13, 14, 17, 18, 25, 26, 27

With two eclipses happening, the month ahead is turbulent and eventful. Aside from the eclipses, Jupiter makes a major move this month from your 5th house to your 6th house of health and work on the 10th. The party is winding down; it is time to focus on your work, on being productive for others. It's like going from being the playboy or playgirl to being the servant. A shift in psychology.

Service, say the sages, is love in action. There are other, hidden, pleasures in productive work and serving others that are not found in the theatre or night club. This is a time (and it continues well into next year) where you explore this.

Jupiter's move into your 6th house is great news for job seekers. A dream job awaits you. It's not going to be 'just another job', but something really wonderful. Even those of you who are already employed will have new and better job opportunities coming. Jupiter is going to show you how to be more productive in your work. Generally new technology or systems come that do this.

The solar eclipse of the 1st occurs in your 5th house and impacts on children or children figures in your life. They experience life-changing kinds of dramas. Sometimes they are quite normal - like sexual awakening, or graduation - but these are still life changing. Good to keep them out of harm's way during the eclipse period. Those of you in the creative arts make important changes to your creative work. Family members tend to be more temperamental during a solar eclipse and need more patience. There can be dramas in the home, with family members and with a parent or parent figure. Flaws in the home are often revealed under this kind of eclipse and often repairs are needed. This eclipse impacts on two other planets - Mars and Saturn. It is always a good idea to reduce your schedule during an eclipse period, but with the ruler of the 8th house involved it becomes even more important. This can bring encounters with death - not literal death but close calls or brushes with it. Many of you will have dreams of death during this period too. This is just a gentle reminder that life, here on earth, is short and it is time to get serious and do our job. With Saturn involved in the eclipse, foreign travel is best avoided - reschedule trips for a better time if you can. Students at college or post-graduate level make important changes in their educational plans.

The lunar eclipse of 16th occurs in your 11th house. This creates disturbances in professional organizations you're involved with. It will also test your high tech and phone equipment. Make sure important files are backed up and that your anti-virus, anti-phishing software is up to date. Cars will also get tested during this period.

October

Best Days Overall: 8, 9, 17, 25, 26
Most Stressful Days Overall: 3, 4, 10, 11, 23, 24, 30, 31
Best Days for Love: 3, 4, 8, 9, 12, 13, 17, 23, 24, 25, 26, 30, 31
Best Days for Money: 1, 10, 18, 19, 20, 27, 28, 30
Best Days for Career: 5, 6, 7, 10, 11, 15, 23, 24

Most of the planets are still in the social Western sector, and Venus (a very important planet in your chart) is in your 7th house of love until the 18th. So, you're right in tune with the stars. You're putting others first, you're there for your friends and the current love. You're basking in social popularity. This is a very nice month for love. On the 23rd the Sun moves into your 7th house and you enter a yearly love and social peak. A very active social month.

All of you seem more aggressive in love these days. You're not waiting for the phone to ring but are proactively shaping and creating the social life that you want. If you like someone they know it. You're not playing coy. Existing relationships are more harmonious and romantic. Singles have very nice love opportunities all month. Love opportunities are still found in educational or religious settings – just as they have been for some years now – but family and family connections are also playing a role here from the 23rd onwards. There will be more socializing from home and with the family. An old flame can be back in the picture, but most likely this is only in order to resolve old issues.

Mars travelling with Pluto from the 18th to the 20th inflames the libido. Both you and the beloved need to reduce your schedules and avoid confrontations and high stress situations. It will be a good idea to take it easy from the 27th to the 29th as well. Parents or parent figures should also do this. There can be some disturbance in your industry or company over that period.

Prosperity is strong this month too. A nice payday happens over the 11th and 12th. Children or children figures in your life also have a nice payday then. Speculations are favourable. Your social connections play an unusual role in finance all month. You have the kind of aspects of someone who likes to do business with friends and who likes to socialize with those you do business with. A partnership or joint venture opportunity is likely this month.

Neptune spends the month camped out on an eclipse point (the solar eclipse of September 1). This indicates dramas in the lives of friends and perhaps the testing of a friendship. Like last month, make sure important files are backed up and your anti-virus software is up to date.

Give more attention to health matters after the 23rd. Overall your health is good, this is a short-term issue. As always be sure to get enough rest. If you feel under the weather a good night's sleep should solve the problem. You can enhance the health further by paying attention to the colon, bladder and sexual organs until the 18th, and to the liver and thighs after that date.

November

Best Days Overall: 4, 5, 13, 14, 21, 22, 23
Most Stressful Days Overall: 1, 6, 7, 8, 19, 20, 26, 27, 28
Best Days for Love: 1, 2, 3, 4, 5, 13, 14, 21, 22, 23, 26, 27, 28
Best Days for Money: 1, 6, 7, 10, 15, 16, 19, 20, 24, 25, 29, 30
Best Days for Career: 2, 3, 6, 7, 8, 11, 12, 19, 20, 29, 30

Last month the planetary power shifted once again. Now the upper half of the Horoscope is overwhelmingly dominant. This sector was strong all year, but now even more so. At least 80 per cent (and sometimes 90 per cent) of the planets are in the upper half. This shows a strong career focus. A focus on the outer, worldly objectives. Your career planet, Uranus, has been in your spiritual 12th house for some years now. On the 9th, Mars, your spiritual planet, crosses the Mid-heaven and enters your 10th house of career. This is a very strong message and it reinforces what we've been seeing for some years now: the spiritual life, the spiritual practice, is ultra-important for the career.

Spiritual insight and understanding will solve many career problems. If you're involved in a worldly career, you enhance it by getting involved in charitable and altruistic activities. These seem more important than your professional achievements.

You're still in the midst of a yearly love and social peak this month. Romance blooms. There is an especially happy romantic or social meeting on the 24th or 25th. Singles are meeting someone significant.

Venus, the ruler of your Horoscope, is 'out of bounds' all month. This shows that you're moving outside your normal sphere this month. This is so on a personal level and in terms of your job. In health matters too you're involved with the 'unorthodox'. Health is more delicate this month – until the 22nd – and this is perhaps why you're exploring unorthodox therapies. A good night's rest will clear up most problems. You just need to maintain a high energy level. You can enhance your health by giving attention to the liver and thighs until the 12th. Thigh massage and a liver cleanse will be wonderful if you feel under the weather. After the 12th the spine, knees, teeth, bones, skin and overall skeletal alignment become important. Regular back and knee massage will do wonders. Good dental health is also important.

We see you going outside your normal sphere in finance too. Mercury is 'out of bounds' from the 19th to the 30th. Going a little 'out of bounds' is healthy for a Taurus. The tendency is to be too conservative – too stuck in your ways – and this often blinds you to opportunities.

Venus, your ruling planet, pauses in the heavens this month. She stays at the same latitude from the 13th to the 16th. This suggests a need for a cosmic pause in your activities. This pause is a good time for festivities, prayer and meditation. It is a pause that refreshes.

December

Best Days Overall: 1, 2, 3, 10, 11, 19, 20, 29, 30
Most Stressful Days Overall: 4, 5, 16, 17, 24, 25, 31
Best Days for Love: 1, 2, 3, 10, 11, 12, 13, 19, 20, 21, 22, 24, 25, 29, 30
Best Days for Money: 4, 5, 10, 11, 12, 13, 19, 20, 21, 22, 29, 30, 31
Best Days for Career: 4, 5, 8, 9, 16, 17, 26, 27, 31

Venus is still 'out of bounds' until December 3. Thereafter she is back in bounds – and so it is with you. You've made a brief excursion to your 'outer limits' and now you're going back to your normal sphere.

The month ahead looks very successful career-wise. The upper half of your Horoscope is still overwhelmingly dominant – often 90 per cent of the planets occupy the upper half. On the 7th Venus crosses the Mid-heaven and enters your 10th house. You're very motivated career-wise. You're focused. You love your career for its own sake. You seem elevated, raised in status. You're recognized not only for your charitable works, but also for who you are. Personal appearance and overall demeanour seem ultra-important in the career. You're the 'image' of success this month. Your good work ethic is noted by your superiors. Your career will be even better next month.

Health is much improved this month. You can enhance it further through back and knee massage (like last month) until the 7th and by ankle and calf massage after that. You're more experimental in health matters after the 7th and are not as conservative as you usually are.

Finances look good too. Mercury, your financial planet, is still 'out of bounds' until the 17th. Thus you pursue earnings outside your normal sphere and perhaps with people outside your normal sphere. Until the 3rd you earn more and you spend more. But after the 3rd, as Mercury enters conservative Capricorn, the financial judgement becomes more sober. You're more careful with your money. You take a step-by-step methodical approach to wealth. You're working to build wealth for the long term. Taureans enjoy savings and investment plans, budgets, etc. and this is a good period – from the 3rd onwards – to set these things up if you haven't already done so. On the 19th

Mercury begins to go backwards again. Try to do your major holiday shopping before the 19th. Afterwards, as always, the goal is to gain mental clarity about finances. It is a period for study and review, not for making major purchases or investments.

Though you ended your yearly social peak last month, the month ahead still looks very social. Your love planet, Pluto, receives positive stimulation from the Sun and Mercury. Thus, there is more socializing from home and with the family. Family members are playing cupid and family connections are important socially.

New Year's Eve is a very spiritual day for you. Try to celebrate it in a more spiritual way.

Gemini

Ⅱ

THE TWINS

Birthdays from
21st May to
20th June

Personality Profile

GEMINI AT A GLANCE

Element – Air

Ruling Planet – Mercury
  Career Planet – Neptune
  Love Planet – Jupiter
  Money Planet – Moon
  Planet of Health and Work – Pluto
  Planet of Home and Family Life – Mercury

Colours – blue, yellow, yellow-orange

Colour that promotes love, romance and social harmony – sky blue

Colours that promote earning power – grey, silver

Gems – agate, aquamarine

Metal – quicksilver

Scents – lavender, lilac, lily of the valley, storax

Quality – mutable (= flexibility)

Quality most needed for balance – thought that is deep rather than superficial

Strongest virtues – great communication skills, quickness and agility of thought, ability to learn quickly

Deepest need – communication

Characteristics to avoid – gossiping, hurting others with harsh speech, superficiality, using words to mislead or misinform

Signs of greatest overall compatibility – Libra, Aquarius

Signs of greatest overall incompatibility – Virgo, Sagittarius, Pisces

Sign most helpful to career – Pisces

Sign most helpful for emotional support – Virgo

Sign most helpful financially – Cancer

Sign best for marriage and/or partnerships – Sagittarius

Sign most helpful for creative projects – Libra

Best Sign to have fun with – Libra

Signs most helpful in spiritual matters – Taurus, Aquarius

Best day of the week – Wednesday

Understanding a Gemini

Gemini is to society what the nervous system is to the body. It does not introduce any new information but is a vital transmitter of impulses from the senses to the brain and vice versa. The nervous system does not judge or weigh these impulses – it only conveys information. And it does so perfectly.

This analogy should give you an indication of a Gemini's role in society. Geminis are the communicators and conveyors of information. To Geminis the truth or falsehood of information is irrelevant, they only transmit what they see, hear or read about. Thus they are capable of spreading the most outrageous rumours as well as conveying truth and light. Geminis sometimes tend to be unscrupulous in their communications and can do both great good or great evil with their power. This is why the sign of Gemini is symbolized by twins: Geminis have a dual nature.

Their ability to convey a message – to communicate with such ease – makes Geminis ideal teachers, writers and media and marketing people. This is helped by the fact that Mercury, the ruling planet of Gemini, also rules these activities.

Geminis have the gift of the gab. And what a gift this is! They can make conversation about anything, anywhere, at any time. There is almost nothing that is more fun to Geminis than a good conversation – especially if they can learn something new as well. They love to learn and they love to teach. To deprive a Gemini of conversation, or of books and magazines, is cruel and unusual punishment.

Geminis are almost always excellent students and take well to education. Their minds are generally stocked with all kinds of information, trivia, anecdotes, stories, news items, rarities, facts and statistics. Thus they can support any intellectual position that they care to take. They are awesome debaters and, if involved in politics, make good orators. Geminis are so verbally smooth that even if they do not know what they are talking about, they can make you think that they do. They will always dazzle you with their brilliance.

Finance

Geminis tend to be more concerned with the wealth of learning and ideas than with actual material wealth. As mentioned, they excel in professions that involve writing, teaching, sales and journalism – and not all of these professions pay very well. But to sacrifice intellectual needs merely for money is unthinkable to a Gemini. Geminis strive to combine the two. Cancer is on Gemini's solar 2nd house of money cusp, which indicates that Geminis can earn extra income (in a harmonious and natural way) from investments in residential property, restaurants and hotels. Given their verbal skills, Geminis love to bargain and negotiate in any situation, and especially when it has to do with money.

The Moon rules Gemini's 2nd solar house. The Moon is not only the fastest-moving planet in the zodiac but actually moves through every sign and house every 28 days. No other heavenly body matches the Moon for swiftness or the ability to change quickly. An analysis of the Moon – and lunar phenomena in general – describes Gemini's financial attitudes very well. Geminis are financially versatile and flexible; they can earn money in many different ways. Their financial attitudes and needs seem to change daily. Their feelings about money change also: sometimes they are very enthusiastic about it, at other times they could not care less.

For a Gemini, financial goals and money are often seen only as means of supporting a family; these things have little meaning otherwise.

The Moon, as Gemini's money planet, has another important message for Gemini financially: in order for Geminis to realize their financial potential they need to develop more of an understanding of the emotional side of life. They need to combine their awesome powers of logic with an understanding of human psychology. Feelings have their own logic; Geminis need to learn this and apply it to financial matters.

Career and Public Image

Geminis know that they have been given the gift of communication for a reason, that it is a power that can achieve great good or cause unthinkable distress. They long to put this power at the service of the highest and most transcendental truths. This is their primary goal, to communicate the eternal verities and prove them logically. They look up to people who can transcend the intellect – to poets, artists, musicians and mystics. They may be awed by stories of religious saints and martyrs. A Gemini's highest achievement is to teach the truth, whether it is scientific, inspirational or historical. Those who can transcend the intellect are Gemini's natural superiors – and a Gemini realizes this.

The sign of Pisces is in Gemini's solar 10th house of career. Neptune, the planet of spirituality and altruism, is Gemini's career planet. If Geminis are to realize their highest career potential they need to develop their transcendental – their spiritual and altruistic – side. They need to understand the larger cosmic picture, the vast flow of human evolution – where it came from and where it is heading. Only then can a Gemini's intellectual powers take their true position and he or she can become the 'messenger of the gods'. Geminis need to cultivate a facility for 'inspiration', which is something that does not originate in the intellect but which comes through the intellect. This will further enrich and empower a Gemini's mind.

Love and Relationships

Geminis bring their natural garrulousness and brilliance into their love life and social life as well. A good talk or a verbal joust is an interesting prelude to romance. Their only problem in love is that their intellect is too cool and passionless to incite ardour in others. Emotions sometimes disturb them, and their partners tend to complain about this. If you are in love with a Gemini you must understand why this is so. Geminis avoid deep passions because these would interfere with their ability to think and communicate. If they are cool towards you, understand that this is their nature.

Nevertheless, Geminis must understand that it is one thing to talk about love and another actually to love – to feel it and radiate it. Talking about love glibly will get them nowhere. They need to feel it and act on it. Love is not of the intellect but of the heart. If you want to know how a Gemini feels about love you should not listen to what he or she says, but rather, observe what he or she does. Geminis can be quite generous to those they love.

Geminis like their partners to be refined, well educated and well travelled. If their partners are more wealthy than they, that is all the better. If you are in love with a Gemini you had better be a good listener as well.

The ideal relationship for the Gemini is a relationship of the mind. They enjoy the physical and emotional aspects, of course, but if the intellectual communion is not there they will suffer.

Home and Domestic Life

At home the Gemini can be uncharacteristically neat and meticulous. They tend to want their children and partner to live up to their idealistic standards. When these standards are not met they moan and criticize. However, Geminis are good family people and like to serve their families in practical and useful ways.

The Gemini home is comfortable and pleasant. They like to invite people over and they make great hosts. Geminis are also good at repairs and improvements around the house – all fuelled by their need to stay active and occupied with something they like to do. Geminis have many hobbies and interests that keep them busy when they are home alone.

Geminis understand and get along well with their children, mainly because they are very youthful people themselves. As great communicators, Geminis know how to explain things to children; in this way they gain their children's love and respect. Geminis also encourage children to be creative and talkative, just like they are.

Horoscope for 2016

Major Trends

Saturn spent all of last year in your 7th house of love. He will be there all of this year too. This is testing marriages and existing relationships. They are getting 'stress tested'. The good relationships will survive almost any kind of stress, but not the flawed ones, and this is the reason for the testing. Only the best will do for you. More on this later.

However, it's not just love relationships that are getting tested. Uranus in your 11th house of friends is testing friendships too. They come suddenly and they go just as suddenly. There's more on this later too.

Jupiter moved into your 4th house of home and family on August 12 last year and will be there until September 9. Thus there are happy moves (if they haven't already happened) in store. There is an expansion of the family circle and happiness from the family. Jupiter will move into your 5th house on September 10 and stay there for the rest of the year. This will be a fun period in life, a period to explore the rapture of life. It will be like a vacation period.

You are always idealistic about your career and your work in the world. But now that Neptune is in your 10th house (as he has been since 2012) the idealism is much stronger. Career has to be more meaningful than just making money or achieving fame. It has to be spiritually meaningful too.

Pluto in your 8th house of transformation and regeneration for many years has forced many of you to get more serious about life. You've been dealing with death and near-death types of experiences – both personally and with those around you. This is sobering, but ultimately good. Many of you are involved in projects of personal transformation, and these projects are going well.

Mercury, the ruler of your Horoscope, will be in retrograde motion four times in the year ahead. Usually this happens only three times in a year and it shows that there is more indecision in your life, more need of review and mental clarity. We will deal with these periods in the monthly reports.

Your most important interests in the year ahead are: home and family (until September 9); children, fun and creativity (from September 10 onwards); love and romance; personal transformation, death and rebirth, occult studies and sex; career; and friends, groups and group activities.

Your paths of greatest fulfilment in the year ahead are home and family; and children, fun and creativity (from September 10 onwards).

Health

(Please note that this is an astrological perspective on health and not a medical one. In days of yore there was no difference, these perspectives were identical. But now there could be quite a difference. For a medical perspective, please consult your doctor or health practitioner.)

Health needs more attention these days. Saturn has been in stressful alignment with you since late December 2014, and Neptune has been in stressful alignment since 2012. By themselves they're not enough to cause sickness, but when other short-term planets join the fray, you become more vulnerable. So make a special point to rest and relax more from February 18 to March 20, August 23 to September 22 and November 22 to December 21. These are your most vulnerable periods.

Your 6th house of health and work is not strong this year. You could have a tendency to ignore your health and this could be a problem. You'll have to force yourself to give it the attention it deserves.

There is a lot that can be done to enhance your health and prevent problems from developing. Give more attention to the following areas (their reflexology points are highlighted in the following chart):

- The heart (especially during the vulnerable periods mentioned above). Many spiritual healers affirm that worry and anxiety are the root causes of heart problems. Replace worry with faith.
- The lungs, small intestine, arms, shoulders and respiratory system. These are always important for a Gemini. Regular arm and shoulder massage will be wonderfully beneficial.
- The colon, bladder and sexual organs. These are also always important for a Gemini. Colon action has been sluggish for some years now. It's a little better since 2015, but needs energy. A colonic or two might be a good idea. Safe sex and sexual moderation are always important.
- The spine, knees, teeth, bones, skin and overall skeletal alignment. These have become important since 2008. Regular back massage is wonderful. There are chairs on the market that automatically massage your back and you might want to invest in one of these

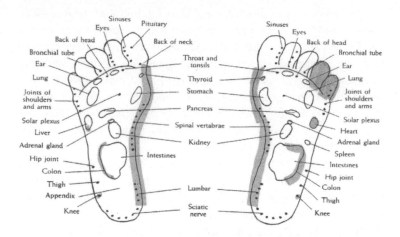

Important foot reflexology points for the year ahead

*Try to massage all of the foot on a regular basis – the top of the foot as well as
the bottom – but pay extra attention to the points highlighted on the chart.
When you massage, be aware of 'sore spots' as these need special attention.
It's also a good idea to massage the ankles and, especially, just below them.*

this year. Knee massage is good too. Give the knees more support
when you exercise. Regular visits to a chiropractor or osteopath are
a good idea.

• The gall bladder.

You have made many sudden and dramatic changes to the health
regime over the past two years, but things are more stable now.

Pluto, your health planet, rules surgery and detox regimes, and you
have an affinity for both. Back and/or knee surgery could be recommended this year, but get a second opinion and don't rush into
anything.

Home and Family

Your 4th house of home and family is a house of power this year and
seems very happy.

Jupiter, as we mentioned, entered your 4th house on August 12 of last year and he is there until September 9 of the current year. As our regular readers know, this transit generally produces a happy move or the fortunate sale or purchase of a home. The home – the living quarters – gets enlarged. Often this is by a physical move, but not necessarily. Sometimes people buy additional homes or renovate the existing home. Often they buy expensive items for the home. The effect is as if one had moved. If this hasn't happened as yet, it is still likely in the year ahead.

Jupiter in the 4th house enlarges the family circle. Generally this happens through birth or marriage, but often one meets people who are 'like' family to you. They give the same kind of emotional support you would expect from a family member.

Geminis of childbearing age are ultra-fertile this year. A pregnancy wouldn't be a surprise.

Jupiter in your 4th house gives us other messages as well. Jupiter is your love planet. So, this reinforces what we said above about marriages in the family. It also shows that your social life is centred in the home and with the family. You are doing more entertaining from home as well.

The ruler of the 7th house being situated in the 4th gives us other messages too. It shows that you're beautifying the home. You are redecorating, perhaps repainting or landscaping and otherwise trans-forming the home. Most likely you're buying objects of art and beauty for the home.

One of the parent figures in your life is in a prosperity cycle (they have been since August last year) and seems generous and supportive. He or she needs to watch the weight these days, though.

Jupiter in your 4th house makes this a year for making psychological progress. It reveals the wealth you possess in your subconscious mind. Your memories are a source of wealth.

A solar eclipse on September 1 occurs in your 4th house. This can make family members more temperamental and volatile, so be more patient with them. Often it produces some family kind of crisis which requires your utmost attention. If there are problems in the home, this is when you find out about them.

Finance and Career

Your 2nd house of finance is not a house of power this year, Gemini. Since the Horoscope aims at a balanced development, it is normal that in certain years different areas of life are emphasized and others de-emphasized. In our culture it is always about money, money, money. But the cosmos has a different perspective. Finance is important – it is one of the twelve houses of the Horoscope – but it's not everything. It is only a part of the whole.

This signals a stable kind of year. I read it as basic contentment with the status quo with no pressing need to make dramatic change. However, should financial difficulties arise (and this can happen because of temporary planetary transits through the house) you probably need to focus more. You will not have been giving finance the attention it deserves.

There has been much instability in the job for some years now. There have probably been multiple job changes – sudden and dramatic. The good news is that this year things are more stable on this front. In fact, ever since August of 2015, your job prospects have been excellent. Very nice job opportunities are happening and these seem much better, much happier, than the previous ones.

There is more good news. When Jupiter enters Libra on September 10, he will start to make wonderful aspects to you. This will help finances – but most especially it will help your writing and communication skills. The final quarter of the year will be more prosperous than the first three quarters.

Your financial planet, the Moon, is the fastest of all the planets – and the most changeable. Every month she moves through all the houses and signs of your chart. Thus, financial fortunes tend to fluctuate with the Moon, with her position and the aspects she receives. So you can be up one day and down the next. One day you're full of enthusiasm and optimism, the next, lethargic. These short-term trends are best covered in the monthly reports.

In general we can say that your best financial days in a given month are the New and Full Moons and when the Moon is in Virgo (until September 9) and Libra (after September 9). A waxing Moon is financially better than a waning Moon.

When Jupiter enters your 5th house on September 10 you can earn from your personal creativity. It becomes more marketable. This transit will also bring luck in speculations. The cosmos doesn't have to prosper you in this way, but this can be one of its avenues. When intuition urges it might be wise to invest harmless sums in a lottery or some other speculation after this date.

Your favourable financial numbers are 2, 4, 7 and 9.

Career – your life work – seems more important than finance this year. You might take a pay cut to get a job with more prestige and status – and not everyone thinks this way. A successful career tends to lead to money. But with you the career comes first.

Neptune, your career planet, spends many months on the South Node of the Moon this year. He also gets eclipsed. So there are career changes afoot and probably for the better. In addition to this there are two eclipses in your 10th house – a solar eclipse on March 9 and a lunar eclipse on September 16. This reinforces what we have said above.

In general you need a spiritual kind of career, as we mentioned. But the glamour industries – film, photography, music and dance – would also fit the bill.

Love and Social Life

The love life is very complicated this year – especially until September 9. Singles will still date and socialize but not as much as usual. The social life is much toned down.

Further, Jupiter, your love planet, is in stressful aspect with you until September 9. A current relationship is being severely tested. If it is fundamentally sound it will survive – though it will take more work and effort. But the flawed ones are likely to dissolve.

Jupiter in the sign of Virgo is not especially good for love. Not in your case, anyway. Love, which is something of the heart, becomes too mental and analytical. If you're not careful you'll overanalyse yourself out of a relationship. Analysis is good later on, but not during romantic moments. Also, the love planet in Virgo can make a person too perfectionistic in love matters. Any little flaw can be magnified out of all proportion. The good points can get lost. Criticism is another issue with the love planet in Virgo. There is nothing that will destroy the feeling of romance faster than destructive criticism. You need to avoid this like the plague. (In many cases it's not you who is like that, but your partner – you can be attracting these kinds of people these days.)

You can make the love life better by avoiding these pitfalls. You deserve perfect love but it is seldom handed to us on a silver platter. It is something that we work on and develop. It's a long-term project. As long as the relationship is better today than it was yesterday, you're on the road to perfect love. If you must criticize the beloved, choose an appropriate time – and do your best to phrase it in a constructive manner.

People get intellectual and analytical about love to avoid pain. But they often create more pain with this approach.

With Jupiter in your 4th house until September 9, love and love opportunities are found close to home – there'll be no need to travel far and wide. Family and family connections play a huge role in love. Family members are playing cupid this year.

You are attracted to people with strong family values, to people with whom you can share feelings. Emotional intimacy seems just as important as physical intimacy. You also seem attracted to older, more settled kinds of people – corporate and managerial types.

When the love planet enters Libra on September 10, the attitude changes. Love becomes more about fun. You gravitate towards the person who can show you a good time. Someone you can laugh with. Love opportunities happen at the normal places – parties, the theatre, resorts and places of entertainment.

Marriage is not likely this year – nor is it advisable. There's no need to rush into anything.

Self-improvement

Saturn in your 7th house of love and Jupiter in Virgo can make you seem cold, distant and unfeeling to others. Even if you aren't like that – they feel this. And this can further dampen the love life. Thus this year it will be good to practise sending love and warmth to others. You will have to work on this consciously. Make it a project.

With Jupiter in your 4th house this year, you're going to experience Nature's therapeutic system. Periodically an emotional spring-cleaning is in order and Nature goes about setting the stage for it. The subconscious mind is filled with untapped riches, with wisdom and knowledge gained by past experience and with abilities unhindered by space and time. But these can't be accessed if there is too much baggage there too: resentment, false ideas, false opinions, etc. These are in need of resolution. So with Jupiter in your 4th house you will feel more nostalgic. Old memories will arise spontaneously. You'll find yourself daydreaming of the past at odd moments. At night you'll have dreams of the past. These are all significant and should be noted. Perhaps most importantly, you'll be remembering old, unresolved love relationships. Don't try to suppress these things. The idea is to look at them from your present perspective, from your present state of consciousness. Things that seemed 'disastrous' when they happened are now seen as perhaps good things. You can laugh about them. Your personal history is not being rewritten – the facts are still the facts – but it is being reinterpreted in the light of greater maturity.

All of this will happen naturally, without a human therapist. However, a good human therapist can be of invaluable assistance to speed the process.

Part of the problem in the love life is that you might be living in the past. You might be trying to duplicate some happy kind of relationship, or trying to duplicate past pleasures. More likely, you're trying to avoid past pains and disappointments. You have a tendency this year to leave the 'now'. Past pleasures were wonderful, but new pleasures and new dimensions in love are constantly unfolding. Things you never imagined. Why block it?

Often with this aspect, an old flame come back into the picture. In many cases it is the actual person. In other cases it is someone with the same physical and psychological patterns as the old flame. Sometimes it is someone who reminds you of a parent figure at a younger age. These things generally don't lead to anything serious, but they help to resolve old issues of the past. When these are resolved you are ready to move on. Nature is very smart.

It's a very good idea to keep a journal of your dreams and experiences – especially this year.

Month-by-month Forecasts

January

Best Days Overall: 1, 2, 3, 11, 12, 19, 20, 29, 30
Most Stressful Days Overall: 6, 7, 13, 14, 26, 27
Best Days for Love: 6, 7, 8, 9, 10, 15, 16, 17, 18, 26, 27
Best Days for Money: 9, 10, 17, 18, 21, 22, 23, 26, 27, 29, 30
Best Days for Career: 4, 5, 13, 14, 21, 22, 31

You begin your year with the Western, social sector of your chart most
dominant. Mercury, your ruling planet, is very distant from you. You're
far away from yourself and focused on the needs of others. This is as it
should be. Personal power, personal self-confidence, is much weaker
this month – Mercury is retrograde most of the month. Perhaps this is
a good thing. Your way is probably not best these days. Let others have
their way, so long as it isn't destructive. Adapt yourself to situations as
best you can. In a few months, when the planetary power shifts to the
East, it will be easier to make changes.

At times like this it's good to remember that 'my strength is made
perfect in your weakness'. When we rely on a Higher Power, our
personal power is of little relevance.

The upper half of your chart is dominant this month. Home and
family is very important, but it is time to shift your focus to the career
and your outer goals. This is the best way to serve the family right now.

The year ahead is not a very strong love year, but this month brings
more social activity than usual. Mercury makes beautiful aspects to
your love planet Jupiter from the 9th onwards. The 14th to the 16th
look especially good. Important romantic or social meetings are
happening. However, there is no need to rush into anything serious.
Saturn is in your 7th house of love and Jupiter is retrograde. Take your
time. Jupiter is near the Moon's North Node and thus you might be
hyperactive socially – more than is necessary. This might make for a
tendency to force things.

Health is good this month and will get even better from the 20th
onwards. Detox regimes are always good for you – especially colonics.
Mars moves into your 6th house on the 4th and spends the rest of the

month there. This indicates that face and scalp massage will enhance the health. Physical exercise is also good: muscles need to be in tone.

Saturn re-stimulates an old eclipse point from the 15th to the 24th. Avoid high stress activities then.

Job seekers have good fortune on the 5th and 6th.

February

Best Days Overall: 7, 8, 15, 16, 17, 25, 26
Most Stressful Days Overall: 2, 3, 4, 9, 10, 22, 23, 24
Best Days for Love: 2, 3, 4, 5, 6, 13, 14, 22, 23, 24, 25
Best Days for Money: 5, 6, 7, 8, 13, 14, 17, 18, 19, 22, 23, 24, 27, 28
Best Days for Career: 1, 9, 10, 18, 19, 27, 28

Health, energy and self-confidence are much improved over last month. You're in a very good period – especially until the 14th – for weight loss regimes. After the 19th, health will need more attention, though. The most important thing is to get enough rest. You're working hard from the 19th onwards; the career is happy and successful, but try not to overdo things. Enhance your health in the ways mentioned last month. Spiritual healing is powerful from the 5th to the 8th.

The love life seems more active this month. The 5th to the 7th and the 9th to the 11th seem especially active and happy times. There are good romantic opportunities for singles, and family and family connections are playing a role here. But again, as was mentioned last month, there's no need to rush into anything. Saturn is still in your 7th house and the love planet is still retrograde.

Your 9th house of religion, travel and ideas became powerful on January 20 and is even more powerful this month – until the 19th. This augurs foreign travel and educational opportunities and is a wonderful transit for college or post-graduate level students – they seem successful in their studies. This is a month for religious, metaphysical and philosophical breakthroughs – a month for widening your understanding of these things.

The main headline, though, is the career. The upper half of your chart is still very dominant. On the 19th the Sun crosses the

Mid-heaven and enters your 10th house of career. You are in a yearly career peak which will continue well into next month. The focus is on the career – as it should be. A very happy career opportunity happens on the 28th and 29th. Superiors are impressed with your verbal and communication skills and seem receptive to your ideas, which are very inspired during that period. If you need to deal with a government department, the 28th and 29th are good days for that.

Saturn is still on an eclipse point from the 1st to the 5th. Avoid risky situations and daredevil-type stunts.

The planetary momentum is forward this month – overwhelmingly forward. Almost all of the planets are in direct motion. This shows a fast-paced kind of month. Rapid progress is made towards your goals.

March

Best Days Overall: 6, 7, 14, 15, 23, 24
Most Stressful Days Overall: 1, 2, 8, 9, 21, 22, 28, 29
Best Days for Love: 1, 2, 3, 4, 6, 7, 12, 13, 16, 21, 22, 26, 27, 28, 29, 31
Best Days for Money: 3, 4, 8, 9, 12, 13, 16, 17, 21, 22, 28, 29, 31
Best Days for Career: 8, 9, 16, 17, 26, 27

March this year is a fast paced, hectic kind of month, with never a dull moment. Mercury, the ruler of your Horoscope, moves speedily through three signs and houses of your Horoscope this month. This shows that you're covering a lot of territory and making good forward progress.

The month ahead is successful, but frenetic. There is good career advancement until the 20th and especially on the 1st and 11th.

There are two eclipses this month, and this adds to the frenzy. The solar eclipse of the 9th (in America it is on the 8th) affects you strongly, so take it easy then, and for a few days before and after. This eclipse occurs in your 10th house and shakes up the career. It shakes up your company, industry and perhaps the corporate hierarchy. But these things seem to work in your favour. Obstructions to progress get removed by these shake-ups. This kind of eclipse tends to bring dramas in the life of a parent, parent figure, boss or superior. Every solar eclipse tests cars and communication equipment and this one is no different. There can be dramas in the lives of siblings and sibling figures in your life. There can be upheavals (often new construction works) in the neighbourhood.

This eclipse impacts on two important planets in your chart – Jupiter, the love planet, and Saturn, the ruler of the 8th house of transformation. Love has been tested since the beginning of 2015, but the eclipse is like a catalyst that triggers more testing. Flawed relationships are in trouble. Good ones will survive. The spouse or current love is forced to make dramatic financial changes. You can have 'encounters' with death – close calls, or dreams of death. These are friendly cosmic reminders to get more serious about life.

The lunar eclipse of the 23rd also has a strong effect on you. Again, reduce your schedule over the period. Since the Moon, the eclipsed planet, is your financial planet it indicates important financial changes – things that have long needed to be done. Now you're forced into doing something about them. Generally this happens through some sudden kind of expense. You will handle it once the changes are made. This eclipse occurs in your 5th house and so it impacts on the children or children figures in your life. It brings life-changing kinds of dramas with them. They too should reduce their schedules. This eclipse is different from normal in that impacts on Mercury – the ruler of your Horoscope. Another reason to take it easy. Be more patient with family members and especially a parent or parent figure. There can be upheavals at home and with family members.

April

    Best Days Overall: 2, 3, 10, 11, 19, 20, 21, 29, 30
    Most Stressful Days Overall: 4, 5, 17, 18, 24, 25, 26
    Best Days For Love: 1, 6, 8, 9, 14, 15, 17, 18, 24, 25, 26, 27, 28
    Best Days For Money: 1, 6, 7, 8, 9, 12, 13, 14, 15, 16, 17, 18, 27, 28
    Best Days For Career: 4, 5, 12, 13, 22, 23

Last month, on the 5th, the planetary power began to shift from the West to the East – from the social sector to the sector of the self. This represents a psychological shift in you. The planetary power is starting to move towards you rather than away from you. This increases your personal power and independence. Self-interest is not evil – so long as it isn't abused and no one is hurt. Self-interest is the enlightened pursuit of happiness. And the cosmos is interested in your happiness. You've had six or so months of adapting to things. By now you know what is uncomfortable and needs changing. Now, for the next few months, it is time to make these changes. They will be easier to implement and with less effort now. The love life is pretty stressed this month. Not much can be done about that (except, try not to make things worse than they need to be) so you might as well please yourself. Make your changes before Mercury goes retrograde on the 28th. After that (and well into next month) give more thought to the changes you want to make. Get more facts. When Mercury moves forward again – on May 22 – you'll be ready to act with power.

Pluto, your health and work planet, goes retrograde on the 18th. Thus job seekers should study job offers more closely. Don't be afraid to ask questions. Resolve all doubts before acting on anything. The same holds true for those of you who hire others – check them out more thoroughly.

Health and energy are much improved this month. If there have been pre-existing conditions they seem much better now. Enhance the health in the ways mentioned in the yearly report. With Pluto retrograde from the 18th onwards (and for many months after), be more cautious with changes in your diet or health regime. Do your homework first.

Last month, on the 20th, your 11th house of friends became powerful. This is the case until the 19th. The romantic life leaves much to be desired, but this is an excellent non-romantic social period. It will be good to be involved with friends and group activities. It is an excellent period for boning up on your high tech skills and for online kinds of activities, and for buying high tech equipment or new software. The New Moon of 7th is especially good for these things. It also brings sudden financial increase. In general, you have greater earning power – more enthusiasm for finance – from the 7th to the 23rd.

May

Best Days Overall: 7, 8, 17, 18, 27, 28
Most Stressful Days Overall: 1, 2, 3, 14, 15, 22, 23, 29, 30
Best Days for Love: 6, 14, 15, 22, 23, 24, 25, 26, 27
Best Days for Money: 6, 10, 11, 14, 15, 24, 25, 27
Best Days for Career: 1, 2, 3, 10, 11, 19, 20, 21, 29, 30

The love life is still very stressed this month. However, there is some improvement after the 9th as Jupiter starts moving forward. At least there is some mental clarity now on the current state of affairs. This is better than confusion. Like last month, try not to make things worse than they need to be.

The good news is that you're entering your period of maximum personal power and independence. The planets are now in their most Easterly position. Love is what it is. You can't please everybody. Time to please yourself. Time to take responsibility for your own happiness. Time to create conditions that make you happy. From the 22nd onwards is best (Mercury moves forward and your 1st house is strong).

Last month on the 19th your 12th house of spirituality became very strong, and remains so until the 20th of this month. So, you're in a period that favours spiritual growth and spiritual studies. From the spiritual perspective there is a blessing in the love problems. It gives the opportunity for more solitude, which you need right now. In solitude there are many answers. The Higher Power can come in and solve things. When the 12th house is strong, we learn through a process of revelation - not from scientific method or reading books. It is as if someone turns on the light in a dark room and suddenly you see - really see - what the reality is. This seeing is a healing.

Many of you have birthdays coming up. This makes it a very good time to review the past year, to acknowledge what has been accomplished and what hasn't, atone for past mistakes and set new goals for the year ahead. Your birthday - your Solar Return - is considered your personal New Year and you want to start it on the right footing.

On the 20th the Sun crosses the Ascendant and enters your 1st house. You begin one of your yearly personal pleasure peaks. It is time to get the body and image in right shape and to pamper yourself a little.

The Sun crossing your Ascendant shows that you're getting new communication equipment – some of you are getting new cars. Venus enters your 1st house on the 24th. There might be problems in love, but your personal appearance doesn't seem the issue. You look good. There is energy and star quality to the image. You're managing to have fun. There are opportunities for non-serious love – love affairs. A good period – from the 24th onwards – for buying clothes and personal accessories. Good for doing things that beautify the personal image.

June

Best Days Overall: 4, 5, 13, 14, 23, 24
Most Stressful Days Overall: 10, 11, 12, 18, 19, 25, 26
Best Days for Love: 2, 3, 4, 5, 10, 11, 14, 18, 19, 20, 21, 25, 26, 29, 30
Best Days for Money: 2, 3, 4, 5, 6, 7, 10, 11, 13, 14, 20, 21, 25, 29, 30
Best Days for Career: 6, 7, 15, 16, 17, 25, 26

The love life is still not what it should be, but there's more improvement happening this month. Mars moved backwards out of your 7th house on the 27th of last month and will be in your 6th house for all of June. Jupiter, your love planet, is now moving forward. There is less intensity to the problems. Jupiter spends the month very near the Moon's North Node. Thus you can be forcing love issues, forcing yourself to socialize or date more than you need to. This can bring short-term results but not long-term happiness.

Leaving the love life aside, this is basically a happy and prosperous month. The great Law of Compensation is certainly at work here. The stress in one area opens doors in other areas. You're still in a personal pleasure peak until the 21st. The personal appearance shines. Self-confidence and personal power are at a yearly high right now. You're enjoying all the physical delights. Family support also looks good.

On the 13th, as Mercury crosses your Ascendant and enters your 1st house, there is a shift in planetary power. Now the lower half of your Horoscope becomes strong. I wouldn't call it dominant, but it is stronger than it has been all year, and stronger than the upper half (for most of the month). Thus it is time to let go of career matters. Do what you have to do, but shift more focus to the family and the emotional life. The idea now is to find and function from your point of emotional harmony. If your emotional life is right, the career will fall into place (as will other areas of life).

On the 21st the Sun moves into your money house, joining Venus and Mercury, and you enter a yearly financial peak. It's a prosperous month. The money house is filled with beneficent planets, helpful planets. Earnings will increase. The Sun in the money house indicates money from intellectual activities, from writing, teaching, sales, marketing and trading. These are your natural strengths. Your intellectual property is worth more. Venus in the money house indicates rich friends and the importance of social contacts. It shows luck in speculations and a sound financial intuition. Spiritual wealth is the root of material wealth – something you learn this month. Mercury in the money house shows good family support. It also shows that you spend on yourself and are seen as prosperous by others. You have a more prosperous appearance.

Drive more carefully on the 8th, 9th, 23rd and 24th. There can be some communication foul-ups on those days too. Avoid high stress activities on the 23rd and 24th as well – Mercury moves over an eclipse point. On the 27th and 28th the intuition is very sharp and the dream life becomes more active. Children or children figures in your life have career success.

July

Best Days Overall: 1, 2, 10, 11, 12, 20, 21, 29, 30
Most Stressful Days Overall: 8, 9, 15, 16, 22, 23
Best Days for Love: 3, 4, 8, 9, 15, 16, 18, 19, 24, 25, 27, 28
Best Days for Money: 3, 4, 8, 9, 13, 14, 18, 19, 24, 27, 28, 31
Best Days for Career: 3, 4, 13, 14, 22, 23, 31

A prosperous and basically successful month ahead with a few little challenges thrown in just so you don't get too bored!

You're still in the midst of a yearly financial peak until the 22nd. So the focus is on financial issues – as it should be. The New Moon of the

4th – a nice payday by the way – occurs in your money house and will clarify many financial conundrums as the month progresses. All the information you need to make good financial decisions will come to you – naturally and normally. Money comes to you from your natural strengths, from writing, teaching, journalism, sales, marketing and PR. The financial intuition is exceptionally good these days and there is luck in speculations.

The happiness continues even after your financial peak. On the 22nd you enter Gemini heaven. The Sun moves into your 3rd house of communication and intellectual interests and this becomes the main focus for the rest of the month. There's never any need to coax Geminis to read more or to study – just give them half an excuse! Geminis are naturally good students, but become even better from the 22nd onwards. Students below college level are doing well in their studies.

Mercury, the ruler of your Horoscope, is 'out of bounds' until the 9th. Thus you're outside your normal sphere in the search for earnings. You're thinking outside the box and doing unconventional kinds of things. Take it easy on the 1st and the 2nd. Avoid high stress activities. (The same goes for family members.) On the 7th Mercury makes a square to Pluto and this can bring a health scare (probably no more than that) personally or with family members. You and family members should take it easy on the 6th and 7th, and it will be best to avoid foreign travel on those days. College level students have dramas at school.

Neptune, your career planet, travels with the South Node of the Moon all month. This suggests career instability, changes in the company your work for or in your industry. With most of the planets still below the horizon, observe all this but keep the focus on the home and family.

Health is good this month. You can enhance it further in the ways mentioned in the yearly report.

August

Best Days Overall: 7, 8, 16, 17, 18, 25, 26
Most Stressful Days Overall: 4, 5, 12, 13, 19, 20, 31
Best Days for Love: 3, 4, 5, 12, 13, 14, 15, 23, 24, 31
Best Days for Money: 1, 2, 3, 4, 5, 12, 13, 14, 15, 23, 24, 27, 28, 31
Best Days for Career: 1, 9, 10, 19, 20, 27, 28

You're always an intellectual star, Gemini, but this month even more so than usual. Your 3rd house of communication and intellectual interests is still powerful. You always absorb information quickly – and especially so nowadays. You only need to glance at a book and you pretty much know what's in it. For students this is a good time to take tests; results should be better than usual.

There is still much career instability and change happening. Only time will sort things out. So, keep the focus on the home and family – especially from the 22nd onwards. Your 4th house of home and family becomes very powerful then. It is the 'midnight hour' of your year – a powerful time. Career is important to you but now it is good to work on it by the methods of night, rather than by the methods of day. Visualize, dream and affirm what you want and allow the power of the universe to make these things happen in its own way. So long as you don't doubt or deny, your visualizations and affirmations must happen.

This is a month for coming to terms with the past, for resolving old traumas and experiences. These are the things that hold a person back. And it is good to give attention here. Those of you involved in psychological therapy should have a good month. Many might find it useful to begin therapy.

Love is very complicated this month. On the one hand, your love planet receives positive stimulation from the 22nd onwards – this should bring romantic opportunity for singles. On the other hand, the 7th house contains maleficent planets – the two biggies in the zodiac: Mars and Saturn. So love opportunity comes, but it gets tested. Existing relationships get tested even further than they have been (this has been going on all year). The testing of love is not a pleasant experience.

However, much good can come from it. It is only through this kind of severe testing that we learn if love is real or not. Good relationships will survive. It will take work and effort but they're likely to survive. It is the mediocre ones – the essentially flawed ones – that are likely to dissolve.

Health needs a lot more watching from the 22nd onwards. Three long-term planets and four short-term ones are in stressful alignment with you. This is no joke. Make sure you get enough rest. It might be wise to spend more time at a health spa or book some massages or reflexology treatments. Keep the focus on the really important things in your life and let go of trivia.

September

Best Days Overall: 3, 4, 13, 14, 21, 22, 30
Most Stressful Days Overall: 1, 2, 8, 9, 15, 16, 28, 29
Best Days for Love: 1, 2, 3, 4, 8, 9, 12, 13, 14, 21, 23
Best Days for Money: 1, 2, 11, 12, 13, 20, 21, 23, 24, 30
Best Days for Career: 5, 6, 7, 15, 16, 23, 24

Health is still very delicate this month, especially until the 27th, and two eclipses this month are adding to the pressure. Keep in mind our discussion of last month.

The solar eclipse of the 1st affects you very much. Take it nice and easy during that period. (Those of you born from June 14–20 are going to feel this eclipse most strongly.) Drive more carefully and more defensively. This eclipse occurs in your 10th house of career, so there are career changes happening – either in your own career or in the lives of people involved in your career. Changes have been going on in your company and industry for some months and these are accelerated now. There are personal dramas in the lives of parents, parent figures and bosses. There can be changes in government regulations that impact on you and your company or industry. Cars and communication equipment get tested and might need replacement. Siblings and sibling figures in your life are also experiencing personal dramas.

The lunar eclipse of the 16th also strongly affects you (here its impact will be strongest on those of you born between June 1 and June

11). So take it nice and easy during this period too. This eclipse occurs in your 4th house, bringing dramas in the home and in the lives of family members – especially parents or parent figures. Be more patient with family members during this period – things are stressed enough and there's no need to make things worse. Often repairs are needed in the home. Since it impacts on your career planet Neptune, the eclipse brings more career turmoil and upheaval. It is almost a continuation of the solar eclipse of the 1st. Every lunar eclipse brings financial changes and this one is no different. It is as if every six months or so, the cosmos forces you to readjust and update your financial thinking and planning. Basically this is a good thing, but it is not always pleasant while it's happening.

There are good things happening this month, in spite of all the drama. Jupiter, the love planet, moves into romantic Libra on the 10th. This is a positive for health (overall) and for love. Jupiter moves away from his stressful aspect with you and with Saturn, which was inhibiting the love life. The worst of the love crises of the past year are over with.

Jupiter now in your 5th house brings more joy and pleasure in life. On the 22nd the Sun moves into your 5th house too, adding to this. Once the turmoil of the eclipses passes, it should be a fun kind of month – a yearly personal pleasure peak. Health improves after the 22nd as well. But be sure to get enough rest until the 27th.

October

Best Days Overall: 1, 2, 10, 11, 19, 27, 28, 29
Most Stressful Days Overall: 5, 6, 7, 12, 13, 25, 26
Best Days for Love: 1, 3, 4, 5, 6, 7, 10, 12, 13, 18, 19, 23, 24, 27, 28
Best Days for Money: 1, 2, 10, 11, 18, 19, 20, 21, 22, 27, 28, 30
Best Days for Career: 3, 4, 12, 13, 21, 22, 30, 31

Health and energy are much improved over last month. It won't hurt though to take it gently on the 15th and 16th as Mercury squares Pluto. Avoid confrontations at work too. Family members should also reduce their schedule a bit then. This is important from the 18th to the

20th as well. (Read the newspapers during those periods and you'll see what we're talking about.)

If you got through the past two months with your health intact, you'll coast through the month ahead.

You're still in a yearly personal pleasure peak – and this is stronger than usual. Overall this is a happy period. You're enjoying life. Your personal creativity is ultra strong right now. And you have the ability – and interest – in dealing with children and children figures in your life.

The love life is much improved over the past year too. Saturn is still in your 7th house, so serious committed love is still not advisable. But with your love planet Jupiter now in your 5th house for the rest of the year there are plenty of 'non-serious' love opportunities. Singles are meeting people they would consider 'marriage material' but actual marriage is not advisable at this time. Next year will be a different story.

In August the planetary power shifted from the East to the social Western sector. The planetary power now moves away from you rather than towards you for the next few months. Hopefully you used your period of personal power to create your personal happiness. If you created well, things are pleasant. If there have been errors, you're learning about it now and should adapt yourself as best you can. Next year, when the planets start to shift to the East again, you'll be able to make the necessary changes. Right now it is about getting on with others and cultivating their grace. It's about taking a vacation from yourself and putting others first. Your social grace will bring you more good than your personal abilities or personal initiative.

On the 23rd the Sun moves into your 6th house. You're temporarily partied out. You're still having fun, but you are a bit more serious and work-oriented during this period. This is a very good time to achieve work-related goals now. Your work ethic is much stronger than usual. It's a very nice period for job seekers – there are many happy opportunities.

The career planet is still on an eclipse point all month (the lunar eclipse of September 16). So career dramas are still happening. Neptune is retrograde to boot. So continue to focus on home and family. The career situation is highly unclear right now.

November

Best Days Overall: 6, 7, 8, 15, 16, 24, 25
Most Stressful Days Overall: 2, 3, 9, 10, 21, 22, 23, 29, 30
Best Days for Love: 2, 3, 6, 7, 13, 15, 16, 21, 22, 24, 25, 29, 30
Best Days for Money: 6, 7, 9, 10, 15, 16, 17, 18, 24, 25, 29
Best Days for Career: 1, 9, 10, 17, 18, 26, 27

On the 22nd, as the Sun enters your 7th house, you enter a yearly love and social peak. You'll have better love peaks in future years, but this is the peak for present. Singles are dating more than usual and attending more parties and gatherings. Those still in relationships are also attending more parties. You still need to be more discriminating about all this. Choose quality over quantity.

It's good that you've been focusing on your health since the 23rd of last month. This will stand you in good stead for later this month when health becomes more delicate. The situation is nowhere near as severe as it was in September and October, but it is still not your best period for energy. So, as always, make sure you get enough sleep and rest. If you're tired take a short nap. If a pre-existing condition acts up, because of low energy, the chances are that a good night's sleep will ease things. The 24th, 25th, 29th and 30th are the most vulnerable days of the month. This is when you really need more rest. Spiritual healing is especially powerful on the 24th and 25th. Continue to enhance the health in the ways mentioned in the yearly report.

Drive more carefully on the 18th, 19th and 30th. Communication glitches are more likely then too.

Mercury goes 'out of bounds' from the 19th to the 30th. So you, and probably family members too, are outside your normal sphere during that period. We see this also with children and children figures – Venus spends all month 'out of bounds'. This would also suggest that in your spiritual life you're moving out of your normal comfort zone and exploring new spiritual territory.

Venus has her 'solstice' from November 13 to 16. She pauses in her movement and stays at the same exact latitude those four days. Children and children figures should pause during that period too – and most likely they will. It is a pause that refreshes. A pause in your spiritual life is also indicated. Let go of your spiritual goals and just allow the Higher Power to have its way.

On the 22nd the planetary power begins to shift to the upper half of the Horoscope. Dawn is breaking in your year. The activities of the day are more important than the activities of the night. It is time to push forward to your outer objectives. Neptune, your career planet, starts moving forward on the 20th – beautiful timing! There is more clarity in career matters and thus your efforts are more directed and powerful.

December

Best Days Overall: 4, 5, 12, 13, 21, 22, 31
Most Stressful Days Overall: 6, 7, 19, 20, 26, 27
Best Days for Love: 2, 3, 4, 5, 12, 13, 21, 22, 26, 27
Best Days for Money: 4, 5, 8, 9, 12, 13, 14, 15, 17, 18, 21, 22, 29, 31
Best Days for Career: 6, 7, 14, 15, 24, 25

The love and social life is still strong until the 21st. You're still in a yearly love and social peak. So it's a socially active month. Review our discussion of this last month. The love planet opposes Uranus from the 19th onwards. This can make love unstable. The good part is that love becomes more exciting. Never a dull moment. Anything can happen at any time.

Finances don't seem a big issue this month. You're more concerned with the finances of others – those of partners, investors or the current love interest – than your own. Your earning power is strongest from the 1st to the 13th and from the 27th onwards. The spouse, partner or current love is having a banner financial month from the 21st onwards. He or she is in a yearly financial peak and is likely to be more generous with you.

Your 8th house of transformation has been powerful all year (and for many years past now) and becomes especially powerful from the 21st onwards. This is excellent for projects involving personal transformation and personal reinvention. It is wonderful for detox and weight loss regimes. It generally indicates a more sexually active kind of period. Libido is stronger than usual.

Our regular readers know that detoxing is not just about physical things. Real detoxes should happen on the emotional and mental levels too. This is a month to purge the mind of negative thoughts and habit patterns; to purge the feeling nature of negative feelings. Just this will bring all kinds of subtle improvements in the outer affairs and conditions. When the mind and feelings are purged the life power can come in much stronger and there will be an increase in well-being.

Health is much improved after the 21st. Yet you still have a strong interest in health. This is all very good for getting involved in disciplined health regimes or for initiating these things. It is also an excellent period for job seekers and for those who employ others. There is good fortune from the 21st onwards.

The career is busy and successful this month, and it will be even more successful in the coming months. Mars conjuncts your career planet Neptune on the 31st. This indicates that friends are succeeding and helping you. They provide career opportunities. Networking is especially powerful during that period.

Cancer

THE CRAB

Birthdays from
21st June to
20th July

Personality Profile

CANCER AT A GLANCE

Element – Water

Ruling Planet – Moon
   Career Planet – Mars
   Love Planet – Saturn
   Money Planet – Sun
   Planet of Fun and Games – Pluto
   Planet of Good Fortune – Neptune
   Planet of Health and Work – Jupiter
   Planet of Home and Family Life – Venus
   Planet of Spirituality – Mercury

Colours – blue, puce, silver

Colours that promote love, romance and social harmony – black, indigo

Colours that promote earning power – gold, orange

Gems – moonstone, pearl

Metal – silver

Scents – jasmine, sandalwood

Quality – cardinal (= activity)

Quality most needed for balance – mood control

Strongest virtues – emotional sensitivity, tenacity, the urge to nurture

Deepest need – a harmonious home and family life

Characteristics to avoid – over-sensitivity, negative moods

Signs of greatest overall compatibility – Scorpio, Pisces

Signs of greatest overall incompatibility – Aries, Libra, Capricorn

Sign most helpful to career – Aries

Sign most helpful for emotional support – Libra

Sign most helpful financially – Leo

Sign best for marriage and/or partnerships – Capricorn

Sign most helpful for creative projects – Scorpio

Best Sign to have fun with – Scorpio

Signs most helpful in spiritual matters – Gemini, Pisces

Best day of the week – Monday

Understanding a Cancer

In the sign of Cancer the heavens are developing the feeling side of things. This is what a true Cancerian is all about – feelings. Where Aries will tend to err on the side of action, Taurus on the side of inaction and Gemini on the side of thought, Cancer will tend to err on the side of feeling.

Cancerians tend to mistrust logic. Perhaps rightfully so. For them it is not enough for an argument or a project to be logical – it must feel right as well. If it does not feel right a Cancerian will reject it or chafe against it. The phrase 'follow your heart' could have been coined by a Cancerian, because it describes exactly the Cancerian attitude to life.

The power to feel is a more direct – more immediate – method of knowing than thinking is. Thinking is indirect. Thinking about a thing never touches the thing itself. Feeling is a faculty that touches directly the thing or issue in question. We actually experience it. Emotional feeling is almost like another sense which humans possess – a psychic sense. Since the realities that we come in contact with during our lifetime are often painful and even destructive, it is not surprising that the Cancerian chooses to erect barriers – a shell – to protect his or her vulnerable, sensitive nature. To a Cancerian this is only common sense.

If Cancerians are in the presence of people they do not know, or find themselves in a hostile environment, up goes the shell and they feel protected. Other people often complain about this, but one must question these people's motives. Why does this shell disturb them? Is it perhaps because they would like to sting, and feel frustrated that they cannot? If your intentions are honourable and you are patient, have no fear. The shell will open up and you will be accepted as part of the Cancerian's circle of family and friends.

Thought processes are generally analytic and dissociating. In order to think clearly we must make distinctions, comparisons and the like. But feeling is unifying and integrative.

To think clearly about something you have to distance yourself from it. To feel something you must get close to it. Once a Cancerian has accepted you as a friend he or she will hang on to you. You have to be really bad to lose the friendship of a Cancerian. If you are related to Cancerians they will never let you go no matter what you do. They will always try to maintain some kind of connection even in the most extreme circumstances.

Finance

The Cancer-born has a deep sense of what other people feel about things and why they feel as they do. This faculty is a great asset in the workplace and in the business world. Of course it is also indispensable in raising a family and building a home, but it has its uses in business. Cancerians often attain great wealth in a family business. Even if the business is not a family operation, they will treat it as one. If the Cancerian works for somebody else, then the boss is the parental figure and the co-workers are brothers and sisters. If a Cancerian is the boss, then all the workers are his or her children. Cancerians like the feeling of being providers for others. They enjoy knowing that others derive their sustenance because of what they do. It is another form of nurturing.

With Leo on their solar 2nd money house cusp, Cancerians are often lucky speculators, especially with residential property or hotels and restaurants. Resort hotels and nightclubs are also profitable for the Cancerian. Waterside properties attract them. Though they are basically conventional people, they sometimes like to earn their livelihood in glamorous ways.

The Sun, Cancer's money planet, represents an important financial message: in financial matters Cancerians need to be less moody, more stable and fixed. They cannot allow their moods - which are here today and gone tomorrow - to get in the way of their business lives. They need to develop their self-esteem and feelings of self-worth if they are to realize their greatest financial potential.

Career and Public Image

Aries rules the 10th solar career house cusp of Cancer, which indicates that Cancerians long to start their own business, to be more active publicly and politically and to be more independent. Family responsibilities and a fear of hurting other people's feelings – or getting hurt themselves – often inhibit them from attaining these goals. However, this is what they want and long to do.

Cancerians like their bosses and leaders to act freely and to be a bit self-willed. They can deal with that in a superior. They expect their leaders to be fierce on their behalf. When the Cancerian is in the position of boss or superior he or she behaves very much like a 'warlord'. Of course the wars they wage are not egocentric but in defence of those under their care. If they lack some of this fighting instinct – independence and pioneering spirit – Cancerians will have extreme difficulty in attaining their highest career goals. They will be hampered in their attempts to lead others.

Since they are so parental, Cancerians like to work with children and make great educators and teachers.

Love and Relationships

Like Taurus, Cancer likes committed relationships. Cancerians function best when the relationship is clearly defined and everyone knows his or her role. When they marry it is usually for life. They are extremely loyal to their beloved. But there is a deep little secret that most Cancerians will never admit to: commitment or partnership is really a chore and a duty to them. They enter into it because they know of no other way to create the family that they desire. Union is just a way – a means to an end – rather than an end in itself. The family is the ultimate end for them.

If you are in love with a Cancerian you must tread lightly on his or her feelings. It will take you a good deal of time to realize how deep and sensitive Cancerians can be. The smallest negativity upsets them. Your tone of voice, your irritation, a look in your eye or an expression on your face can cause great distress for the Cancerian. Your slightest gesture is registered by them and reacted to. This can be hard to get used to, but stick by your love – Cancerians make great partners once you learn how to deal with them. Your Cancerian lover will react not so much to what you say as to the way you are actually feeling at the moment.

Home and Domestic Life

This is where Cancerians really excel. The home environment and the family are their personal works of art. They strive to make things of beauty that will outlast them. Very often they succeed.

Cancerians feel very close to their family, their relatives and especially their mothers. These bonds last throughout their lives and mature as they grow older. They are very fond of those members of their family who become successful, and they are also quite attached to family heirlooms and mementos. Cancerians also love children and like to provide them with all the things they need and want. With their nurturing, feeling nature, Cancerians make very good parents – especially the Cancerian woman, who is the mother *par excellence* of the zodiac.

As a parent the Cancerian's attitude is 'my children right or wrong'. Unconditional devotion is the order of the day. No matter what a family member does, the Cancerian will eventually forgive him or her, because 'you are, after all, family'. The preservation of the institution – the tradition – of the family is one of the Cancerian's main reasons for living. They have many lessons to teach others about this.

Being so family-orientated, the Cancerian's home is always clean, orderly and comfortable. They like old-fashioned furnishings but they also like to have all the modern comforts. Cancerians love to have family and friends over, to organize parties and to entertain at home – they make great hosts.

Horoscope for 2016

Major Trends

Many of the trends written of in past years are still very much in effect. Long-term planets are involved here. Long-term planets indicate long-term projects – things that can't be done in a year or two years or three years. They take much time.

Uranus is still in your 10th career house. He has been there for many years and will be there for another few years. This shows much ferment and change in your career. There is much instability there.

However, the career is definitely interesting and exciting. Instability is the price we pay for excitement.

Neptune has been in your 9th house for some years now and will also be there for many years to come. Your personal religion – your personal philosophy of life – is becoming spiritualized, more elevated. Neptune's action is to 'dissolve' old ideas and philosophies; he doesn't shatter them like Uranus does, or Pluto, instead they sort of just 'melt away' gradually. This is a very good time to pursue the mystical traditions of your own religion.

Pluto, in your 7th house for many years now, is purifying the marriage and social life. Purging it of impurities, bad attitudes and bad people. Through this process you're giving birth to the ideal love and social life. There's more on this later.

Saturn has been in your 6th house since December 2014 and will be there for the year ahead. It shows that you're getting more serious about your health and are taking on disciplined health regimes. Your work situation could be better, though.

Jupiter spends most of the year in your 3rd house of communication. Many of you are getting new cars and communication equipment these days. (It could have happened last year too.) This is an excellent aspect for students (below college level). It shows success in their studies. It is a good year to expand your mind – to read more and take courses in subjects that interest you.

Jupiter will move into your 4th house on September 10. This often indicates a move or renovation of the home. The family circle gets enlarged. More on this later.

Your strongest interests in the year ahead are: communication and intellectual interests (until September 9); home and family (from September 10 onwards); health and work; love, romance and social activities; religion, philosophy, higher education and foreign travel; and career.

Your paths of greatest fulfilment this year are communication and intellectual interests; and home and family (from September 10 onwards).

Health

(Please note that this is an astrological perspective on health and not a medical one. In days of yore there was no difference, these perspectives were identical. But now there could be quite a difference. For a medical perspective, please consult your doctor or health practitioner.)

Health needs more attention paying to it this year – especially from September 10 onwards. Happily, your 6th house of health is strong and you're on the case. You're willing to do whatever is necessary to maintain good health.

We should mention that if you got through 2014 in reasonable shape, the year ahead will not be too trying. This year is much less severe than 2014 was.

There is much you can do to enhance your health, as our regular readers know. Give more attention to the vulnerable areas of your chart, detailed below (the relevant reflexology points are shown in the

Important foot reflexology points for the year ahead

Try to massage all of the foot on a regular basis – the top of the foot as well as the bottom – but pay extra attention to the points highlighted on the chart. When you massage, be aware of 'sore spots' as these need special attention. It's also a good idea to massage the ankles and the middle of the top of the foot.

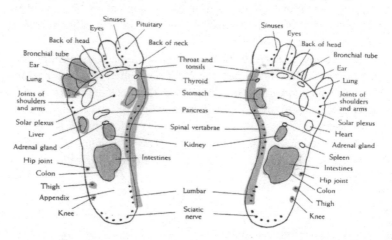

diagram). This is where problems would most likely happen. Keeping these areas healthy and fit is sound preventive medicine.

- The stomach and breasts. These are always important for you, Cancer, and this year is no different. Diet is always an important issue for you. Keep in mind that *how* you eat is perhaps as important as *what* you eat. Meals should be taken in a calm and relaxed way. It is good to have nice soothing music playing as you eat, and to say grace (in your own words) and express appreciation for the food. Do your best to make the act of eating a ritual of worship rather than just the fulfilling of an animal appetite.
- The liver and thighs. These too are very important for you. Liver action is more sluggish than usual this year and needs more energy. Avoid foods that stress the liver (too much alcohol for example). A herbal liver cleanse/detox is a good idea if you feel under the weather.
- The small intestine. This area is only important until September 9. Right diet will help the intestine.
- The kidneys and hips. These become important from September 10 onwards. The hips should be regularly massaged, and if you feel under the weather a herbal kidney cleanse would be a good idea.
- The spine, knees, teeth, bones, skin and overall skeletal alignment. These became important last year. Regular back and knee massage will be very helpful and it is a good idea to give the knees more support when you exercise. Regular visits to a chiropractor or osteopath will prove beneficial. The vertebrae need to be kept in right alignment. Protect the teeth with good dental hygiene. If you're out in the sun remember to use a good sun screen.

We have discussed the purely physical aspects of health, but as regular readers know, the body is only where disease manifests – it is not the cause. The causes are always on the more subtle levels – the levels of mind and feeling.

So, good emotional health is always important for you. Keep your moods positive and constructive and avoid depression like the plague.

Meditation will be a big help here. Good health for you means good emotional health.

Of late, though, good social health has also become important. Your love planet, Saturn, is in your 6th house all year (and was there last year), and your health planet, Jupiter, moves into the love sign of Libra on September 10. So problems in love, in the marriage or with friends, can be a spiritual root cause of health problems. Should such problems arise (God forbid), restore the social harmony as quickly as you can. The same is true for family discords.

Home and Family

Home and family are always important for the Cancerian. For them, they are the very meaning of life itself. In raising a family and dealing with these issues the Cancerian finds meaning and purpose in life.

Of late, they have not been as important as usual. But this changes on September 10 as Jupiter moves into your 4th house, making it a house of power. This, as we mentioned, often brings a move or an enlargement of the present home. Sometimes it indicates the purchase of an additional home, sometimes the purchase of expensive items for the home. The whole effect is as if one had moved.

Those of you of childbearing age are more fertile, and a pregnancy this year wouldn't be a surprise. The family circle is expanding. It is almost like a clan or tribe rather than just a family. This is one way that the clan could expand. But other members of the family could give birth too – this would fit the symbolism of the Horoscope. Your extended family will be enlarged as well.

Jupiter is your health planet. His move into your 4th house shows that you're very concerned with the health of the overall family and with family members. You are working to make the physical home healthier. If there are toxic paints or other unhealthy environmental materials in your home, you're spending to clear them up. There will also be a tendency to install exercise equipment, back massagers and other health equipment in the home. The home will become as much a health spa as a home.

Jupiter is also your work planet. Thus many of you are working more from home this year. With all the new technology available, this is not the problem that it used to be. So, if you don't already have one, you're setting up a home office. You are making the home a work place as much as a home.

A sibling or sibling figure in your life is in a strong prosperity cycle this year and seems more attached to the family than usual. He or she should probably not move this year, though they may want to. Next year will be better for that than now.

A parent or parent figure begins a prosperity cycle from September 10 onwards. Until then he or she is in a strong spiritual period, with many spiritual breakthroughs and supernatural kinds of experiences happening.

Children and children figures in your life have had a rough few years, but things are getting better for them this year. They seem more emotionally stable than in the past. Those of appropriate age have had multiple moves in recent years – and this trend continues in the year ahead.

Grandchildren (if you have them) are having a stable kind of family year. There's no need for them to make any dramatic changes.

Finance and Career

You're coming out of two wonderful financial years, Cancer, and by now most of your important financial goals have been achieved. Money, of itself, is not that interesting. Your money house is basically empty this year. (Only short-term planets will move through the 2nd house – they will do their job and then move on.)

This I read as a good thing. You seem basically content with the status quo and have no need to make dramatic changes or pay undue attention here. Of course, you're free to make changes, but there's no compelling urge.

There will be two solar eclipses this year. One on March 9 and the other on September 1. These will shake up the financial life and if changes are needed, you'll make them. We'll discuss these events in greater detail in the monthly reports.

Career is much more interesting to you than mere money. You understand that if the career is good, money follows naturally. A good career opportunity is more important than a financial opportunity. If you can have both, all the better.

The Sun is your financial planet and during the course of the year he will move through all the signs and houses of your Horoscope. Thus money and financial opportunity happen through a variety of ways and means. These short-term trends are best discussed in the monthly reports.

With Jupiter in your 3rd house until September 9, you can earn through your communication skills – through writing, teaching, sales, marketing and PR. Those of you involved in these fields should have a banner year.

Jupiter in Virgo until September 9 makes you lucky in speculations. It also shows enhanced personal creativity.

Children or children figures in your life are prospering and seem supportive. In many cases they inspire you to earn more. In many cases they have good financial ideas.

Jupiter in the 3rd house often indicates a new car (and a good one, and sometimes a second car) and the purchase of good, high-end communication equipment.

Job seekers have opportunities close to home this year. Until September 9, those opportunities can be found in the neighbourhood and perhaps through the recommendation of neighbours or siblings. It is good also to look for opportunities through the 'usual channels' – through the wanted ads in the media and online. After September 9 there will be job opportunities at home. But family members or family connections can also play a role.

Favourable financial numbers are 5, 6, 8 and 19.

The career has been unstable for many years, as we have mentioned. Learning to deal with this has been one of your life lessons of late, Cancer. But along with that is the excitement of knowing that career opportunity can happen at any time in any place – and often in the most unexpected kind of way.

Uranus in your 10th house shows someone who needs a lot of change – variety – in the career. Thus it favours freelance kinds of career. Media and online businesses would fit the bill. But even a conventional corporate career could work if it allowed you much freedom and change.

With Uranus in your 10th house it is dangerous to form any kind of opinion of your career status – high or low. It can change in a flash. It just is what it is, in the 'now'.

Those of you interested in astrology or science might consider these as career paths.

Love and Social Life

Pluto has been in your 7th house for many years, as was mentioned above. This shows a 'cosmic purge' – a detox – of the whole love and social life. This has been going on for years and will continue for many more. This purge has taken many forms. Some old relationships died. Friends have died – in some cases literally, in others, the friendship itself. It's as if they were dead to you. Many a marriage or serious relationship has gone down the tubes. Even the good ones have had 'near death' kinds of experiences.

This will go on for many more years. It is a long-term project.

Saturn, your love planet, has been in Sagittarius since December 2013. In general this is good for love. It shows an expansion of the social sphere. New friends and new love relationships are happening (and they too will get detoxed in due course).

With Saturn as your love planet you tend to be cautious in love matters. It takes time to fall in love. You like to test things and make sure everything is right before you commit yourself. But these days you are less cautious. Love happens more quickly. You're more spontaneous about it.

Saturn in Sagittarius shows an attraction to foreigners, members of the clergy and professor types – mentor types. With these aspects one can fall in love with the minister, rabbi or imam. Also with the professor or guru. You're attracted to people you can learn from and a good theological discussion these days is a form of foreplay. Your place of worship or your college is the venue for romance these days. Romance can happen through the intervention of your worship leader or people in your place of worship. Likewise through your professor or at university functions.

Saturn is ruling your love life from your 6th house of health and work. This shows many things. First, you're also attracted to health professionals. Romance can happen as you pursue your normal health goals – perhaps at the doctor's office, the lab, the gym or the health spa. Perhaps with people involved in your health. (If you go to school with them or attend the same church or place of worship, all the better.)

You yearn for a healthy love life and a healthy marriage.

Don't let this urge, which is basically good, make you too critical or judgemental, however. This can do more harm than good. Don't let it make you search for pathology either – a tendency with this kind of aspect. If there are pathologies in your relationship they will arise quite naturally without you trying to force them out. When they arise naturally, that will be the time to deal with them.

There are plenty of opportunities for love affairs this year. Jupiter is making fabulous aspects to Pluto, the ruler of your 5th house of fun and love affairs. But serious love is more likely after September 10, as Jupiter moves into better aspect with your love planet.

Your best love and social periods will be from March 21 to April 19, July 23 to August 23 and November 22 to December 21.

Self-improvement

The detox going on in your love life sounds gloomy and sombre. But behind all this is great love. You've been praying for the ideal love life, the ideal relationship. The cosmos has heard and is responding. In order to give you what you want, it first has to remove the obstructions to it. And this is what is going on. It is much like what happens when the body gets detoxed. While it's happening it's not very pleasant. All kinds of toxins, effete material, things that have weighed the body down have to come out. Then and only then can the natural healing forces of the body come into play, and heal.

It is not just people that the cosmos is detoxing, but ideas, concepts, attitudes and opinions about love, relationships and even gender. Anything that stands in the way of your ideal love life, your ideal relationship, is being removed.

You're giving birth to your ideal love life. The pains you feel are not pathology but birth pangs. If you understand things in this way, the process will go much easier.

There's more to say about health issues too. Jupiter, your health planet, will be in your 4th house from September 10 onwards. Thus, health problems, should they happen (God forbid) could be coming from a re-stimulation of the memory body. The triggering of old memories can produce real symptoms. They feel real. But they are not what they seem to be. Since, on the outside, they seem real, the tendency is to treat them in the normal medical way. But in these cases it is best to treat the memory body. To go back to the origin of the bad memory and transform it. Sometimes these memories are from past lives, in such cases past-life regression can be a big help. Normally past-life regression is not advisable – there's no reason for it except to satisfy idle human curiosity – however, if health is involved, it's a different story and it is a valid way to proceed.

In the spiritual life, it is fashionable these days to look for the foreign and exotic. People feel that their own religion (whatever it is) has no mystical value. But every religion has its mystical side – its esoteric side – and this will be best for you. Your job now is to uncover the mystical-experiential roots of your native religion.

Month-by-month Forecasts

January

Best Days Overall: 4, 5, 13, 14, 21, 22, 23, 31
Most Stressful Days Overall: 1, 2, 3, 9, 10, 15, 16, 29, 30
Best Days for Love: 6, 7, 8, 9, 10, 15, 16, 24, 25, 26
Best Days for Money: 9, 10, 17, 18, 24, 25, 26, 27, 29, 30
Best Days for Career: 2, 3, 4, 13, 15, 16, 21, 22

You begin your year with the planetary power concentrated in the social, Western sector of the Horoscope. Not only that, but you're right in the midst of a yearly love and social peak. This began on December 21. So the focus is on others these days. Your own needs, though important, take a back seat to others' needs. Take a low profile and let others have their way, so long as it isn't destructive. If conditions are not to your liking, adapt to them as best you can. The time for making changes will come in a few months. It is your social grace, your social skills that will bring you your good, not your personal abilities or personal initiative. There is nothing especially noble about either serving self or serving others. It all depends on the cycle you're in. Your happiness is no less important than the happiness of others. But right now, it takes a back seat. With these kinds of aspects, self-knowledge is gained through relationships.

The love and social landscape is undergoing many changes, sudden shocks and disruptions. Saturn, the love planet, is on an old eclipse point from the 15th to the 24th. This can bring crises to the lives of friends, partners or the current love – and you're needed there. If you're in a relationship, be more patient with the beloved over this period. He or she will tend to be temperamental. In spite of all this the love life is basically happy. Singles are dating more and meeting 'significant' people. Your social skills are helping the career as well – and this has now become more important. A lot of your socializing is business or career related. Sexual magnetism seems the main turn-on in love, but as our regular readers know, this is not enough for a lasting relationship.

Health needs watching this month. The energetic stresses are nowhere near as severe as they were in 2013 or 2014. And if you went through those stresses, you'll easily go through the month ahead. Still, when energy is low, a person becomes more vulnerable to disease. Pre-existing conditions tend to flare up as well. The cure, in most cases, is a good night's sleep or a lazy weekend. Enhance the health in the ways mentioned in the yearly report. Until the 24th, neck, throat and hip massage will also be a help. A herbal kidney detox might also be good. Health improves dramatically after the 20th.

The social life and social skills are important on a financial level as well. Your own financial interest is important, but always keep in mind the financial interest of the other person – and put that first. Your own financial good will happen naturally. There are opportunities for business partnerships and joint ventures. Spousal support is stronger than usual.

February

Best Days Overall: 1, 9, 10, 18, 19, 27, 28, 29
Most Stressful Days Overall: 5, 6, 11, 12, 25, 26
Best Days for Love: 2, 3, 5, 6, 11, 12, 13, 14, 20, 21, 25
Best Days for Money: 5, 6, 7, 8, 13, 14, 17, 20, 21, 22, 23, 24, 27, 28
Best Days for Career: 1, 9, 10, 11, 12, 18, 19, 28, 29

Your 8th house of transformation became powerful last month on the 20th and is still strong until February 19. This has important financial implications. Until the 19th continue to focus on the wealth of others – on prospering others. Money can come to you through insurance claims, trust funds or tax refunds. If you have estate, tax or insurance claims, this is a good month to deal with those things. Spousal support still seems strong. The spouse, partner or current love is in a yearly financial peak and is likely to be more supportive. Those of you of appropriate age should do your estate and tax planning now.

This is an excellent period to pay down debts or to borrow money, depending on your need. Debt used wisely and properly can make you rich. Used unwisely it can destroy. This is a month to learn the difference between constructive and destructive debt. If you have a good business idea this is an excellent period for attracting outside money to your projects, for meeting with investors or bankers.

This is also a good month for a financial 'detox'. Get rid of possessions you don't use or need. Get rid of redundant bank or brokerage accounts and in general get rid of non-essential expenses. This is a month where you prosper by 'cutting back'. These redundancies clog up the financial energy and slow down earnings. Make room for the new good that wants to come in.

The financial intuition is especially sharp on the 28th and 29th – looks like a nice payday.

The planetary power has been in the upper half of the chart since the beginning of the year. Thus it is a period to focus on your outer goals – your career objectives. Home and family are always important to you, but you can serve them best by being successful in the world. Children and children figures in your life are especially good career motivators this month. And often 'out of the mouth of babes' good career ideas come.

Health is good this month and gets even better after the 19th. With more energy there are more possibilities. The horizons expand. Continue to enhance the health in the ways mentioned in the yearly report.

On the 19th, as the Sun enters your 9th house, foreign lands call to you. There is more business-related travel. There are financial opportunities in foreign countries and with foreign companies.

March

Best Days Overall: 8, 9, 16, 17, 26, 27
Most Stressful Days Overall: 3, 4, 10, 11, 23, 24, 31
Best Days for Love: 1, 2, 3, 4, 6, 7, 10, 11, 16, 18, 19, 26, 27, 28, 29, 31
Best Days for Money: 3, 4, 8, 9, 12, 13, 16, 17, 18, 19, 21, 22, 28, 29, 31
Best Days for Career: 10, 11, 18, 19, 28, 29

Your 9th house remains powerful until the 20th. This is a wonderful aspect for college-level students. They succeed in their studies. There are educational disruptions and perhaps changes in educational plans – this comes from the solar eclipse of the 9th – but the changes will be good.

We have two eclipses this month – both of them impact on you strongly. Of the two, the lunar eclipse of the 23rd is stronger (especially on those of you born from June 21 to June 25). So, take it nice and easy during the eclipse periods – a few days before and after.

The solar eclipse of the 9th (in America it is the 8th) occurs in your 9th house. This brings the educational changes that we mentioned above. It is probably not advisable to travel during this time; if you must, try to schedule flights around the eclipse period. The eclipse indicates shake-ups in your place of worship and dramas in the lives of your worship leaders: life-changing kinds of dramas. Often, this kind of eclipse produces 'crises of faith' – a testing of your personal religion and personal philosophy of life. These testings are actually good – there is much that we believe that is mere superstition. These things need to be cleared out and other ideas might need modification.

Every solar eclipse brings financial changes and this one is no different. This is also good. Twice a year the cosmos gives you opportunity to make the changes and adjustments (usually in thinking and planning) that need to be made. It's usually not pleasant while it's happening – often there is great fear and insecurity – but the end result is good.

The lunar eclipse of the 23rd occurs in your 4th house of home and family. The eclipsed planet, the Moon, naturally rules this domain. So the family (and especially a parent or parent figure in your life) is affected and there are likely to be family dramas. Dramas in the home. Flaws in the home (if there are any) are usually revealed under this kind of eclipse and repairs need to be made. Be more patient with family members now. There's no question that passions are running high.

The dream life will most likely be negative during this period. But not too much weight should be placed on it. The eclipse is stirring up the emotional plane. This eclipse affects you on a personal level too. Your sense of self, of identity gets challenged by people or events. There is a need to redefine yourself, your self-concept and the way you want others to see you. This is generally a six-month process. Generally it leads to changes in hair-style and wardrobe. You present a new look to the world. You need to rest and relax more from the 20th onward, but especially around this lunar eclipse period. Spend more quiet time at home, read some good books or watch some films. The best thing would be to meditate more.

April

Best Days Overall: 4, 5, 12, 13, 22, 23
Most Stressful Days Overall: 1, 6, 7, 19, 20, 21, 27, 28
Best Days for Love: 1, 6, 14, 15, 25, 26, 27, 28
Best Days for Money: 1, 6, 7, 8, 9, 14, 15, 16, 17, 18, 27, 28
Best Days for Career: 6, 7, 14, 15, 24, 25

Health became more delicate on the 20th of last month, and remains so until the 19th. You're working hard and seem very successful, but try to schedule rest periods wherever possible. If you keep your focus on the really essential things and let go of trivia, it will be easier to get the rest that you need. Enhance the health in the ways mentioned in the yearly report. In addition, it might be good to exercise more and to massage the head, face and scalp.

Career is the main headline this month. On March 20 you entered a yearly career peak and this continues until the 19th. You have a good work ethic and this is noted by the powers that be. Pay rises – real or 'in kind' – are likely this month. You have the financial favour of elders, bosses, parents and parent figures. Government payments could come too.

Now that the eclipses are over and the Sun is in Aries, this is a good time to launch new products or ventures. The only problem is that there are many retrograde planets this month. Proceed slowly and cautiously.

Finances are good this month. You have confidence and much planetary support. The problem is that you might jump into purchases or investments too quickly. Sleep on things more. On the 19th you take this advice. You're more deliberate, more conservative, in your financial judgement. The Sun, your financial planet, will start making very nice aspects to Jupiter, the planet of abundance, so there is prosperity and good fortune happening.

Your love planet, Saturn, started to travel backwards on March 25 and he will be in retrograde motion for many more months. Love is basically happy this month, but there is no need to rush into anything. There are romantic opportunities with superiors and people of higher social and professional standing. You have the aspects for the 'office romance', but let things develop as they will. The retrograde of Saturn doesn't stop dating or socializing, but it does slow things down a bit. Social judgement is not up to its usual standard. It is time to get more mental and emotional clarity on love – to decide what you need and what you want.

It will be best to avoid unnecessary foreign travel this month. There can be more family dramas on the 7th and 8th – be more patient with family members then. There are also sudden financial changes on the 9th and 10th, but the problem passes quickly.

May

Best Days Overall: 1, 2, 3, 10, 11, 19, 20, 21, 29, 30
Most Stressful Days Overall: 4, 5, 17, 18, 24, 25, 31
Best Days for Love: 4, 5, 6, 12, 13, 14, 15, 22, 23, 24, 25, 26, 27, 31
Best Days for Money: 2, 3, 4, 6, 12, 13, 14, 15, 24, 25
Best Days for Career: 4, 5, 12, 21, 22, 30, 31

Last month – on April 5 – the planetary power began to shift from the West to the East. The planetary power now moves towards you instead of away from you. You've spent many months adapting to things, and pleasing others; now it's time to please yourself. As we mentioned, your happiness and self-interest are no less important than others'. It is time to take responsibility for your own happiness. Personal power is getting stronger day by day. Now – and for the next few months – is the time to make the personal changes you need to make. You don't need to worry about what others think or feel. Create pleasant conditions for yourself. They will, in due course, come around to your way of thinking.

Your 11th house became strong on the 19th of last month and remains so until the 20th. This has important financial implications. Your social connections are important these days. Who you know is probably more important than how much you have. You have the financial favour of friends. You're realizing financial 'fondest hopes and wishes' – and will most likely form new hopes and wishes. It is a never-ending process. From the 2nd to the 4th the Sun trines Jupiter – a very nice payday. Job seekers will have very nice opportunities then too. The financial planet in the 11th house favours online activities and online kinds of businesses. It is good for networking and for being involved in groups and organizations. These bring bottom-line benefits.

The financial planet in the 11th house indicates a need to be more experimental in finance. It is a time when the rule books are thrown out and one learns what works through trial and error. Conservative experimentation is good. Reckless experimentation, however, is not so good.

On the 20th the financial planet enters the spiritual 12th house. This indicates good financial intuition. Psychics, astrologers and other spiritual channels will have good financial guidance for you. Financial guidance will come through dreams as well. Financial problems could be coming from spiritual disconnection. Being 'prayed up' and in a state of grace is always good – but with you it has financial implications. This is a period to go deeper into the spiritual dimensions of wealth.

Mars, your career planet, is retrograde this month. This doesn't stop the career but it does slow things down a bit. New career opportunities need to be looked at closely – things might not be as they seem. Mars will have his 'solstice' from the 7th to the 14th. He will pause in his movement during that period and will occupy the same latitude for seven days. This shows a need to pause in the career. It is a good pause – a pause that refreshes. You come out of it with greater clarity. During this pause nothing seems to be happening – but many things *are* happening behind the scenes.

June

Best Days Overall: 6, 7, 15, 16, 17, 25, 26
Most Stressful Days Overall: 1, 13, 14, 20, 21, 22, 27, 28
Best Days for Love: 1, 4, 5, 8, 9, 14, 18, 19, 20, 21, 22, 25, 26, 27, 28
Best Days for Money: 2, 3, 4, 5, 8, 9, 10, 11, 13, 14, 20, 21, 25, 29, 30
Best Days for Career: 1, 7, 16, 17, 25, 26, 27, 28

The planetary power is now at its maximum Eastern position in your chart. This will be the case next month too. So, personal power is now at its maximum. There is strong planetary support for your personal goals. Strong support for your personal happiness. The cosmos is grand and lofty and involved in huge undertakings. Yet, it cares that you have the right clothing, shoes and personal conditions. These things are not too trivial for it. So create the conditions that please you. In a few months' time it will be more difficult to do.

Your 12th house of spirituality became strong last month (on the 20th) and is strong until the 21st. So you're in a spiritual period. A period for interior growth and spiritual breakthroughs. Those already on a spiritual path will find their progress accelerated. Those not on a path will have supernatural kinds of experiences that make them scratch their heads. Events happen that cast doubt on the whole physical 3D model of the universe. Seeds are being planted for future growth. So, the month ahead is good for studying sacred literature, for attending spiritual seminars or lectures, and for getting more involved in charities or good causes. (These are not only good for their own sake but will aid your bottom line.)

On the 21st the Sun (also your financial planet) crosses the Ascendant and enters the 1st house, instituting a very happy kind of period – one of your yearly personal pleasure peaks. All the physical delights become available. The interior growth of the past month now becomes more visible. The body shines. The physical appearance is at a yearly high. Money comes to you. Windfalls. Financial opportunity seeks you out and happens naturally with little fuss. You look wealthy. You spend on yourself – invest in yourself. Others see you as prosperous. This prosperity image that you have draws prosperity opportunities to you. Venus in your sign from the 18th onwards brings beautiful women to men. In a woman's chart she enhances her own beauty. Thus it is good to buy those personal accessories or clothing that you need. The taste is super and the choices will be good.

Though you're more attractive and alluring to the opposite sex, love needs more caution. Saturn is still retrograde all this month. There is no need to rush into anything. Love will be much better next month.

Health and energy are excellent these days. You can enhance them further in the ways mentioned in the yearly report.

July

Best Days Overall: 3, 4, 13, 14, 22, 23, 31
Most Stressful Days Overall: 10, 11, 12, 18, 19, 24, 25
Best Days for Love: 3, 4, 6, 7, 15, 16, 18, 19, 24, 25
Best Days for Money: 3, 4, 6, 7, 8, 9, 13, 14, 18, 19, 24, 27, 28
Best Days for Career: 3, 4, 13, 14, 22, 23, 24, 25, 31

A happy and successful month ahead, Cancer. Enjoy!

Like last month you're at the peak of personal power right now. Make the changes that need to be made. Have things your way. You know what's best for you, so go for it. The 'Force' (the planetary power) is with you now.

One of the problems with too much ease is boredom. So, the cosmos, in its infinite wisdom, throws in a few challenges to keep things interesting and to keep you on your toes. Drive more carefully on the 1st, 2nd, 7th, 10th and 11th. Cars and communication equipment get tested. The dream life can be foreboding during this period too.

This is not such a great month for foreign travel – do it only if you must. Neptune is camped out on the Moon's South Node. College-level students have to work harder in school. Legal issues can swallow you up.

You're still in the midst of a yearly personal pleasure peak. Good for pampering the body and enjoying the physical delights. Very good for getting the body and image in right shape. And it is still good – until the 12th – for buying clothing and personal accessories. Personal appearance shines. Love is much happier from the 12th onwards, but like last month there is no need to rush into anything.

The month ahead is prosperous. Until the 22nd, money and financial opportunity pursue you. There is not much that you need to do: money will find you wherever you are. Just go about your daily business. On the 22nd the Sun, the financial planet, enters the money house and you begin a yearly financial peak. The focus is on finance then. And, by the cosmic law, we get what we focus on.

Last month (on the 21st) the planetary power shifted from the upper to the lower half of your Horoscope. Your career goals have been more or less achieved and now it is time to focus on the home, family and your emotional well-being. You're in the night time of your year. During the night we gather strength for the next day. If you want your next career push to go well, get a good night's rest now.

August

Best Days Overall: 1, 9, 10, 19, 20, 27, 28
Most Stressful Days Overall: 7, 8, 14, 15, 21, 22
Best Days for Love: 2, 3, 12, 13, 14, 15, 21, 22, 23, 24, 29, 30
Best Days for Money: 2, 3, 4, 5, 12, 13, 14, 15, 23, 24, 29, 30, 31
Best Days for Career: 1, 2, 12, 21, 22, 29, 30

You're still in a yearly financial peak until the 22nd. Earning power is at its maximum right now. Friends and family seem unusually supportive. Good high tech skills and equipment are very important now and most likely you're spending more on these things. By the 22nd, as the Sun leaves the money house, financial goals – at least the short-term ones – are achieved and your focus shifts to mental and intellectual interests. On a financial level, sales, marketing, advertising and PR seem very important. Neighbours and siblings seem helpful. There are happy financial opportunities close by in your neighbourhood.

Mars, the career planet, moves into your 6th house on the 2nd. This is an excellent time for job seekers. Career is boosted by a good work ethic.

Health is good this month, but Mars in the 6th house suggests a need for more physical exercise. Good muscle tone is important. In addition to what was mentioned in the yearly report, head, face and scalp massage will enhance the health and energy level.

Career is important but can be downplayed this month. Emotional wellness lays the groundwork for future career success. Focus on this.

Mars is 'out of bounds' from the 9th to the 31st. This gives us many messages. Your company or industry is exploring new and strange paths. Parents, parent figures or bosses are outside their normal sphere.

Retrograde activity is strong this month; 40 per cent of the planets are retrograde until the 18th and after the 30th – a high percentage.

Make haste slowly. Try to be perfect in all that you do – no need to make matters worse.

There are great improvements in the love life this month. Saturn receives wonderful aspects which show romantic opportunity. More importantly, the love planet starts moving forward on the 18th, bringing sorely needed clarity to the love life. Social and romantic decisions will be much better from the 18th onwards.

Venus travels with Jupiter from the 26th to the 28th. This indicates prosperity for the family as a whole. Perhaps new and expensive items come into the home – it seems like high tech or health equipment. Happy job opportunities come from the family (and for family members).

September

Best Days Overall: 5, 6, 7, 15, 16, 23, 24
Most Stressful Days Overall: 3, 4, 10, 11, 12, 17, 18, 30
Best Days For Love: 3, 4, 8, 9, 10, 11, 12, 13, 14, 19, 20, 23, 25, 26, 27
Best Days For Money: 1, 2, 11, 12, 13, 20, 21, 25, 26, 27, 30
Best Days For Career: 8, 9, 17, 18, 25, 27, 28

The planetary power is now at the nadir (lowest point) of your chart. It is the 'midnight hour' in your year – the magical, mystical midnight hour. A new day is being born in the darkest point of night. So the focus is on home, family and your emotional wellness. Career can be (and will be) downplayed. Mars, your career planet, has his 'solstice' from the 19th to the 28th. He will more or less stay in one position of latitude that whole period. This shows a 'pause' in the career. Career activity more or less stops for a while. Don't be alarmed by this pause. These pauses bring heightened career activity later on. The pause leads to positive change.

We also have two eclipses this month. These are more benign to you than the ones we had in March, but they still bring disruptions – both personal and in those around you and to the world at large.

The solar eclipse of the 1st occurs in your 3rd house. Drive more carefully over this period. Cars and communication equipment will get tested and will often be found wanting, and needing to be replaced. There are dramas in the lives of siblings, sibling figures and neighbours. Often there are disruptions in the neighbourhood. Dramatic kinds of events. Every solar eclipse brings financial changes – the Sun is your financial planet. Though it might not be pleasant while it is happening – it often brings a sudden expense – it forces changes that have long needed to be made. The solar eclipse impacts on Mars and Saturn – your career and love planets. Thus career changes are afoot. By now, you're pretty good at handling these things. Uranus has been in your 10th house for many years. The impact on Saturn shows the testing of a current relationship. It puts the relationship in crisis. The good relationships survive, but the flawed ones are in danger.

The lunar eclipse of the 16th occurs in your 9th house, but near the cusp of your 10th house. Thus there are more career changes. Foreign travel should be avoided during that period. Students at college or post-graduate level make important changes in their educational plans. Sometimes they change schools or courses. There are dramas in your place of worship and in the lives of your worship leaders. Every lunar eclipse has quite an effect and you feel them more than most. This is because the eclipsed planet, the Moon, is your ruling planet. So, as in March, you're once again forced by events to redefine yourself – your image, your look and your self-concept. If you don't define yourself for yourself, others will – and that's not so pleasant.

October

  Best Days Overall: 3, 4, 12, 13, 21, 22, 30, 31
  Most Stressful Days Overall: 1, 2, 8, 9, 15, 27, 28, 29
  Best Days for Love: 3, 4, 5, 6, 8, 9, 12, 13, 15, 23, 24
  Best Days for Money: 1, 2, 10, 11, 18, 19, 20, 23, 24, 27, 28, 30
  Best Days for Career: 8, 9, 14, 15, 17, 25, 26

Last month, on the 10th, Jupiter entered your 4th house of home and family. He will be there for the rest of the year ahead and well into next year. On September 22, the Sun also entered this house. So it is a happy period. Home and family issues are happy. Moves could happen – either this month or in the next twelve or so months. The family circle is being expanded too, generally though birth or marriage. For a Cancerian this is Nirvana.

Health needs more watching, however. This has been the case since September 22. Happy things (especially a move, birth or marriage) can be as stressful as negative things. Make sure you get enough rest. Spend more time in a spa, schedule in more massages or reflexology treatments. Enhance the health in the ways mentioned in the yearly report. Now that your health planet, Jupiter, has changed signs, your needs in health are different. The kidneys and hips are important health areas for you now, and hip massage will do wonders for you. (Venus, the planet that rules the kidneys and hips, moves into your 6th house on the 8th – reinforcing what we say here.) Neck massage is also good. Emotional wellness is always important for you, but now even more so. Keep the moods positive and constructive. Do your best to maintain family harmony.

Health and energy improve after the 23rd but health is still delicate for the rest of the year.

The month ahead looks prosperous. Money comes from the family or through family connections. Money is earned from home. September 25–26 brought a nice payday and you're in the glow of that this month. On the 22nd the Sun enters your 5th house. Speculations are more favourable. You spend on children and leisure activities. You enjoy your wealth more. Children are financially supportive as well – sometimes through actual financial contributions, sometimes though ideas and inspiration. Money is earned in happy ways.

Unnecessary foreign travel is not advisable this month. Neptune is camped out on an eclipse point all month.

Sales and marketing people have a fortunate sale on the 11th or 12th. Traders do well on those days too. For others that time can bring happy reading material or communication equipment. It is a good period for job seekers.

November

Best Days Overall: 1, 9, 10, 17, 18, 26, 27, 28
Most Stressful Days Overall: 4, 5, 11, 12, 24, 25
Best Days for Love: 2, 3, 4, 5, 11, 12, 13, 19, 20, 21, 22, 29, 30
Best Days for Money: 6, 7, 9, 10, 15, 16, 18, 19, 20, 24, 25, 29
Best Days for Career: 4, 5, 11, 12, 15, 24, 25

Last month, on the 7th, the planetary power shifted from the East to the West – from the sector of self to the sector of others. The shift actually began September 22, but it was strengthened last month. The planetary power is now moving away from you and towards others. Thus your personal independence and personal power are beginning to decline. The reason for this is so you can cultivate your social skills – your ability to get on with others and obtain their cooperation. You have considerable personal skills and gifts, but these are not what counts now. Your good comes through others now and you need their good will. Your way might not be the best way these days. Let others have their way, so long as it isn't destructive.

Last month on the 23rd you entered another of your yearly personal pleasure peaks. This goes on until the 22nd of this month. This is a time to have fun, to enjoy life and engage in creative pursuits. This is a very good month for being involved with children and children figures in your life. When it comes to the joy of life, children are the best teachers.

Health still needs watching and you seem on the case – a good thing. Your 6th house of health is strong all month. Health can be enhanced in the ways mentioned in the yearly report, but also by giving more attention to the lungs, small intestine, arms, shoulders and respiratory system. Arm and shoulder massage is important. After the 22nd give more attention to the heart. Don't let financial ups and downs impact on your health. Money is money, health is health. They're two separate things. The good news is that finances are excellent all month. They're especially good after the 22nd when the Sun enters Sagittarius – the sign of expansion. You earn more and you spend more. You're 'happy go lucky' when it comes to money; the main danger is overspending. Money comes happily until the 22nd, perhaps while you're on the tennis court or golf course – while you're out having fun. After the 22nd it comes through work.

Even if you're already employed, extra work assignments are likely that will bring in cash. Sometimes it happens through overtime. Those of you seeking jobs have many good opportunities.

The love life is happy this month. The love planet has been moving forward for some months now and this month it receives much positive stimulation. It looks like an active social month – enjoy.

December

Best Days Overall: 6, 7, 14, 15, 24, 25
Most Stressful Days Overall: 1, 2, 3, 8, 9, 21, 22, 29, 30
Best Days for Love: 1, 2, 3, 8, 9, 12, 13, 16, 17, 21, 22, 26, 27, 29, 30
Best Days for Money: 4, 5, 8, 9, 12, 13, 16, 17, 18, 21, 22, 29, 31
Best Days for Career: 4, 5, 8, 9, 12, 13, 24

The planetary power is now at its most Western position – furthest away from you. The month ahead is all about others and their needs. People will see you as unselfish, putting others ahead of yourself. But really it's just the cycle you're in. If conditions are irksome, reconcile yourself to them as best you can. Now is not the time to make changes or to overly assert yourself. Plan the changes that need to be made and in a few months – when the planets shift to the East again – it will be easier to implement them.

Personal power is lessened, but your social power is much increased. The month ahead is a banner love and social month. On the 21st the Sun enters your 7th house (which is already strong) and you begin a yearly love and social peak. You're in the mood for love (and that's the most important thing) – you're focused here. And, according to the spiritual law, we get what we focus on.

Singles attract all kinds of people this month – there are the money people, the spiritual types, the intellectuals and the 'play around' types. With so many planets in the 7th house (half of the planets are either there or moving through there this month) you get along with all kinds of different people.

Finances are good this month but there are a few bumps in the road. Financial intuition needs some verification on the 1st. Financial decisions need more study. Be careful of overspending on the 9th and 10th. The 11th and 12th bring some financial disturbance – most likely an unexpected expense or development. Changes need to be made. There is luck in speculations on the 7th and 8th. There are opportunities for business partnerships or joint ventures all month. Social connections are important financially, especially from the 21st onwards. This is a time when you learn that wealth of friendships is an important form of wealth. It's not so much about how much you have, but about who you know and how others feel about you.

Health needs serious attention being paid to it from the 21st onwards. Five, and at times six, planets are in stressful aspect with you. So, enjoy yourself, but allow more time for rest. If you're tired take a nap. Avoid worry and anxiety – the emotions that can create heart problems. Enhance the health in the ways mentioned in the yearly report.

Leo

♌

THE LION

Birthdays from
21st July to
21st August

Personality Profile

LEO AT A GLANCE

Element – Fire

Ruling Planet – Sun
  Career Planet – Venus
  Love Planet – Uranus
  Money Planet – Mercury
  Planet of Health and Work – Saturn
  Planet of Home and Family Life – Pluto

Colours – gold, orange, red

Colours that promote love, romance and social harmony – black, indigo,
  ultramarine blue

Colours that promote earning power – yellow, yellow-orange

Gems – amber, chrysolite, yellow diamond

Metal – gold

Scents – bergamot, frankincense, musk, neroli

Quality – fixed (= stability)

Quality most needed for balance – humility

Strongest virtues – leadership ability, self-esteem and confidence, generosity, creativity, love of joy

Deepest needs – fun, elation, the need to shine

Characteristics to avoid – arrogance, vanity, bossiness

Signs of greatest overall compatibility – Aries, Sagittarius

Signs of greatest overall incompatibility – Taurus, Scorpio, Aquarius

Sign most helpful to career – Taurus

Sign most helpful for emotional support – Scorpio

Sign most helpful financially – Virgo

Sign best for marriage and/or partnerships – Aquarius

Sign most helpful for creative projects – Sagittarius

Best Sign to have fun with – Sagittarius

Signs most helpful in spiritual matters – Aries, Cancer

Best day of the week – Sunday

Understanding a Leo

When you think of Leo, think of royalty – then you'll get the idea of what the Leo character is all about and why Leos are the way they are. It is true that, for various reasons, some Leo-born do not always express this quality – but even if not they should like to do so.

A monarch rules not by example (as does Aries) nor by consensus (as do Capricorn and Aquarius) but by personal will. Will is law. Personal taste becomes the style that is imitated by all subjects. A monarch is somehow larger than life. This is how a Leo desires to be.

When you dispute the personal will of a Leo it is serious business. He or she takes it as a personal affront, an insult. Leos will let you know that their will carries authority and that to disobey is demeaning and disrespectful.

A Leo is king (or queen) of his or her personal domain. Subordinates, friends and family are the loyal and trusted subjects. Leos rule with benevolent grace and in the best interests of others. They have a powerful presence; indeed, they are powerful people. They seem to attract attention in any social gathering. They stand out because they are stars in their domain. Leos feel that, like the Sun, they are made to shine and rule. Leos feel that they were born to special privilege and royal prerogatives – and most of them attain this status, at least to some degree.

The Sun is the ruler of this sign, and when you think of sunshine it is very difficult to feel unhealthy or depressed. Somehow the light of the Sun is the very antithesis of illness and apathy. Leos love life. They also love to have fun; they love drama, music, the theatre and amusements of all sorts. These are the things that give joy to life. If – even in their best interests – you try to deprive Leos of their pleasures, good food, drink and entertainment, you run the serious risk of depriving them of the will to live. To them life without joy is no life at all.

Leos epitomize humanity's will to power. But power in and of itself – regardless of what some people say – is neither good nor evil. Only when power is abused does it become evil. Without power even good things cannot come to pass. Leos realize this and are uniquely qualified to wield power. Of all the signs, they do it most naturally. Capricorn, the other power sign of the zodiac, is a better manager and administrator than Leo – much better. But Leo outshines Capricorn in personal grace and presence. Leo loves power, whereas Capricorn assumes power out of a sense of duty.

Finance

Leos are great leaders but not necessarily good managers. They are better at handling the overall picture than the nitty-gritty details of business. If they have good managers working for them they can become exceptional executives. They have vision and a lot of creativity.

Leos love wealth for the pleasures it can bring. They love an opulent lifestyle, pomp and glamour. Even when they are not wealthy they live as if they are. This is why many fall into debt, from which it is sometimes difficult to emerge.

Leos, like Pisceans, are generous to a fault. Very often they want to acquire wealth solely so that they can help others economically. Wealth to Leo buys services and managerial ability. It creates jobs for others and improves the general well-being of those around them. Therefore – to a Leo – wealth is good. Wealth is to be enjoyed to the fullest. Money is not to be left to gather dust in a mouldy bank vault but to be enjoyed, spread around, used. So Leos can be quite reckless in their spending.

With the sign of Virgo on Leo's 2nd money house cusp, Leo needs to develop some of Virgo's traits of analysis, discrimination and purity when it comes to money matters. They must learn to be more careful with the details of finance (or to hire people to do this for them). They have to be more cost-conscious in their spending habits. Generally, they need to manage their money better. Leos tend to chafe under financial constraints, yet these constraints can help Leos to reach their highest financial potential.

Leos like it when their friends and family know that they can depend on them for financial support. They do not mind – and even enjoy – lending money, but they are careful that they are not taken advantage of. From their 'regal throne' Leos like to bestow gifts upon their family and friends and then enjoy the good feelings these gifts bring to everybody. Leos love financial speculations and – when the celestial influences are right – are often lucky.

Career and Public Image

Leos like to be perceived as wealthy, for in today's world wealth often equals power. When they attain wealth they love having a large house with lots of land and animals.

At their jobs Leos excel in positions of authority and power. They are good at making decisions – on a grand level – but they prefer to leave the details to others. Leos are well respected by their colleagues and subordinates, mainly because they have a knack for understanding and relating to those around them. Leos usually strive for the top positions even if they have to start at the bottom and work hard to get there. As might be expected of such a charismatic sign, Leos are always trying to improve their work situation. They do so in order to have a better chance of advancing to the top.

On the other hand, Leos do not like to be bossed around or told what to do. Perhaps this is why they aspire so for the top – where they can be the decision-makers and need not take orders from others.

Leos never doubt their success and focus all their attention and efforts on achieving it. Another great Leo characteristic is that – just like good monarchs – they do not attempt to abuse the power or success they achieve. If they do so this is not wilful or intentional. Usually they like to share their wealth and try to make everyone around them join in their success.

Leos are – and like to be perceived as – hard-working, well-established individuals. It is definitely true that they are capable of hard work and often manage great things. But do not forget that, deep down inside, Leos really are fun-lovers.

Love and Relationships

Generally, Leos are not the marrying kind. To them relationships are good while they are pleasurable. When the relationship ceases to be pleasurable a true Leo will want out. They always want to have the freedom to leave. That is why Leos excel at love affairs rather than commitment. Once married, however, Leo is faithful – even if some Leos have a tendency to marry more than once in their lifetime. If you are in love with a Leo, just show him or her a good time – travel, go to casinos and clubs, the theatre and discos. Wine and dine your Leo love – it is expensive but worth it and you will have fun.

Leos generally have an active love life and are demonstrative in their affections. They love to be with other optimistic and fun-loving types like themselves, but wind up settling with someone more serious, intellectual and unconventional. The partner of a Leo tends to be more political and socially conscious than he or she is, and more libertarian. When you marry a Leo, mastering the freedom-loving tendencies of your partner will definitely become a lifelong challenge – and be careful that Leo does not master you.

Aquarius sits on Leo's 7th house of love cusp. Thus if Leos want to realize their highest love and social potential they need to develop a more egalitarian, Aquarian perspective on others. This is not easy for Leo, for 'the king' finds his equals only among other 'kings'. But perhaps this is the solution to Leo's social challenge – to be 'a king among kings'. It is all right to be regal, but recognize the nobility in others.

Home and Domestic Life

Although Leos are great entertainers and love having people over, sometimes this is all show. Only very few close friends will get to see the real side of a Leo's day-to-day life. To a Leo the home is a place of comfort, recreation and transformation; a secret, private retreat – a castle. Leos like to spend money, show off a bit, entertain and have fun. They enjoy the latest furnishings, clothes and gadgets – all things fit for kings.

Leos are fiercely loyal to their family and, of course, expect the same from them. They love their children almost to a fault; they have to be careful not to spoil them too much. They also must try to avoid attempting to make individual family members over in their own image. Leos should keep in mind that others also have the need to be their own people. That is why Leos have to be extra careful about being over-bossy or over-domineering in the home.

Horoscope for 2016

Major Trends

The year ahead looks happy and successful, Leo. Enjoy. The long-term planets are either in harmony with you or leaving you alone. There is little obstruction to your plans and you should achieve your goals rather easily. Sure, there will be periods in the year where life is less easy than usual. These come from the transits of the planets, which are temporary, and are not trends for the year. When the difficult transits pass, your life resumes its normal ease.

You will have some challenges, to be sure, but you have much help in dealing with them.

The main headline is Saturn in Sagittarius, your 5th house. He has been there since late 2013 and will remain there for the entire year. Leo is the fun lover *par excellence* of the zodiac, but lately you've needed to tone this down a bit. Instead of irrational exuberance, let it be rational exuberance. There is another message too. Saturn is your planet of work. Learn to enjoy your work. Make it pleasurable. Use your creativity. As you do so you'll achieve more and still have fun.

Pluto has been in your 6th house of health for some years now and he will be there for many years to come. This creates a tendency to surgeries. But it also indicates that detoxes are very effective. Your attitudes about health are being transformed too. More on this later.

Neptune has been in your 8th house for some years now and will be there for many more years. This indicates the spiritualization of your sexuality. You are going deeper into the spiritual side of sex – sex as an act of worship rather than an act of lust.

The year ahead is prosperous too. Jupiter has been in your money house since August 12 of last year and will remain there until September 9 of this year. A classic signal of prosperity. More details later.

Last year was an excellent love year and many of you are with someone special now. This is probably why love is not such a major interest in the year ahead. There's nothing against it, but nothing especially supporting it.

Jupiter will enter your 3rd house of communication on September 10 and spend the rest of the year in this house. This is a wonderful transit for students, teachers, writers and journalists. It shows success and good fortune.

Your areas of greatest interest in the year ahead are: finance (until September 9); communication and intellectual interests (from September 10 onwards); children, fun and creativity; health and work; sex, occult studies, personal transformation, taxes and estates; and religion, philosophy, higher education and foreign travel.

Your paths of greatest fulfilment are finance; and communication and intellectual interests (from September 10 onwards).

Health

(Please note that this is an astrological perspective on health and not a medical one. In days of yore there was no difference, these perspectives were identical. But now there could be quite a difference. For a medical perspective, please consult your doctor or health practitioner.)

Health and energy look excellent in the year ahead. There are no long-term planets stressing you out. There will be times, due to the short-term transits, when health and energy are not at their optimum. But these are temporary things, not trends for the year ahead. If you have a pre-existing condition you should see good improvement this year.

Health is good, yet your 6th house is strong this year. There are various ways to read this. Perhaps you are over-focusing on your health, perhaps magnifying little things into big things (hypochondria). Or, and this is more likely, you are involved in disciplined daily health regimes. And, it seems, these involve detox or purification regimes. With Pluto being in your 6th house for so many years, you seem expert at detoxes and they work well for you.

Good though your health is, you can make it even better. Give more attention to the following – the vulnerable areas of your chart (the relevant reflexology points are shown in the following diagram):

- The heart. This is always important for Leo. Worry and anxiety, the side effects of lack of faith, are the main root causes of heart problems. Avoid them.
- The spine, knees, teeth, bones, skin and overall skeletal alignment. These areas are also very important for Leo, as Saturn

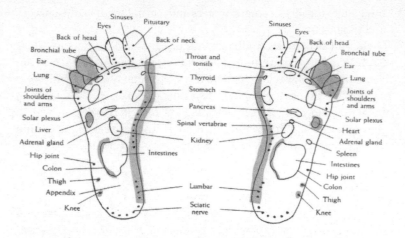

Important foot reflexology points for the year ahead

*Try to massage all of the foot on a regular basis – the top of the foot as well as
the bottom – but pay extra attention to the points highlighted on the chart.
When you massage, be aware of 'sore spots' as these need special attention.
It's also a good idea to massage the ankles, and below them especially.*

(who has a special care for them) is your health planet. Regular
back and knee massage is always advisable. There are chairs that
massage the back mechanically and this might be a good
investment if you don't already have one. Regular visits to a
chiropractor or osteopath will help keep the vertebrae in right
alignment. Regular dental hygiene will help the teeth. Use a good
sun screen when out in a strong sun and give the knees more
support when exercising.

- The colon, bladder and sexual organs. These have become more
  important ever since Pluto moved into your 6th house at the end of
  2008. If you feel under the weather a good herbal colon cleanse
  might be in order. Safe sex and sexual moderation are important.
- The liver and thighs. These have only become important since last
  year. The liver needs more energy as it seems sluggish these days.
  If you feel under the weather a herbal liver cleanse will be
  beneficial. Massage the thighs regularly.

Pluto, the ruler of surgery, in your 6th house suggests a predisposition to this. No doubt this has happened for many of you in recent years. It can be recommended again. However, keep in mind that in many cases a good detox will achieve the same result.

Pluto is your family planet. Thus problems at home – discord with family members – can be a root cause of problems. Should problems arise (God forbid), restore harmony at home as quickly as possible.

Emotional health is very important these days. Work to keep the moods positive and constructive.

Home and Family

Your 4th house of home and family will become strong next year, but this year it is basically empty. Only short-term planets will move through there – and briefly. This suggests a stable kind of year.

There has been much turmoil and drama in the family in recent years – especially in 2013 and the first half of 2014. There could have been deaths in the family or near-death kinds of experiences in the lives of family members. Happily things seem much more peaceful now.

Pluto, the family planet, has been in Capricorn for some years. This suggests that you're running the family in a traditional kind of way. Rebellion breaks out every now and then (much less often than in recent years, though!) but basically, the family is a traditional, conservative one.

Pluto has been in your 6th house of health since late 2008. Thus you've been working to make the home 'healthier'. You have probably been spending on health equipment, spas, exercise equipment and other such health products. If there are environmental problems in the home – old paint, furniture with toxic materials in, etc. – this is a good time to have a clean-up. (In all probability you have already done so.) You are spending on these things lately.

Since Pluto is also your work planet, Pluto's position indicates working from home. Home offices are being set up or expanded. Family members seem eager to work for you. They can be a good source of employees (if you hire others) or they can recommend people. If you're looking for work, the family circle is a good place to start.

Jupiter is making very nice aspects to the family planet this year. Sometimes this indicates a move. However, next year might be better for that.

The health of one of the parent figures in your life is improved. He or she benefits from new and cutting-edge kinds of therapies. Another parent figure in your life has a very spiritual kind of year, especially from September 10 onwards.

The family – and perhaps a parent figure – is at odds with the current love. This has been a problem for some time. If you are unattached this would relate to your friends and social life in general.

A parent figure (the mother figure if you're male, the father figure if you're female) seems to have been more temperamental – more emotionally volatile – in recent years. This trend continues in the year ahead.

Siblings and sibling figures in your life are prospering in the year ahead. They seem to be making major repairs or renovations in the home.

Children and children figures are more serious about life this year. They are taking on extra responsibility. They seem to have had multiple moves in recent years and this trend continues. They seem restless on the emotional level.

If you're embarking on heavy construction work or major repairs to your house, January 4 to March 6 will be a good time. If you're beautifying the home – redecorating, etc. – September 23 to November 21 is a good period for this.

Finance and Career

You have been in a prosperity cycle for two years now and it continues in the year ahead. Benevolent Jupiter is still in your money house, at least until September 9. So, you're catching the lucky financial breaks. Assets that you already own increase in value. There is luck in speculations – and Leos are great speculators. There is good family support most of the year too. And, you're probably spending more on the home and family.

Jupiter in your money house shows other things too. You're earning in happy ways. It shows 'happy money'. Not only that but you're enjoying your wealth, spending on leisure and fun kinds of things. You earn freely and you spend freely.

Many Leos are involved in the creative arts. Leo is one of the most creative signs in the zodiac. So, the Horoscope is telling us that your personal creativity is more marketable these days.

Often in finance, we are our own worst enemies. We have a certain attitude or plan that might not be realistic. Often, in order to reach our full potential, this needs some 'shaking up'. The cosmos does this on September 1 as a solar eclipse occurs in your money house. It forces the changes that need to be made.

By September 10, as Jupiter leaves your money house, your major (short-term) financial goals should be achieved. You'll be able to shift attention to other things – such as your mind and your knowledge base. Wealth is not the purpose of life. It is important and we should have it. But wealth is a means to an end and not an end in itself. This you'll discover in the year ahead. Wealth means freedom to develop oneself, to pursue interests that are enjoyable, to learn and study.

Mercury, your financial planet, is fast moving. During the course of a year he will move through your entire chart. This shows that money and financial opportunity can come to you in a variety of ways and through a variety of people. These short-term trends are best discussed in the monthly reports.

This year Mercury will go into retrograde motion four times. This is highly unusual; generally he moves backwards only three times in a year. This shows a greater need for review and for attaining financial clarity than usual. Often we need to go backwards in order to move forward and this year especially so.

The year ahead is a strong financial year, but not especially strong for career. Some years are like that. Money, the bottom line, is more important than status or prestige this year. Your 10th house of career is basically empty (only short-term, fast-moving planets will move through there) while your money house is very strong.

Venus is your career planet. She is a fast-moving planet and this year she moves even faster than usual. Thus there are many short-term career trends that are best dealt with in the monthly reports.

Venus's speedy motion shows you have confidence in career matters and that you're someone who makes speedy progress. The only problem this year is lack of interest.

Love and Social Life

Your 7th house of love is not a house of power this year. This tends to the status quo. There's nothing against the social life – the social aspects are neutral this year – but there's nothing especially strong supporting it. The last two years were banner love years. Many of you entered into serious, committed kinds of relationships then. You now seem satisfied with the status quo. In a sense this is a good message. You're content and have no need to make dramatic changes.

However, with Uranus as your love planet, you like the 'soap opera' kind of relationship. You like the ups and downs and changes. You might be more in love with the 'dramas of love' than with the actual person. Contentment can be boring for a Leo. Without drama life is not worth living. Drama implies change and conflict. So even in a relatively quiet social period there will always be some drama.

Many of the love trends that we have discussed in recent years are still in effect now. Uranus has been in Aries, your 9th house of religion and ideas, for some years now. Thus love and social opportunities happen at university or your place of worship, at educational or religious functions. Love could also happen in foreign lands or with foreigners.

You gravitate to educated and refined people, to mentor types. Being able to learn from someone is a romantic turn-on, and a juicy philosophical or theological discussion is a form of foreplay these days. This attraction to mentor types often shows as love with a professor, minister or guru.

Leos are generally 'love at first sight' people. For them love is instantaneous. These days it is even more so than normal: one glance or gesture is all it takes. There is good and bad in this tendency. When your intuition is working well, you save a lot of time and hassle. However, when your intuition is a bit off, there can be much pain. There is a need to slow things down a bit. There's no need to jump into serious relationships so quickly.

Our regular readers know that Uranus is the planet of sudden change. He is like the lightning flash in the sky. It illuminates the darkest hour. But its illumination is generally short lived. This is a good description of your love life. Love can happen in the darkest hour. It can happen at any time in any place. This makes it exciting. The only issue is the stability of this love – generally it isn't stable.

With Uranus involved in love, you can be attracting unserious people into your life. Their interest is for the moment, not the long term. Singles are better off not marrying this year. In a few years' time when Uranus moves into Taurus, love will be more stable. (It is never completely stable with you, but it will be more stable than it is now.)

Self-improvement

Leo, with the possible exception of Scorpio, is the most highly sexed of all the signs. It is said that the male Lion can mate forty to fifty times in a day. Leo is a storehouse of creative power – which is sexual by nature.

But now (and for the past few years) Neptune, the most spiritual of all the planets, is in your 8th house of transformation and regeneration. This, as was mentioned, spiritualizes the sex life and raises it to a higher, healthier and better level.

Secular science understands the physiological aspects of sex. Of late there is a greater understanding of the psychological aspects as well. But beyond that secular science cannot go. But you most likely will go there. Most likely you'll be exploring the spiritual side of it.

The sexual force, the sexual act, is capable of much more than just physical ecstasy. It can heal. It can open up new powers of the mind. It not only creates physical babies but can create mental and emotional babies as well – new projects, businesses or institutions. And, if used correctly, can actually bring a person close to the Divine – it can bring spiritual illumination. So what is happening now is the elevation of the sexual act from mere animal lust to an act of worship.

Leos are now strong candidates for systems like Kundalini Yoga, Tantra Yoga, karezza or Hermetic Science. All of these deal with the spiritualization of the sexual force. It is good to read all you can about these things.

This will also have a positive impact on your health. With Pluto, the planet of the family, in your 6th house for many years, misuse or wrong use of the sex force could be a spiritual root cause for problems here.

When the spiritual/energetic aspects of sex are better understood, it will be easier to practise safe sex. The normal methods only protect against physical things. They have no impact on negative energy vibrations. But with spiritual practice, the whole energy vibration of the act can be changed, and thus sex will be safer.

Month-by-month Forecasts

January

Best Days Overall: 6, 7, 15, 16, 24, 25
Most Stressful Days Overall: 4, 5, 11, 12, 17, 18, 31
Best Days for Love: 6, 7, 8, 11, 12, 15, 16, 24, 25, 26
Best Days for Money: 9, 10, 17, 18, 26, 27
Best Days for Career: 6, 7, 8, 15, 16, 17, 18, 26

Generally spring, when the Sun is in Aries, is considered the best starting energy of the year – best for launching new products or projects. But for you, the current month is excellent for this. Probably better than spring. First off, both your personal solar cycle and the universal solar cycle are waxing (growing). The planetary momentum is overwhelmingly forward this month. *All* the planets are moving forward until the 5th, and from the 9th to the 25th 80 per cent of them are moving forward. So, there is likely to be fast progress. The Moon will wax from the 10th to the 24th – and this period would be the best.

You begin your year with much of the planetary power in the social Western sector. On the 4th, as Mars moves westward, the Western sector becomes even stronger. Indeed, between the 4th and the 16th 90 per cent of the planets will be in the West (and even after the 16th the Western sector will have 80 per cent of the planets in it). This gives a very clear message: the planetary power is far from you and focused on others. It is time to tone down personal interests and personal desires and focus on others. Others come first. You have great gifts and abilities, but these are not what count now. It's your ability to get on with others that matters. You're distant from yourself but present with others. On the 20th, you enter a yearly love and social peak. You're at the height of personal popularity. Love goes well.

The planetary power is still mostly below the horizon as the year begins, but this is soon to change. Continue to focus on the home, family and your feeling of emotional wellness. Very soon (next month in fact) you'll start to translate this emotional wellness into outer success.

Health needs some attention after the 20th. This is only a short-term issue, however; your overall health is good. Enhance the health in the ways mentioned in the yearly report. Until the 24th, hip massage and perhaps a kidney cleanse will be beneficial. Most importantly, get enough rest.

Jupiter is in your 2nd money house, so prosperity is strong. The 13th and 14th bring a nice payday. There is luck in speculations during that period too. The period from the 14th to the 16th will also bring a nice payday. The only complication is Mercury's retrograde movement from the 5th to the 25th. This isn't going to stop your prosperity, but it will slow things down a bit. There are more delays and glitches in the financial life then, but nothing more than that. Try to make important purchases or financial decisions before the 5th or after the 25th.

February

Best Days Overall: 2, 3, 4, 11, 12, 20, 21
Most Stressful Days Overall: 1, 7, 8, 13, 14, 27, 28, 29
Best Days for Love: 2, 3, 5, 6, 7, 8, 11, 12, 13, 14, 20, 21, 25
Best Days for Money: 5, 6, 13, 14, 15, 16, 22, 23, 24, 25, 26
Best Days for Career: 5, 6, 13, 14, 25

This is another excellent month for starting new projects or launching new products into the world. Your personal solar cycle is at its 'Full Moon' phase and the universal solar cycle is waxing. Virtually all of the planets are in forward motion all month. If you're starting something new – now is the time to do it. You have a lot of planetary support now. The 8th to the 19th is the best time this month.

You're still distant from yourself, but present with others this month. Still in the midst of a yearly love and social peak. Still at the height of personal popularity. Since the Sun is furthest from his natural home, a part of you feels in 'exile' – but the social popularity makes up for it. Health still needs watching until the 19th. Enhance the health in the ways mentioned in the yearly report. Most important, get more rest. With high levels of energy your spiritual immune system – the aura – is strong and this will repel most problems.

Now that your financial planet, Mercury, is moving forward again, finances are much improved. The money is rolling in. There is some financial disturbance on the 1st and changes have to be made, but the changes are good. The 5th to the 7th are excellent paydays. There is luck in speculations during that period too. Financial judgement is sound this month – and cautious – especially until the 14th. This is a good period to start a savings or investment programme (and you're more in the mood for doing such a thing too).

On the 14th the financial planet moves into Aquarius, your 7th house of love and social activities. Your social popularity and social contacts help the bottom line now. Often opportunities for business partnerships or joint ventures happen under this transit. You seem very generous with others – especially the spouse, partner or current love. You're there for your friends personally and financially. You attract richer friends. A good period – from the 14th onwards – to spend on the high tech equipment that you need. Online activities increase earnings.

On the 19th the Sun moves into your 8th house. This favours weight loss regimes (if you need them) and detox programmes. The body needs to be purified of extraneous – effete – material. It is a good period to 'resurrect' the body – to reinvent it – to give birth to your ideal.

This will be a sexually active kind of period as well, especially on the 28th and 29th.

March

Best Days Overall: 1, 2, 10, 11, 18, 19, 28, 29
Most Stressful Days Overall: 6, 7, 12, 13, 26, 27
Best Days for Love: 1, 2, 6, 7, 10, 11, 16, 18, 19, 26, 27, 28, 29
Best Days for Money: 3, 4, 8, 12, 13, 16, 17, 21, 22, 28, 29, 31
Best Days for Career: 6, 7, 12, 13, 16, 26, 27

The 8th house of transformation is where the action is this month; 40 per cent (and sometimes 50 per cent) of the planets are there or moving through there. So, the spouse, partner or current love is prospering these days. He or she is in the midst of a yearly financial peak and is likely to be more generous with you. Your already legendary libido is even stronger than usual. This will be a great month to borrow or to pay down debt – according to your need – especially from the 5th to the 22nd. A great month to go through your possessions and get rid of what you don't need or use. This is just clutter. Make room for the new things that want to come in.

The other headline this month are the two eclipses that happen. This is guaranteed to create turmoil in the world and in the people around you. When humans create things that are not part of the cosmic plan, these things get exploded by the eclipses.

The solar eclipse of the 9th (in America it is on the 8th) occurs in your 8th house. Thus there can be more dealing with death and death issues now. Generally this is not literal death but encounters with it. Sometimes near-death kinds of experiences happen. Sometimes one has dreams about death, or dreams of people who have passed on. There is a need to understand death on a deeper level. The spouse, partner or current love has some financial upheaval now and needs to make dramatic changes. Every solar eclipse tends to affect Leos more strongly than most people. This is because the eclipsed planet, the Sun, is your ruling planet. Thus twice a year the cosmos gives you opportunity to redefine yourself – your image and self-concept. This is basically a healthy thing. We are always changing and we need to redefine ourselves in light of these changes. So, over the next six months the hair-style and wardrobe will change. You'll present a 'new look' to the world. Reduce your schedule during this eclipse and take it a bit easier than normal.

The lunar eclipse of the 23rd is more benign for you. It occurs in your 3rd house of communication and mostly affects siblings, sibling figures and neighbours in your life. Dramatic, life-changing events happen for them. It will be a good idea to drive more carefully at this time. Cars and communication equipment get tested. Every lunar eclipse brings spiritual changes to you. Generally it happens through some revelation or spiritual breakthrough. There are changes in the spiritual practice, attitude and even the teachings. There are dramas and upheavals in spiritual organizations you're involved with, and in the lives of gurus and spiritual teachers.

April

Best Days Overall: 6, 7, 14, 15, 16, 24, 25, 26
Most Stressful Days Overall: 2, 3, 8, 9, 22, 23, 29, 30
Best Days for Love: 2, 3, 6, 7, 14, 15, 24, 25, 26, 29, 30
Best Days for Money: 1, 8, 9, 17, 18, 27, 28
Best Days for Career: 6, 8, 9, 14, 15, 25, 26

A happy and successful month, Leo. Enjoy.

Health right now is excellent. The dust of last month's eclipses is more or less settled. The Fire element, your native element, is very strong this month, with at least 50 per cent (and sometimes 60 per cent) of the planets in Fire signs. This gives energy, enthusiasm, courage and the 'can do' spirit. There is great optimism. Nothing gets you down. You feel there's nothing that can't be overcome. A happy time. However, there is much retrograde activity this month. You will have to learn some patience. Power in Fire makes one want things 'yesterday' – things have to be done quickly. But increased retrograde activity slows things down and introduces delays. Patience. Patience. Patience.

The power this month is in the 9th house. This was the case since March 20. So, foreign lands are calling to you. There are happy travel opportunities. This is a very nice period for college or post-graduate students; there is success in their studies. It is a month for religious and philosophical breakthroughs for those who want them. Leos love the night life, but this month a juicy theological or philosophical discussion is as much fun as a night out on the town.

The love life is also happy this month. Uranus, the love planet, is receiving positive aspects. This will be a socially active kind of month. We could label this a second yearly love and social peak. The 9th, 10th, 22nd and 23rd bring happy romantic meetings, which can happen in foreign countries or at religious or educational functions.

On the 19th the Sun crosses your Mid-heaven and enters your 10th house. You begin a yearly career peak. The timing of this is good as your family planet, Pluto, starts to retrograde on the 18th. Only time will clarify family issues; in the meantime, focus on the career.

You're succeeding this month. You're on top, where you belong. Your star quality, personal appearance and overall demeanour are recognized. You're recognized for who you are more than for your professional achievements. Promotions and pay rises are likely too, although there could be delays associated with these pay rises as Mercury retrogrades on the 28th. But they will happen – either overtly or covertly. You have the financial favour of bosses, elders and parent figures this month. They're supporting your financial goals. The 15th or 16th brings a nice payday.

May

Best Days Overall: 4, 5, 12, 13, 22, 23, 31
Most Stressful Days Overall: 6, 19, 20, 21, 27, 28
Best Days for Love: 4, 5, 6, 12, 13, 14, 15, 22, 23, 26, 27, 28, 31
Best Days for Money: 6, 14, 15, 24, 25
Best Days for Career: 6, 14, 15, 26, 27

Career is still the main headline this month. It is going great guns. There is much success and advancement happening. Pay rises can still happen this month, if they haven't already happened. The 10th and 11th bring special career success and advancement.

There was a Grand Trine in Earth last month and this continues in the month ahead. This shows that you're more practical these days. You've got both feet on the ground. You never lose your creative nature, but you're more practical about things – especially about money and career.

Health became more delicate on April 20 and needs watching until the 20th of this month. This is nothing serious, just a short-term phenomenon. When energy is high we can burn the candle at both ends and seem to get away with it. But when energy is lowered, as it is until the 20th, we can't. Enhance the health in the ways mentioned in the yearly report and give more attention to the heart.

Finances are good this month, though still prone to glitches and delays. Try not to make things worse than they need to be. Make sure all the little details of financial transactions are handled properly. When doing online transactions make sure you click the right buttons and that your spelling is correct. Make sure your cheques are dated and signed properly. Slip-ups in these little things can cause much havoc later on. Still prosperity is happening. Your financial planet, Mercury, is part of the Grand Trine in Earth all month. This means he receives a lot of positive support. You have the financial favour of elders, bosses, parent figures, family members, children and children figures in your life. Your personal creativity is marketable. The 2nd to the 4th and the 22nd to the 25th seem exceptionally good financial days. There is luck in speculations in those periods too (though May 22–25 would be better for this than the earlier period). Mercury starts to move forward on the 22nd bringing financial clarity and direction. The financial judgement is sound and practical.

Mars has been retrograde since April 17 and is retrograde all of this month. Best to avoid unnecessary foreign travel. If you absolutely must travel, allow more time for the trip and don't schedule connecting flights too closely.

June

Best Days Overall: 1, 8, 9, 18, 19, 27, 28
Most Stressful Days Overall: 2, 3, 15, 16, 17, 23, 24, 29, 30
Best Days for Love: 1, 4, 5, 8, 9, 14, 18, 19, 23, 24, 25, 26, 27, 28
Best Days for Money: 2, 3, 10, 11, 12, 13, 20, 21, 23, 24, 29, 30
Best Days for Career: 2, 3, 4, 5, 14, 25, 26, 29, 30

Ever since April 19 the planetary power has been moving in your direction – supporting you. The Eastern sector of the chart is now more powerful than the social Western sector. You've spent many months developing your social skills, so now it's time – by the law of cosmic balance – to develop your personal skills – your personal initiative and independence. Others might attack you as selfish, but your self-interest is no less important than theirs. Now, and for the next few months, is the time to create conditions as you want them – to have your way in life. Your way is the best these days. If others don't go along, go on anyway. The cosmos wants your happiness.

Though your yearly career peak is over with, career is still active. The Moon spends double her usual time in your 10th career house. Mercury, your financial planet, is in the career house until the 13th. Pay rises can still happen – either overtly or covertly. You still have the financial favour of the authority figures in your life – bosses, elders, parents and parent figures – even the government. Prosperity seems strong in the month ahead. Mercury is the most elevated planet in the Horoscope. This shows that you deem prosperity important. It shows your aspiration to wealth. It shows a reverence for the money people in your life.

Your career planet, Venus, spends a good deal of the month 'out of bounds' – from the 13th to the 29th. This shows that career demands carry you outside your normal sphere. Sometimes it shows the necessity of 'thinking outside the box' in order to advance the career. Venus has one of her solstices from the 19th to the 23rd. She stands still (in her latitude motion) over that period. This indicates a pause in the career. Don't panic over the pause. It is in these pauses that mighty changes and developments happen. These are seen later on.

Venus enters your spiritual 12th house on the 18th. The Moon, your spiritual planet, spends much time in your 10th house. Thus, this is a month where you can advance the career by being involved in charities or altruistic causes. On a deeper level, your spiritual understanding advances your career.

Love is happy this month, but the month is more about friendship than romance. It is about being involved with groups and group activities. There's nothing against romance, but your interests lie elsewhere.

Health is excellent.

July

Best Days Overall: 6, 7, 15, 16, 24, 25
Most Stressful Days Overall: 13, 14, 20, 21, 27, 28
Best Days for Love: 3, 4, 6, 7, 15, 16, 20, 21, 24, 25
Best Days for Money: 3, 4, 8, 9, 14, 15, 18, 19, 24, 25, 27, 28
Best Days for Career: 3, 4, 15, 24, 25, 27, 28

Your 12th house of spirituality became powerful on June 21 and is still powerful until the 22nd. So this is a good month to focus on spiritual studies and practices. Those of you who meditate will have better experiences. The dream life will be more active. Many of you will have supernatural kinds of experiences.

Many think that spiritual practice is 'impractical' and 'other worldly'. Perhaps. But these practices have profound impact on the practical affairs of life. This you will learn in the month ahead. Spiritual practice impacts on the career, finances and the personal appearance. How much more practical can you get? The message of this month's Horoscope is that if you're right spiritually all the practical affairs will just fall into place.

The month ahead is prosperous and happy. On the 12th Venus crosses the Ascendant and enters your 1st house. This gives many messages. First of all it brings happy career opportunities to you. There's nothing much that you need to do to seek these opportunities, they just come. They find you. Perhaps more importantly, you look and feel successful. Others see you that way. This transit has a positive impact on your personal appearance too. There is more grace and style to the image. Your movements are more graceful. In a woman's chart this enhances her beauty. In a man's chart it shows more involvement with beautiful women – they come into your sphere.

On the 14th, Mercury, your financial planet, crosses the Ascendant and enters your 1st house, bringing financial windfalls and financial opportunity. These are things that are 'do-able' – not 'pie in the sky'. You have the favour of the money people in your life. You look and feel rich and others see you this way. You have an 'air of prosperity' about you.

On the 22nd the Sun, the ruler of your Horoscope, crosses the Ascendant and enters your 1st house. This will enlarge your already strong 'star quality' and charisma. The transit brings self-confidence and self-esteem. You are the king or queen that you were destined to be. You have a royal air about you.

The love life improves after the 22nd as well. There are many romantic opportunities. Those already in a relationship are in harmony with the beloved from the 22nd onwards.

August

Best Days Overall: 2, 3, 12, 13, 21, 22, 29, 30
Most Stressful Days Overall: 9, 10, 16, 17, 18, 23, 24
Best Days for Love: 2, 3, 12, 13, 14, 15, 16, 17, 18, 21, 22, 23, 24, 29, 30
Best Days for Money: 4, 5, 14, 15, 23, 24, 31
Best Days for Career: 3, 14, 15, 23, 24

Last month on the 22nd the planetary power moved to its maximum Eastern position, and it will stay like that till the 22nd. So, personal power and independence are at their maximum. This is a time to have things your way; to create the conditions of your own happiness. You're at your maximum personal creativity now. So make those changes that need to be made. Later on it will be more difficult.

It is wonderful to be strong and powerful. A great gift. But there's a downside to it. If personal power is abused, it can bring faster and stronger karmic kickbacks. Most of the ills that we see in the world are not due to 'disempowerment' but rather the reverse – to the abuse of power. So use your power wisely and lawfully.

Love is still happy this month. For singles there is a significant meeting on the 15th or 16th. But this month is happy even for those in a relationship. There is more romance with the beloved. Your love planet Uranus went retrograde at the end of last month, but this is the only complication in love right now. The love life is happy but there are a few glitches and delays. Still, there's no need to rush into anything just yet. Let love develop as it will.

The month ahead is very prosperous as well. This is really the headline of the month. Jupiter has been in your money house all year. Mercury entered the money house on July 31. Venus will enter on the

5th and the Sun will enter on 22nd. Thus the money house is chock full of beneficent planets. There's a cosmic conspiracy to prosper you. Great geniuses are scheming, plotting and planning the best ways to achieve this. You are in a yearly financial peak and for many of you this will be a lifetime peak. You have the Midas touch this month. From the 22nd onwards the focus is on finance, as it should be. However, Mercury goes retrograde at the end of the month – on the 30th – so try to wrap up important purchases or investments before then. Prosperity will happen even during the retrograde, just a bit slower.

Health was excellent last month and is excellent in the month ahead. You can enhance it further in the ways mentioned in the yearly report.

September

Best Days Overall: 8, 9, 17, 18, 25, 26, 27
Most Stressful Days Overall: 5, 6, 7, 13, 14, 19, 20
Best Days for Love: 3, 4, 8, 9, 13, 14, 17, 18, 23, 25, 26, 27
Best Days for Money: 1, 2, 10, 11, 12, 13, 19, 21, 20, 28, 29
Best Days for Career: 3, 4, 13, 14, 19, 20, 23

The month ahead is turbulent in the world at large, but nice things are happening for you personally. You're still in a yearly financial peak until the 22nd, and overall health is still excellent. You can handle the turmoil.

We have two eclipses this month – a solar eclipse on the 1st and a lunar eclipse on the 16th. Of the two, the solar eclipse of the 1st has a stronger impact on you. Your health is good, but reduce your schedule over this period; there's no need to tempt the fates.

The solar eclipse occurs in your money house. This shows dramatic financial changes. With all the prosperity that's happening, changes in thinking and planning are inevitable. The eclipse forces the issue. Mars, the ruler of the 9th house, is impacted by this eclipse. Thus avoid foreign travel over that period. If you must travel, schedule your trip around the eclipse period. Students at college or post-graduate level are affected too. There could be dramatic changes in their educational plans. Often there is turmoil or shake-ups at the school they attend. Saturn, your work planet, is also affected by the eclipse. This indicates job changes – this could be with your present employer or with another one. It shows changes in the work environment and the rules of the workplace. Sometimes this kind of eclipse will produce a health scare. However, your health is good and this is likely to be no more than a scare. Every solar eclipse forces you to redefine yourself. To redefine your image, personality and self-concept. This one is no different. In coming months you will present a new image to the world, a new look.

The lunar eclipse of the 16th occurs in your 8th house of transformation. So, stay out of harm's way during that period. Often an eclipse here produces near-death kinds of experiences – close calls and encounters with the dark angel. Dreams of death would not be a surprise either. One is forced to confront one's mortality. In the confrontation positive changes happen. This eclipse brings important financial changes for the spouse, partner or current love. Usually this happens through some unexpected expense or upheaval, which forces the change. Generally the change is good. Every lunar eclipse brings spiritual changes – changes in practice and attitude and sometimes even changes in teachings and teachers. There are likely to be dramas in the lives of guru figures and upheavals in spiritual or charitable organizations you're involved with.

October

Best Days Overall: 5, 6, 7, 15, 23, 24
Most Stressful Days Overall: 3, 4, 10, 11, 17, 30, 31
Best Days for Love: 3, 4, 5, 6, 7, 10, 11, 12, 13, 15, 16, 23, 24
Best Days for Money: 1, 10, 18, 19, 20, 25, 26, 27, 28, 30
Best Days for Career: 3, 4, 12, 13, 16, 17, 23, 24

The month ahead is still prosperous, but the focus on finance is tapering off. Jupiter left the money house on September 10, as did the Sun on September 22. Mercury, the financial planet, remains there until October 7. Financial goals are more or less achieved (for the present) and you're moving on to other interests – mental development, communication and intellectual interests. (There is a nice payday on the 11th or 12th, however.) Jupiter is now in your 3rd house for the rest of the year ahead, and well into next year. This is a wonderful aspect for writers, teachers, journalists, sales and marketing people. Your innate creative abilities are much enhanced. It is also wonderful for students below the college level – there is success in their studies now. Learning is pleasurable and easy. Many of you would rather read a good book – something juicy – than go out on the town.

If you need a new car or communication equipment this is a good month in which to buy these things. Your judgement will be good. Whether you buy these things now or not, you will be acquiring these things in the next twelve months.

Siblings and sibling figures in your life are having a prosperous year. If they are students they're doing well in school. They too are getting new cars and communication equipment, either now or sometime over the coming year.

The planetary power is moving to its nadir (low point) in your Horoscope. It is moving away from your career and towards the home and family. Outer objectives are becoming less important. Your duty now is to the family and to your emotional wellness. This is a time to build the infrastructure that makes further career progress possible. Without emotional and domestic stability, career progress can't really happen – not as it should.

Your 4th house of the home and family becomes powerful on the 23rd and is really the centre of your life now. Even career and financial opportunities happen through the family and family connections. The message is simple: get the emotional life in order and everything else will fall into place.

Health becomes more delicate after the 23rd. Overall health is good, this is just a short-term issue that will pass next month. The main thing is to get enough rest. Don't allow yourself to get overtired.

November

Best Days Overall: 2, 3, 11, 12, 19, 20, 29, 30
Most Stressful Days Overall: 1, 6, 7, 8, 13, 14, 26, 27, 28
Best Days for Love: 2, 3, 6, 7, 8, 11, 12, 13, 19, 20, 21, 22, 29, 30
Best Days for Money: 1, 6, 7, 10, 15, 16, 19, 20, 21, 22, 23, 24, 25, 29, 30
Best Days for Career: 2, 3, 13, 14, 21, 22

Neptune, the ruler of your 8th house, is camped out on an old eclipse point all month. This shows turbulence – and perhaps a crisis – in the financial affairs of the spouse, partner or current love. Many financial changes are happening here. There are more confrontations with your personal mortality as well. You're more involved with death and death issues. Insurance and tax issues seem rocky and unstable, but they will work themselves out in the end.

Your 4th house is still powerful until the 22nd. Thus the focus should be on home, family and emotional wellness rather than on the career. We see more evidence of this with Venus having one of her solstices from the 13th to the 16th. This indicates a pause in the career.

This is a great month for those of you in therapy. There is much progress and insight gained. Even those of you not in formal therapy will receive counselling by nature this month. Past memories will come up spontaneously. There will be dreams of the past (also spontaneous). These are cosmic opportunities to review past things from your present state of consciousness. The opinions formed by a three-year-old traumatized child are not the opinions you would form today. Just looking at these things without judgement will bring emotional healing.

We were not intended to be victims of mood or feeling, but to have emotional freedom. This is a good month to become more emotionally free. This doesn't mean the expression of negativity, but the ability to feel whatever you choose to feel and to be in any mood that you choose to be in.

When emotional harmony comes – and it will – it's time to move on to fun – to the enjoyment of life. A new surge of creativity will come.

This begins on the 22nd, when you enter another one of your yearly personal pleasure peaks. With Mercury also in your 5th house from the 12th onwards you will have the wherewithal to enjoy life and for leisure activities. It's a happy, much less serious, period.

Health and energy will also improve after the 22nd. Health is generally good, but reduce your schedule on the 30th and spend more quiet time at home.

December

Best Days Overall: 8, 9, 16, 17, 26, 27
Most Stressful Days Overall: 4, 5, 10, 11, 24, 25, 31
Best Days for Love: 2, 3, 4, 5, 8, 9, 12, 13, 16, 17, 21, 22, 26, 27, 31
Best Days for Money: 4, 5, 10, 11, 12, 13, 19, 20, 21, 22, 29, 30, 31
Best Days for Career: 2, 3, 10, 11, 12, 13, 21, 22

This time of year is a party time in the world at large, and you're in the thick of it. What's not to be happy about? Health and energy are wonderful this month. Love is going well. Singles have the option of something serious or some fun 'flings' in their relationships. Many of you will be travelling from the 1st to the 3rd and it looks happy. Life is good.

It is only in finance that you seem sober and serious. The financial planet is in Capricorn from the 3rd onwards, so you're thinking more about your financial future – even on to old age. You're more careful of how you spend now and want value for your money. The good news is that the financial judgement is sound and conservative. On the 19th Mercury goes retrograde once more, so try to do your holiday shopping before then. Earnings are good but they happen with delays.

The planetary power has been in the Western, social sector of your chart since October 23. The planets are approaching their maximum Western position this month. Thus the era of personal independence is well and truly over with and you're busy cultivating your social skills. It is much more difficult now to change conditions to your liking or to have things your way. Now is the time to adapt to situations as best you can. The planetary power is flowing towards others and away from you and so others come first now. Let others have their own way, so long as it isn't destructive.

By the 21st you're about partied out. No one can sustain a party atmosphere for too long – not even Leo, the supreme party animal of the zodiac. You're actually in the mood for work, for productivity, for being practical and serious. Though your health is good you want to keep things that way and involve yourself in daily health regimes. It is good to use this mood to your advantage to achieve work-oriented goals, to do mundane, boring, detailed tasks that you usually dislike. If you're looking for a job this is a good period for you, and there are many opportunities out there.

The love life becomes more delicate after the 21st. You and the beloved need to work harder on the relationship. You seem in disagreement.

The focus this month is still on home, family and emotional wellness. But you can advance your career through social means from the 7th onwards. Attend or host the right parties.

Virgo

♍

THE VIRGIN

Birthdays from
22nd August to
22nd September

Personality Profile

VIRGO AT A GLANCE

Element – Earth

Ruling Planet – Mercury
  Career Planet – Mercury
  Love Planet – Neptune
  Money Planet – Venus
  Planet of Home and Family Life – Jupiter
  Planet of Health and Work – Uranus
  Planet of Pleasure – Saturn
  Planet of Sexuality – Mars

Colours – earth tones, ochre, orange, yellow

Colour that promotes love, romance and social harmony – aqua blue

Colour that promotes earning power – jade green

Gems – agate, hyacinth

Metal – quicksilver

Scents – lavender, lilac, lily of the valley, storax

Quality – mutable (= flexibility)

Quality most needed for balance – a broader perspective

Strongest virtues – mental agility, analytical skills, ability to pay
   attention to detail, healing powers

Deepest needs – to be useful and productive

Characteristic to avoid – destructive criticism

Signs of greatest overall compatibility – Taurus, Capricorn

Signs of greatest overall incompatibility – Gemini, Sagittarius, Pisces

Sign most helpful to career – Gemini

Sign most helpful for emotional support – Sagittarius

Sign most helpful financially – Libra

Sign best for marriage and/or partnerships – Pisces

Sign most helpful for creative projects – Capricorn

Best Sign to have fun with – Capricorn

Signs most helpful in spiritual matters – Taurus, Leo

Best day of the week – Wednesday

Understanding a Virgo

The virgin is a particularly fitting symbol for those born under the sign of Virgo. If you meditate on the image of the virgin you will get a good understanding of the essence of the Virgo type. The virgin is, of course, a symbol of purity and innocence – not naïve, but pure. A virginal object has not been touched. A virgin field is land that is true to itself, the way it has always been. The same is true of virgin forest: it is pristine, unaltered.

Apply the idea of purity to the thought processes, emotional life, physical body and activities and projects of the everyday world, and you can see how Virgos approach life. Virgos desire the pure expression of the ideal in their mind, body and affairs. If they find impurities they will attempt to clear them away.

Impurities are the beginning of disorder, unhappiness and uneasiness. The job of the Virgo is to eject all impurities and keep only that which the body and mind can use and assimilate.

The secrets of good health are here revealed: 90 per cent of the art of staying well is maintaining a pure mind, a pure body and pure emotions. When you introduce more impurities than your mind and body can deal with, you will have what is known as 'dis-ease'. It is no wonder that Virgos make great doctors, nurses, healers and dieticians. They have an innate understanding of good health and they realize that good health is more than just physical. In all aspects of life, if you want a project to be successful it must be kept as pure as possible. It must be protected against the adverse elements that will try to undermine it. This is the secret behind Virgo's awesome technical proficiency.

One could talk about Virgo's analytical powers – which are formidable. One could talk about their perfectionism and their almost superhuman attention to detail. But this would be to miss the point. All of these virtues are manifestations of a Virgo's desire for purity and perfection – a world without Virgos would have ruined itself long ago.

A vice is nothing more than a virtue turned inside out, misapplied or used in the wrong context. Virgos' apparent vices come from their inherent virtue. Their analytical powers, which should be used for healing, helping or perfecting a project in the world, sometimes get misapplied and turned against people. Their critical faculties, which should be used constructively to perfect a strategy or proposal, can sometimes be used destructively to harm or wound. Their urge to perfection can turn into worry and lack of confidence; their natural humility can become self-denial and self-abasement. When Virgos turn negative they are apt to turn their devastating criticism on themselves, sowing the seeds of self-destruction.

Finance

Virgos have all the attitudes that create wealth. They are hard-working, industrious, efficient, organized, thrifty, productive and eager to serve. A developed Virgo is every employer's dream. But until Virgos master some of the social graces of Libra they will not even come close to fulfilling their financial potential. Purity and perfectionism, if not handled correctly or gracefully, can be very trying to others. Friction in human relationships can be devastating not only to your pet projects but – indirectly – to your wallet as well.

Virgos are quite interested in their financial security. Being hard-working, they know the true value of money. They do not like to take risks with their money, preferring to save for their retirement or for a rainy day. Virgos usually make prudent, calculated investments that involve a minimum of risk. These investments and savings usually work out well, helping Virgos to achieve the financial security they seek. The rich or even not-so-rich Virgo also likes to help his or her friends in need.

Career and Public Image

Virgos reach their full potential when they can communicate their knowledge in such a way that others can understand it. In order to get their ideas across better, Virgos need to develop greater verbal skills and fewer judgemental ways of expressing themselves. Virgos look up to teachers and communicators; they like their bosses to be good communicators. Virgos will probably not respect a superior who is not their intellectual equal – no matter how much money or power that superior has. Virgos themselves like to be perceived by others as being educated and intellectual.

The natural humility of Virgos often inhibits them from fulfilling their great ambitions, from acquiring name and fame. Virgos should indulge in a little more self-promotion if they are going to reach their career goals. They need to push themselves with the same ardour that they would use to foster others.

At work Virgos like to stay active. They are willing to learn any type of job as long as it serves their ultimate goal of financial security. Virgos may change occupations several times during their professional lives, until they find the one they really enjoy. Virgos work well with other people, are not afraid to work hard and always fulfil their responsibilities.

Love and Relationships

If you are an analyst or a critic you must, out of necessity, narrow your scope. You have to focus on a part and not the whole; this can create a temporary narrow-mindedness. Virgos do not like this kind of person. They like their partners to be broad-minded, with depth and vision. Virgos seek to get this broad-minded quality from their partners, since they sometimes lack it themselves.

Virgos are perfectionists in love just as they are in other areas of life. They need partners who are tolerant, open-minded and easy-going. If you are in love with a Virgo do not waste time on impractical romantic gestures. Do practical and useful things for him or her – this is what will be appreciated and what will be done for you.

Virgos express their love through pragmatic and useful gestures, so do not be put off because your Virgo partner does not say 'I love you' day in, day out. Virgos are not that type. If they love you, they will demonstrate it in practical ways. They will always be there for you; they will show an interest in your health and finances; they will fix your sink or repair your video recorder. Virgos deem these actions to be superior to sending flowers, chocolates or Valentine cards.

In love affairs Virgos are not particularly passionate or spontaneous. If you are in love with a Virgo, do not take this personally. It does not mean that you are not alluring enough or that your Virgo partner does not love or like you. It is just the way Virgos are. What they lack in passion they make up for in dedication and loyalty.

Home and Domestic Life

It goes without saying that the home of a Virgo will be spotless, sanitized and orderly. Everything will be in its proper place – and don't you dare move anything about! For Virgos to find domestic bliss they need to ease up a bit in the home, to allow their partner and children more freedom and to be more generous and open-minded. Family members are not to be analysed under a microscope, they are individuals with their own virtues to express.

With these small difficulties resolved, Virgos like to stay in and entertain at home. They make good hosts and they like to keep their friends and families happy and entertained at family and social gatherings. Virgos love children, but they are strict with them – at times – since they want to make sure their children are brought up with the correct sense of family and values.

Horoscope for 2016

Major Trends

When Jupiter entered your sign in August of last year, you entered a multi-year period of prosperity. This trend gets even stronger in the year ahead. More on this later.

Jupiter is still in your sign in 2016. If you are of childbearing age, fertility is much greater than usual. In general, you're leading the good life these days, so you need to watch your weight!

When Saturn entered your 4th house of home and family late in 2014, you entered a period of psychological discipline. The cosmos is bringing right order to the emotional life, and to the home and family. You're in a great period for making psychological progress, but you need to work harder. Family relations are bitter-sweet these days. There's more on this later.

The love and social life was active – and happy – in 2013 and 2014. 2015 was less active, presumably because love goals were more or less

achieved. Many of you married or entered serious kinds of relationships. This year the love life is less active. The planetary transits at any
given time will either make love easy or challenging. Neptune, your
love planet, remains in your 7th house this year, and thus the whole
love and social life is being raised and spiritualized. You always tend to
be idealistic in love, but these days more so than usual.

Uranus has been in your 8th house of transformation for some years
now and will be there for a few more years. This indicates sexual
experimentation. As long as it isn't destructive, this is a good way to
gain more knowledge. The rule books about sex are being thrown out.
You're learning what works for you through trial, error and experimentation. For the spouse, partner or current love this transit shows great
financial change and instability. Learning how to deal with this has
been his or her main life lesson for the past several years.

Pluto has been in your 5th house since 2008. Thus there is a detox
going on in your attitudes about children. Also in your creative life.
Often, if you're of appropriate age, it shows complications in childbirth
– perhaps the birth happens through surgery or some other complicated method.

Your major interests in the year ahead are: the body, image and
personal pleasure (until September 9); finance (from September 10
onwards); home and family; children, fun and creativity; love and
romance; sex, occult studies, personal transformation, debt and taxes.

Your paths of greatest fulfilment in the year ahead are: the body,
image and personal pleasure; finance (from September 10 onwards).

Health

*(Please note that this is an astrological perspective on health and not a
medical one. In days of yore there was no difference, these perspectives
were identical. But now there could be quite a difference. For a medical
perspective, please consult your doctor or health practitioner.)*

Virgo will always be focused on health, but with your 6th house of
health mostly empty this year, the focus is less than usual. Two long-
term planes are in stressful alignment with you, but two others are
making nice aspects – the transits of the planets at any given time will
determine the issue. When they are kind, health and energy will be

good. When they're unkind, the situation becomes more challenging.

In the year ahead May 21 to June 20 and November 22 to December 21 are the most vulnerable periods. These are the times to rest and relax more and give more attention to your health.

As our regular readers know, there is much that can be done to enhance the health and prevent problems from developing. Give more attention to the following areas (the reflexology points are shown in the following chart):

- The small intestine. This is always an important area for Virgo.
- The ankles and calves. These are also always important for you. Both areas should be regularly massaged, and you should give the ankles more support when your exercise.
- The head, face and scalp. These became important when your health planet Uranus entered Aries for the long haul in 2011. Regular scalp and face massage will be powerful for you and you'll

Important foot reflexology points for the year ahead

Try to massage all of the foot on a regular basis – the top of the foot as well as the bottom – but pay extra attention to the points highlighted on the chart. When you massage, be aware of 'sore spots' as these need special attention. It's also a good idea to massage the ankles.

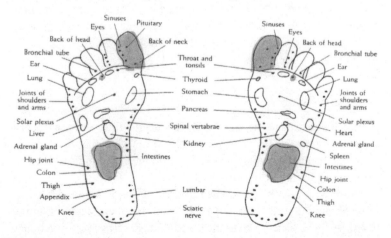

respond well to this. Craniaosacral therapy would also be beneficial.

- The adrenals. These have also become important since 2011. The important thing with the adrenals is to avoid anger and fear, the two emotions that stress them out.
- The musculature. Another area that has become important since Uranus entered Aries. Good muscle tone is important, Virgo. Flabby or weak muscle tone can knock the skeleton out of alignment and cause all kinds of other problems. Vigorous physical exercise – according to your age and stage in life – is good.

Since these are the most vulnerable areas this year, problems, if they happened (God forbid) would most likely begin there. So it's important to keep them healthy and fit.

Since Uranus's move in 2011 good health for you means more than just 'no symptoms'. It means physical fitness – the ability to jog or run X number of miles, or lift X pounds or kilos. Thus, a day at the gym will often do as much good as a visit to the doctor.

With Uranus as your health planet, you tend to gravitate to alternative medicine. But the new cutting-edge (and perhaps untried) technologies of orthodox medicine could also be appealing to you. With your kind of chart, healing comes from new kinds of therapies.

Your attraction to the new and untried can lead to 'health faddism' if you're not careful. There can be a tendency to chase after every new fad or trend in the health field simply because it is new and modern. There is a need to do more homework on these things. Otherwise it can get quite expensive!

Home and Family

Your 4th house of home and family has been strong since late 2014 when Saturn moved in there. When your family planet, Jupiter, moved into your 1st house in August of last year, home and family has become even more prominent in your chart.

This area seems bitter-sweet this year. On the one hand there is good family support. Family members (and especially a parent figure) seem very devoted to you. On the other hand, Saturn in your 4th house shows that you're taking on extra burdens and responsibilities – things that you can't really avoid. These are generally difficult things.

You will probably have opportunities to move in the coming year, but it doesn't seem advisable. Saturn in this house suggests that you make better use of the existing space you have, rather than move home.

Those of you of childbearing age are unusually fertile this year. A pregnancy or new birth would fit the symbolism we see here. It is both a blessing and a chore at the same time. But there are other ways to read this too. Existing children or children figures in your life could require extra care and attention, but you'll have help.

You're working to make the home more of a 'fun' kind of place. Almost like an entertainment centre. The symbolism of the Horoscope indicates home theatres, musical instruments or equipment, toys and games, etc.

On September 10 your family planet Jupiter enters your money house. This suggests earning money from home. The home as a place of business. It indicates spending money on the home and family and earning from them as well. A family business would fit the symbolism. Family connections could be important financially – and as we mentioned, it shows good financial support from the family.

A parent or parent figure prospers. He or she could be moving in or spending long periods with you. He or she is not so keen on the spouse, partner or current love; however, this will ease after September 10.

Children and children figures in your life seem emotionally volatile these days. They seem restless too. If they are of an appropriate age there could be moves this year – perhaps multiple moves. They have had this tendency for some years now.

Siblings and sibling figures have a stable, static kind of family year.

Grandchildren (if you have them) have moved recently, but the year ahead is stable here.

If you're doing major repairs or construction work on the home, August 3 to September 27 would be a good time. If you're repainting, decorating or otherwise beautifying the home, October 18 to November 12 and November 22 to December 21 are good times.

Finance and Career

As we mentioned earlier, you're in a banner financial year. A year of prosperity and financial growth. The financial horizons are much expanded.

Jupiter in your own sign until September 9 ushers in the 'high life'. One lives on a higher standard. One lives as if one were rich (each according to their own concept of wealth). The cosmos is indulging your sensual desires – the desires of the flesh. So, without any conscious effort on your part, you eat in the better restaurants, you drink the finer wines, you travel more, you dress more expensively, etc. People see you as wealthy. You project the image of wealth and prosperity.

There is a deep magic – a deep metaphysical principle – in cultivating the image of wealth. It puts you in that vibration. You start to attract wealthier people into your life. You attract financial opportunity as well. Further, when you project this image, you tend to 'feel' wealthier and the feeling of wealth always precedes the actual manifestation.

On September 10, as Jupiter enters your money house, the actual, tangible, touchable wealth starts to happen. Financial opportunities come. Things that you already own are worth more. You catch lucky financial breaks. You have a feeling of financial optimism.

Jupiter involved in finance shows good family support, as we have mentioned. It shows earnings from real estate, the food business, hotels and industries that cater to the home – such as interior design, furniture providers, landscaping and things of this nature. It favours earning from home and a family-type business.

But Jupiter is not the only factor influencing your financial life. Venus is your financial planet and in order to really understand the financial picture we must study her. However, she is a fast-moving planet – and this year more so than usual. Thus there are many short-term trends in finance that are best dealt with in the monthly reports.

Venus's speedy motion this year – she will visit some of your houses twice, when she usually only does so once – is also a good financial signal. It shows confidence, rapid progress and good forward momentum.

This is not an especially strong career year. Most of the long-term planets are below the horizon of your chart. Your 10th house of career is basically empty and only short-term planets will move through there. Sure, there will be periods where career is important, but these are short lived. Your focus is more on money and home and family issues.

You tend to be ambitious by nature, but this year less so than usual. Mercury, your career planet, is also a fast-moving planet (usually faster than Venus, but not this year). Thus there are many short-term trends in the career that we will cover in the monthly reports.

Because Mercury will go into retrograde motion four times this year – more than usual – there is more review needed in the career. There is a greater need too for mental clarity on this subject. Things are not as they seem.

Love and Social Life

Love is a bit more complicated than usual this year. However, the planetary strength in your 7th house shows that you're focused here. It is important to you and thus you're willing to deal with the complications and challenges. This focus tends to success.

The first complication is that you're more self-centred this year – especially until September 9. You tend to want things your own way. You're focused on personal fulfilment. Your spouse, partner or current love is pretty much the same. Neither is right or wrong. Sometimes one is, sometimes the other. There is a need to bridge your competing interests. Sometimes you lean one way, sometimes the other.

The second complication is your idealism in love. You have always had high ideals in love, but with Neptune, your love planet, now in your 7th house of love, these ideals have grown exponentially. It is good to have high ideals in love. It is good to want the highest and the best. You deserve it – everyone deserves it. However, one needs to know where to look for this. If we are looking outside ourselves there is always a feeling of disappointment – disillusion. For, though some people have a greater capacity for love than others, no mortal can live up to such high ideals. So a subtle sense of disappointment is felt even in the best of relationships. There is a cosmic agenda here. You're being led to spiritual love – the Divine Love – Agape as the Greeks called it. Many will find it in the coming years. It is the only power that can love you perfectly and can fulfil every need in love.

The third complication is getting the family – and especially a parent or parent figure – to be in harmony with the current love and to accept him or her. The reverse is also true. The current love might not be accepting of the family. This is going to be a challenge. But you will handle it.

Two eclipses will occur in your 7th house of love this year. The first is a solar eclipse on March 9 (in America it is on March 8) and the second a lunar eclipse on September 16. These will test your current relationships. Dirty laundry will be revealed so that it can be cleansed. Good relationships will survive and get even better, but flawed ones could dissolve.

If you're single and working towards your first marriage, this is not advisable this year. Even a good relationship will need more time. Those working towards their second or third marriage have a static kind of year. But those working towards their fourth marriage have excellent prospects. Romance is happening.

Your best love and social periods will tend to be February 18 to March 20, June 21 to July 23, and October 23 to November 21.

The most stressed-out love periods will tend to be from May 21 to June 20 and November 22 to December 21. This is when more patience is needed with the beloved.

Self-improvement

Jupiter in your sign for the first half of the year, and then moving into your money house, brings prosperity as we mentioned. But more important than the actual material prosperity is the revelation that he brings. Too often we think of wealth as material, tangible things – the cars, homes, money, jewellery – and the tendency is to worship these objects of wealth. This is 'Mammon Worship' – a form of idolatry. It's good to be wealthy and to have all the material things we want, but we must worship the power that produces these things and not the things themselves. Jupiter's real gift is the insight he gives into the spiritual laws of prosperity. It is good to be open to this. If you receive this revelation, you will have a more permanent kind of wealth. You will know how to operate the spiritual law at any time – even when Jupiter moves away from you next year. You can produce what the world calls 'good luck' whenever you want.

Uranus in your 8th house shows sexual experimentation, as we have mentioned. Of itself this is a good thing. Through this experimentation we learn our own sexual nature and what works for us. However, sexual experimentation can take destructive forms if we are not careful. And this can lead to all kinds of negative experiences. So long as you keep things positive and non-destructive, you're OK.

Astrologers understand Neptune in the 7th house as the 'search for spiritual love'. This is the agenda this year and for many years to come. While this brings both highs and lows in love – and often disappointments – the end result is good. Through the disappointments we arrive at the Divine Love – Agape. When this is discovered – and it is an amazing discovery – you will never lack for love or companionship. Whether you're in a relationship or not, you'll always feel like you're on your honeymoon. Every love need – whatever it is – will be fulfilled at the right time and in right order. As with money, the tendency is to worship the object of love, rather than the power that produces it. Neptune, in coming years, will straighten this out.

Saturn's presence in your 4th house since last year shows a need to get the emotional life in right order. Disordered emotions created a disordered life. There is nothing that will sabotage a life more than negative emotions. Saturn in the 4th house tends (if you're not careful) to repression of feeling. One doesn't feel safe in expressing real feelings and so they get repressed. Repression can't go on for too long, however – it is like trying to repress the urge to go to the bathroom. Eventually the feelings get expressed and generally in a much more destructive way than they should be. What is needed is a safe way to express negative emotion and then to transform these things into positives. Work with a therapist would be advisable. However, there are many spiritual techniques that can be used to deal with this. Some of you might want to look at *A Technique for Meditation*, by yours truly, for methods to proceed.

Month-by-month Forecasts

January

Best Days Overall: 9, 10, 17, 18, 26, 27
Most Stressful Days Overall: 6, 7, 13, 14, 19, 20
Best Days for Love: 4, 5, 6, 7, 8, 13, 14, 15, 16, 21, 22, 26, 31
Best Days for Money: 1, 2, 3, 6, 7, 8, 9, 10, 15, 16, 17, 18, 26, 27,
  29, 30
Best Days for Career: 10, 17, 18, 19, 20, 26, 27

Right now you're in an excellent period for starting new projects or launching new products into the world. Both your personal and universal solar cycles are waxing. The planetary momentum is forward – there will never be more than two planets retrograde at this time. If you can schedule your launch between the 10th and the 24th you have the added 'oomph' of a waxing moon. Next month should also be good for these things. But don't wait too much longer.

You begin your year with the planetary power moving away from you. It is concentrated in the Western, social sector of your chart. Your needs are important, but right now focus on others. Cultivate your relationships and your social skills. Learn about who you are through your relationships. If conditions are irksome, make a note of what needs to be changed and when the planets shift to the East – as they start moving towards you – it will be easier to make those changes.

The planetary power is mostly in the bottom half of your chart this month. Your career planet, Mercury, is retrograde most of the month – from the 5th to the 25th. So, career moves and goals need more study and clarity before being pursued. Career issues need time to resolve. Give your attention to the home, family and your emotional wellness instead.

This is a happy month, Virgo. Health needs watching this year, but for now it is good. You're in a strong party period as the year begins. You're enjoying your life and involved in all kinds of fun activities. And, even when the Sun moves into your 6th house of work on the 20th – it is still fun. For a Virgo work is fun. An unemployed or underemployed Virgo is a most miserable creature.

The Sun is your spiritual planet. His move into your 6th house shows an affinity for spiritual healing. This is a good period to go deeper into this. If you feel under the weather try seeing some sort of spiritual healer and work with the methods discussed in the yearly report.

There are happy career and financial opportunities from the 14th to the 16th, but study them carefully.

The Sun had its solstice on the 21st of last month. This month Venus, your financial planet, is on one of her solstices from the 25th to the 30th. This shows a financial pause. This is not to be feared but should be welcomed – let go of financial worries and cares for a while. When Venus resumes her latitude motion the financial life moves forward – and is better than before.

February

Best Days Overall: 5, 6, 13, 14, 22, 23, 24
Most Stressful Days Overall: 2, 3, 4, 9, 10, 15, 16, 17
Best Days for Love: 1, 5, 6, 9, 10, 13, 14, 18, 19, 25, 27, 28
Best Days for Money: 5, 6, 13, 14, 22, 23, 24, 25, 26
Best Days for Career: 5, 6, 15, 16, 17, 25, 26

As we mentioned last month, the month ahead is wonderful for starting new projects, for launching a new business or product. The personal and universal solar cycles are still waxing and 90 per cent of the planets are in forward motion. You should see fast progress towards your goals. The 8th to the 22nd, as the Moon waxes, is the best period of a good month.

Saturn re-stimulates an old eclipse point from the 1st to the 5th. Advise children and children figures in your life to take it easy and avoid stressful kinds of activities. Be more patient with them as well – they are probably more temperamental.

Another happy month ahead. Your 6th house of work and health – your favourite house – is powerful until the 19th, which makes this a good period to achieve work-oriented goals. If you're a job seeker you have many good opportunities now. Likewise if you employ others.

On the 19th the Sun enters your 7th house of love and you begin a yearly love and social peak. The Sun, the actual spiritual planet in your chart, and Neptune, the generic spiritual planet, both occupy the 7th house. A clear message. You're meeting spiritual and artistic kinds of people. Other types don't interest you very much. Spiritual compatibility is perhaps just as important as physical magnetism at the moment. Love awaits you at spiritual or charitable events – perhaps at the yoga studio or meditation class or at a spiritual lecture given by a visiting guru. Guru-type figures are playing cupid from the 19th onwards, and there is a romantic meeting with a spiritual person on the 28th or 29th.

Learn as much as you can about spiritual healing until the 19th. This knowledge will stand you in good stead for when your health becomes more stressful. Enhance the health in the ways mentioned in the yearly report and, most importantly, maintain high energy levels. A strong aura will repel any disease. Health can be further enhanced through arm and shoulder massage from the 14th onwards, and through hip and neck massage from the 17th onwards.

Finance doesn't seem a major interest this month. If there are problems they probably come about through lack of attention. Until the 17th money is earned in happy ways – perhaps while you're out enjoying yourself. From the 17th onwards money is earned through work. Often there is overtime or extra jobs that bring in more cash.

March

Best Days Overall: 3, 4, 12, 13, 21, 22, 31
Most Stressful Days Overall: 1, 2, 8, 9, 14, 15, 28, 29
Best Days for Love: 6, 7, 8, 9, 16, 17, 26, 27
Best Days for Money: 3, 4, 6, 7, 12, 13, 16, 21, 22, 23, 24, 26, 27, 31
Best Days for Career: 8, 14, 15, 16, 17, 28, 29

Health and energy are delicate in March, and two eclipses this month – both of which affect you strongly – only add to the pressure. So, take it nice and easy this month – especially around the eclipse periods. Make sure, as always, that you get enough rest. Let go of the trivial things in your life and focus on what's really important. It would be wonderful to schedule massages in this month or spend more time in a health spa, if possible. Until the 5th health can be enhanced through arm and shoulder massage; until the 12th through hip and neck massage. In addition, refer to the ways to maintain health mentioned in the yearly report.

The solar eclipse of the 9th (in America it is on the 8th) occurs in your 7th house of love and will test current relationships. The social life has become very active these days. New relationships have been formed. Now it is time they get tested and only the good ones will remain. Often a solar eclipse brings dramatic, life-changing events to the lives of partners and friends – this too can test a relationship. An eclipse in the 7th house often announces a change in marital status. Singles can decide to marry and married couples can decide to split. But a good marriage will survive the eclipse. Every solar eclipse brings spiritual changes to you and this one is no different. Usually this happens because of interior revelation. The practice, the attitudes and perhaps even the teachings of your spiritual path change. There are dramas and upheavals in spiritual or charitable organizations you're involved with, and in the lives of guru figures. This eclipse impacts on Jupiter and Saturn. Thus there are family dramas, and dramas with the children or children figures in your life.

The lunar eclipse of the 23rd occurs in your money house and announces dramatic financial changes – changes in thinking, planning and strategy. Often this happens because of some financial disruption such as an unexpected expense or obligation. This is the catalyst for the change. These changes are also necessary for other reasons. You are in a strong prosperity period and you need to make the changes that allow this to happen. This kind of eclipse often brings dramas in the lives of the money people in your life.

Since the eclipsed planet, the Moon, rules friendships, there are more dramas in the lives of friends. Friendships get tested. Mercury, the ruler of your Horoscope and your career planet, is impacted by this eclipse too, so career changes are happening. There are upheavals in your company or industry. There are dramas in the lives of bosses, parents or parent figures. Also, there is a need now to redefine yourself – to redefine your image, personality and self-concept. Usually events force the issue. Over the next six months you'll present a 'new look' to the world.

April

Best Days Overall: 1, 8, 9, 17, 18, 27, 28
Most Stressful Days Overall: 4, 5, 10, 11, 24, 25, 26
Best Days for Love: 4, 5, 6, 12, 13, 14, 15, 22, 23, 25, 26
Best Days for Money: 1, 6, 8, 9, 14, 15, 17, 18, 19, 20, 21, 25, 26, 27, 28
Best Days for Career: 8, 9, 10, 11, 17, 18, 27, 28

Health still needs watching but is much improved over last month. Last month was a 'critical' health month. If you got through it with your health and sanity intact you did very well. Pat yourself on the back.

The eclipses are over with but there are still some lingering effects. Venus, your financial planet, re-stimulates an eclipse point on the 7th and 8th, bringing some financial disturbance and more change. On the 22nd and 23rd Venus travels with Uranus, bringing more of the same. However, this latter period can also (and often does) bring 'unexpected money'.

Your 8th house of transformation became powerful on March 20 and is still powerful until the 19th of this month. This is a wonderful time for detox and weight loss regimes. This period favours getting rid of the extraneous, the non-essential things in your life, whether they be in the physical body, your possessions or in your mental and emotional life. Most people see a detox as something purely physical. But a real detox should include the mind and feelings too. We all walk around with ideas and concepts that are either not true or irrelevant. These should be purged. There are also old emotional patterns that serve no useful purpose (and are generally harmful) – these too should be purged and replaced with more positive ones.

Power in the 8th house favours projects of personal transformation and reinvention. We all have an 'ideal' self – the self that we want to be. This is a good month to let that come through, to give birth to it.

The spouse, partner or current love is having a banner financial month – a yearly peak. You seem very involved with this. He or she is likely to be more generous with you.

The Sun in Aries (since March 20) is considered the best time to start new projects. Aries is starting energy. However, there is a lot of retrograde activity this month, with 40 per cent of the planets retrograde from the 18th to the 25th, increasing to 50 per cent retrograde after the 25th. January and February were much better for starting new things than now – especially for you, Virgo.

Last month the planetary power shifted from the lower to the upper half of your Horoscope. It is morning in your year and time for you to focus on your career and outer goals. Hopefully, you have attained emotional harmony over the past six months as it is now time to translate that into outer success.

May

Best Days Overall: 6, 14, 15, 24, 25
Most Stressful Days Overall: 1, 2, 3, 7, 8, 22, 23, 29, 30
Best Days for Love: 1, 2, 3, 6, 10, 11, 14, 15, 19, 20, 26, 27, 29, 30
Best Days for Money: 6, 14, 15, 17, 18, 24, 25, 26, 27
Best Days for Career: 6, 7, 8, 14, 15, 24, 25

Travel – foreign travel – has been in your chart all year, and this month it is indicated even more than before. Happy travel opportunities are happening. With the 9th house strong and filled with beneficent planets, college or post-graduate level students are doing well. They are interested in their studies and highly motivated – and this is 90 per cent of success. In general, even those who are not students are more interested in higher learning this month. Happy opportunities come and you should take them. It will be especially good to take courses or seminars that are career related. This will boost your career and bring advancement.

The 9th house, which rules religion, philosophy and metaphysics, is one of the most important houses in the zodiac – and yet it is often overlooked. The Hindus consider it the *most* important house for our personal religion, our personal philosophy, shaping our view of the world, our view of life, and our interpretation of the events that happen to us. It is much more important than psychology, in that affairs of the 9th house will mould a person's psychology. Philosophy and world view are cause, psychology is effect. So this is a great month for metaphysical and philosophical studies. A great month to examine personal belief systems. A great month to attain philosophical purity.

On the 20th the Sun crosses the Mid-heaven and enters your 10th house of career. This is noon time in your year. You are in a yearly career peak and will make much career progress. On the 24th Venus, the financial planet, also enters the 10th house, creating a good financial transit. It shows that money is high on your agenda. You admire the rich and aspire to be like them. It shows that your good professional reputation is especially important in your financial life – more so than usual. Pay rises, either monetary ones or 'remuneration in kind', can happen now. You have the financial favour of bosses, elders, parents and parent figures.

The Sun, your spiritual planet, in the 10th house of career shows that you can advance your career – your professional standing – by being more involved with charities and altruistic causes. Indeed, these might be more important than your professional achievements. Gurus, psychics, astrologers and other spiritual channels have important career guidance for you. Career guidance can come in dreams too.

Make sure to get enough rest from the 20th onwards when health becomes more delicate. Enhance the health in the ways mentioned in the yearly report.

June

Best Days Overall: 2, 3, 10, 11, 12, 20, 21, 22, 29, 30
Most Stressful Days Overall: 4, 5, 18, 19, 25, 26
Best Days for Love: 4, 5, 14, 25, 26
Best Days for Money: 2, 3, 4, 5, 10, 11, 13, 14, 20, 21, 25, 26, 29, 30
Best Days for Career: 2, 3, 4, 5, 12, 13, 23, 24

An active and hectic month, but a successful one.

You're still in the midst of a yearly career peak until the 21st. Review our discussion of this in last month's report. On the 13th Mercury, your ruling planet, crosses the Mid-heaven and enters the 10th house. You are above everyone in your world – for now anyway. You're in charge. Elevated. Promotions are likely (official or unofficial). You seem involved in large and complicated undertakings. These things are always delicate and challenging.

The family life seems more challenging now and perhaps those close to you want more of your attention, but with the career so dominant this is difficult for you. The focus on the career creates challenges in love too. Somehow – and there are no rules for this – you have to bring all these areas into balance. Now you will lean one way, now another. Keeping everyone pleased is the challenge.

Health needs keeping an eye on even more carefully than last month. You're very busy, but schedule in more rest periods. Take a break from work and get a massage. Make sure you get enough sleep. This is not a time to burn the candle at both ends. Continue to enhance the health in the ways mentioned in the yearly report. Health will improve after the 21st.

Your financial planet, Venus, is in your 10th house until the 18th. Review our discussion of this from last month. Venus spends a good part of the month 'out of bounds'. This shows that in finance you're moving outside your normal sphere, your normal habitat. You're taking roads that you generally don't travel. Venus has one of her solstices from the 19th to the 23rd. She pauses in her latitudinal motion and occupies the exact same latitude during these five days. This indicates a financial pause for you. A pause that refreshes. It shows a change of direction happening in your financial life – it will be good. During this pause it is good to set new financial goals for the future. The financial intuition is excellent on the 1st, 27th and 28th. The 1st looks like a nice payday. Be careful of overspending on the 3rd and 4th.

The eclipses of March have long passed, but we still have lingering after-effects even in this month. The Sun and Venus transit an eclipse point on the 8th and 9th. The financial intuition needs verification before being acted upon, and there can be some financial disturbance.

The Sun and Mercury move over an eclipse point on the 23rd and 24th. Avoid stressful activities then and spend more quiet time at home.

July

Best Days Overall: 8, 9, 18, 19, 27, 28
Most Stressful Days Overall: 1, 2, 15, 16, 22, 23, 29, 30
Best Days for Love: 3, 4, 13, 14, 15, 22, 23, 24, 25, 31
Best Days for Money: 3, 4, 8, 9, 10, 11, 12, 15, 18, 19, 24, 25, 27, 28
Best Days for Career: 1, 2, 3, 4, 14, 15, 24, 25, 29, 30

The love life is active but complicated this month. First off your love planet, Neptune, is retrograde all month, which weakens your social confidence. Neptune spends the month conjunct to the Moon's South Node. This can give a feeling of lack or deficiency even where none exists. You feel 'something is missing here'. Yet love and social opportunities are happening. The only question is how satisfying are they?

The other complication is that the planetary power is now in the independent Eastern sector. The shift happened on the 13th of last month. The planets are moving towards you and away from others. While this gives you more personal power and independence, it's not always good for relationships. Not everyone can handle an independent lover. The good news is that you can start creating conditions as you want them to be, you can start to create your own happiness. The pursuit of happiness is not selfish but a God-given right. As long as the rights of others are respected it's a wonderful thing.

Friendships, which is what the month is about, seem more satisfying than romance. July is a socially active kind of month. This is a month for networking and being involved with groups and organizations. There is increased online activity too. These activities boost the bottom line until the 12th. After that the financial intuition becomes important. Financial guidance will come in dreams or through psychics, astrologers or spiritual channels. From the 12th onwards it will be a good period to go deeper into the spiritual dimensions of wealth. A parent or parent figure is prospering this month. He or she is having a yearly financial peak and seems more supportive. Car or communication problems can create expenses on the 1st. A sudden expense forces some financial change on the 6th or 7th – but unexpected money can occur to cover it.

Mercury, both your ruler and career planet, is 'out of bounds' from the 1st to the 9th, indicating that you are outside your normal habitat in the pursuit of career goals. Another way to read this is that the demands of your career pull you outside your normal sphere.

Health is good this month but take it easy on the 1st and 2nd. There can be career changes or upheavals then too. There's no need for high stress kinds of activities. Drive more carefully on the 7th, 10th and 11th.

August

Best Days Overall: 4, 5, 14, 15, 23, 24, 31
Most Stressful Days Overall: 12, 13, 19, 20, 25, 26
Best Days for Love: 1, 3, 9, 10, 14, 15, 19, 20, 23, 24, 27, 28
Best Days for Money: 3, 4, 5, 7, 8, 14, 15, 23, 24, 31
Best Days for Career: 4, 5, 14, 15, 23, 24, 25, 26, 31

Last month on the 22nd your 12th house of spirituality became powerful, and remains so until August 22. This is a spiritual period. Many people fear solitude, but there are times when it is necessary and good. This is that kind of time. People tend to feel naturally reclusive when the 12th house is strong. There are spiritual reasons for this. It is in the solitude that spiritual breakthroughs and insights happen. Rest assured, this solitude is not for ever and not a trend for the year or for life.

The month ahead is happy and successful. The planetary power is now at its maximum Eastern position. The cosmos supports you and your personal goals. It is a time for being independent, for standing on your own two feet and for having your way in life. Make the changes necessary that bring you happiness. This may stress a current relationship, but this stress is also temporary. You and the beloved have to work harder to bridge your differences. You're seeing things from opposite perspectives. Neither of you is always right or wrong; sometimes one is right, sometimes the other. If these opposite perspectives can be bridged the relationship will be more powerful than before.

Mercury is going retrograde at the end of the month – on the 30th. Make your changes before then.

The Sun enters your sign on the 22nd. This gives a supernatural, otherworldly kind of glamour to the image. It gives power to shape the body and image as you desire it to be. Those of you into yoga or other spiritual-type exercises are better at them this month. A guru or guru figure is coming into your life.

Venus will move into your sign on the 5th. This adds beauty, style and grace to the image, and it also brings financial windfalls and opportunity. There are very nice paydays happening between the 20th and the 24th, and between the 26th to the 28th. The 20th to the 24th brings career success too.

Mercury is in your sign all month. This increases your confidence and self-esteem. His presence also brings career opportunities. You look rich and successful this month. You dress that way and others see you that way too.

Health is good all month, but especially after the 22nd.

September

   Best Days Overall: 1, 2, 10, 11, 12, 19, 20, 28, 29
   Most Stressful Days Overall: 8, 9, 15, 16, 21, 22
   Best Days for Love: 3, 4, 5, 6, 13, 14, 15, 16, 23, 24
   Best Days for Money: 1, 2, 3, 4, 12, 13, 14, 21, 23, 30
   Best Days for Career: 8, 9, 10, 11, 17, 18, 27, 28

We have two eclipses this month; both affect you strongly but the month ahead won't be as challenging as March was. You have more energy supporting you now. Still, it is advisable to take it easy and relax more during the eclipse periods.

The solar eclipse of the 1st occurs in your own sign. Those of you born between September 25 and October 5 will feel it most strongly but all of you will feel it to some degree. This eclipse brings a redefinition of the self, your personality and self-concept. Generally outer events force you to do this. If people are slandering or misrepresenting you, you have to define yourself for yourself, or allow others to do it. This latter scenario is not so pleasant. Over the next six months you will present a new 'look' to the world and this often involves wardrobe and hairstyle changes. Sometimes this kind of eclipse prompts a detox of the body (and this is especially likely if you haven't been careful in dietary matters).

This solar eclipse impacts on Mars and Saturn. Thus it can bring near-death experiences or close calls with death, dreams of death, etc. (Another good reason to reduce your schedule this during this period.) Sometimes surgery is recommended. The spouse, partner or current love is forced to make dramatic financial changes and there can be disturbances in issues involving taxes, estates or insurance claims. The impact on Saturn can bring dramas in the lives of children and children figures in your life. They should stay out of harm's way during this period too. Every solar eclipse brings spiritual changes and this one is no different. It brings turbulence in spiritual or charitable organizations you're involved with and dramas in the lives of guru figures.

The lunar eclipse of the 16th occurs in your 7th house of love and will test your current relationship or partnership. Dirty laundry, long suppressed, surfaces for cleansing and resolution. Good relationships tend to survive this testing, but weaker ones are in danger. Friendships are again getting tested. There are life-changing kinds of dramas in the lives of your friends. There is upheaval in a professional or trade organization you belong to, or that you're involved with. High tech equipment also gets tested. Make sure important files are backed up and that anti-virus, anti-hacking and anti-phishing software is up to date.

October

Best Days Overall: 8, 9, 17, 25, 26
Most Stressful Days Overall: 5, 6, 7, 12, 13, 19
Best Days for Love: 3, 4, 12, 13, 21, 22, 23, 24, 30, 31
Best Days for Money: 1, 2, 3, 4, 10, 12, 13, 18, 19, 23, 24, 27, 28, 29
Best Days for Career: 10, 19, 20, 30

Last month, on the 10th, Jupiter entered your money house at the start of a beautiful financial transit. Finances have been good this year and from here on in they get even better. On September 22, the Sun also entered your money house and you began a yearly financial peak. For many of you (much depends on your age) this is a lifetime financial peak. There is good family financial support now. Money can be earned from home or through the home – often this indicates a fortunate purchase or sale of a home. The real estate industry is good. The Sun in the money house shows the importance of your financial intuition. There is financial guidance in dreams or from psychics, astrologers and other spiritual channels. Miracle money happens for you.

The month ahead is financially active in other ways too. The Moon, which normally spends two days in a sign or house each month, will spend five days in the money house – two-and-a-half times longer than usual. This suggests the financial cooperation of friends and social contacts. Technology – and your skills in this area – play a huge role in earnings.

Your financial planet Venus will be 'out of bounds' from the 17th to the 31st. This shows that you're going outside your normal sphere in pursuit of earnings. You're not afraid to do unconventional kinds of things.

Last month's eclipses are over with, but there are still lingering effects – especially in your love life. Neptune, your love planet, spends the month camped out on the solar eclipse point of September 1, and so there is still turbulence in your relationships. The spouse, partner or current love could be going through a challenging period – he or she should avoid high risk activities. Neptune is still retrograde, so this is not a time to make important love decisions, one way or the other. There is still much distance between you and the beloved. The challenge will be to bridge your differences and your opposite perspectives on things.

Job changes can happen this month as your work planet, Uranus, receives some stressful aspects. This stressful period is especially severe from the 27th to the 29th. Job safety is an important issue during that time.

Health is basically good this month, but it won't hurt to drive more carefully on the 15th, 16th, 19th and 20th. Enhance the health in the ways mentioned in the yearly report.

November

Best Days Overall: 4, 5, 13, 14, 21, 22, 23
Most Stressful Days Overall: 2, 3, 9, 10, 15, 16, 29, 30
Best Days for Love: 2, 3, 9, 10, 13, 17, 18, 21, 22, 26, 27
Best Days for Money: 2, 3, 6, 7, 13, 15, 16, 21, 22, 24, 25
Best Days for Career: 1, 10, 15, 16, 19, 20, 29, 30

The planetary power is at its nadir (lowest point) this month. The bottom half of the Horoscope is dominant and you are approaching the mystical midnight hour of your year. It is an hour of darkness and mystery, but this is where change happens. It is at midnight, the darkest hour, that the old day dies and a new one is born. Many, many miracles happen at the midnight hour. This is a time where you achieve your goals by the methods of night – by dreaming, visualizing and speaking the word. At midnight the body is still, but the deeper mind is active and we have better access to its powers. The deeper mind is not limited by time or space, it is not limited by your present condition. This is a time to avail yourself of these gifts.

On a more mundane level, this is a time to focus on the home, family and your personal emotional wellness. Too often we think of this as unimportant when compared to our outer goals. But this is not true. Career success is founded upon a stable and harmonious home life and a sense of emotional wellness. This is your real career – your real mission – in the month ahead. If your emotions are in right order, everything else will fall into place.

You have been in a prosperity cycle all year and it continues in the month ahead. Venus, your financial planet, spends the whole month (very unusually) 'out of bounds'. So you're outside your normal sphere in search of earnings. You are doing unusual kinds of things. Venus is in your 4th house of home and family until the 12th, showing that you're earning money from home. It shows a family kind of business and good family support. You are spending more on the home and family too. There is good financial cooperation between you and the family. On the 12th Venus enters Capricorn, your 5th house. This indicates happy money – money that is earned in happy ways – and that you spend more on leisure activities. Speculations are more favourable during this period, but they are more the calculated kind – not the casino kind.

Venus has one of her solstices from the 13th to the 16th. She pauses in her heavenly motion. She occupies the exact degree and minute of latitude for those days. This suggests a financial pause in your life. There's nothing to be alarmed about, it is only a temporary pause. She is changing direction – and this is happening in your financial life.

Health is more delicate after the 22nd so make sure you get enough rest. Enhance the health in the ways mentioned in the yearly report.

December

Best Days Overall: 1, 2, 3, 10, 11, 19, 20, 29, 30
Most Stressful Days Overall: 6, 7, 12, 13, 26, 27
Best Days for Love: 2, 3, 6, 7, 12, 13, 14, 15, 21, 22, 23, 24
Best Days for Money: 2, 3, 4, 5, 12, 13, 21, 22, 31
Best Days for Career: 10, 11, 12, 13, 19, 20, 29, 30

Your 4th house is still powerful this month, keeping the focus on the home, family and your personal emotional wellness. Ignoring your emotional wellness is like not having a good night's sleep. The coming day is not what it should be. Those of you involved in psychological kinds of therapy should make good progress this month. You will find that psychological breakthroughs are happening.

Psychological breakthroughs will happen even for those of you not in formal therapy. Nature will see to that. Old memories and perhaps old traumas will surface spontaneously so that they can be resolved. Look at them impersonally and much of the negative power they had will dissolve. A person becomes more aware of the vast universe of mood and feeling under this transit and becomes more able to navigate it. You're more moody than usual during this period. Through meditation and spiritual practice, however, you can learn to harness the power of mood for your benefit.

The natural result of a psychological breakthrough, of emotional wellness, is joy and increased creativity. The 5th house of fun comes after the 4th house of mood and feeling. Thus by December 21 you enter a yearly personal pleasure peak. A fun kind of month. The Sun has his solstice then. There is a pause in the affairs of the world. A pause that refreshes. Life is meant to be enjoyed. Even the challenges of life are meant to be enjoyed. And this is a period where you explore this dimension. Your financial planet has been in your 5th house since November 12 and is there until the 7th of this month. Thus resources are there for fun. Venus has deposited the funds into your 5th house.

On the 7th Venus enters your 6th house of work, and money is earned through hard work now. It not only comes from your present job, but from other 'side jobs' or through overtime opportunities that come. The 7th onwards is a highly prosperous time, as Venus makes nice aspects to Jupiter. There is good family support during that period.

Health is much improved after the 21st. You can enhance it further in the ways mentioned in the yearly report.

Love is still stormy, but improving. Neptune, the love planet, started to move forward, after many months of retrograde motion, on November 20. So at least there is mental clarity in love now. However, Mars moves into your 7th house of love on the 20th and this can endanger a present relationship. Be careful of power struggles in love from the 20th onwards.

Libra

THE SCALES

Birthdays from
23rd September to
22nd October

Personality Profile

LIBRA AT A GLANCE

Element – Air

Ruling Planet – Venus
   Career Planet – Moon
   Love Planet – Mars
   Money Planet – Pluto
   Planet of Communications – Jupiter
   Planet of Health and Work – Neptune
   Planet of Home and Family Life – Saturn
   Planet of Spirituality and Good Fortune – Mercury

Colours – blue, jade green

Colours that promote love, romance and social harmony – carmine, red, scarlet

Colours that promote earning power – burgundy, red-violet, violet

Gems – carnelian, chrysolite, coral, emerald, jade, opal, quartz, white marble

Metal – copper

Scents – almond, rose, vanilla, violet

Quality – cardinal (= activity)

Qualities most needed for balance – a sense of self, self-reliance, independence

Strongest virtues – social grace, charm, tact, diplomacy

Deepest needs – love, romance, social harmony

Characteristic to avoid – violating what is right in order to be socially accepted

Signs of greatest overall compatibility – Gemini, Aquarius

Signs of greatest overall incompatibility – Aries, Cancer, Capricorn

Sign most helpful to career – Cancer

Sign most helpful for emotional support – Capricorn

Sign most helpful financially – Scorpio

Sign best for marriage and/or partnerships – Aries

Sign most helpful for creative projects – Aquarius

Best Sign to have fun with – Aquarius

Signs most helpful in spiritual matters – Gemini, Virgo

Best day of the week – Friday

Understanding a Libra

In the sign of Libra the universal mind – the soul – expresses its genius for relationships, that is, its power to harmonize diverse elements in a unified, organic way. Libra is the soul's power to express beauty in all of its forms. And where is beauty if not within relationships? Beauty does not exist in isolation. Beauty arises out of comparison – out of the just relationship between different parts. Without a fair and harmonious relationship there is no beauty, whether it in art, manners, ideas or the social or political forum.

There are two faculties humans have that exalt them above the animal kingdom: their rational faculty (expressed in the signs of Gemini and Aquarius) and their aesthetic faculty, exemplified by Libra. Without an aesthetic sense we would be little more than intelligent barbarians. Libra is the civilizing instinct or urge of the soul.

Beauty is the essence of what Librans are all about. They are here to beautify the world. One could discuss Librans' social grace, their sense of balance and fair play, their ability to see and love another person's point of view – but this would be to miss their central asset: their desire for beauty.

No one – no matter how alone he or she seems to be – exists in isolation. The universe is one vast collaboration of beings. Librans, more than most, understand this and understand the spiritual laws that make relationships bearable and enjoyable.

A Libra is always the unconscious (and in some cases conscious) civilizer, harmonizer and artist. This is a Libra's deepest urge and greatest genius. Librans love instinctively to bring people together, and they are uniquely qualified to do so. They have a knack for seeing what unites people – the things that attract and bind rather than separate individuals.

Finance

In financial matters Librans can seem frivolous and illogical to others. This is because Librans appear to be more concerned with earning money for others than for themselves. But there is a logic to this financial attitude. Librans know that everything and everyone is connected and that it is impossible to help another to prosper without also prospering yourself. Since enhancing their partner's income and position tends to strengthen their relationship, Librans choose to do so. What could be more fun than building a relationship? You will rarely find a Libra enriching him- or herself at someone else's expense.

Scorpio is the ruler of Libra's solar 2nd house of money, giving Libra unusual insight into financial matters – and the power to focus on these matters in a way that disguises a seeming indifference. In fact, many other signs come to Librans for financial advice and guidance.

Given their social grace, Librans often spend great sums of money on entertaining and organizing social events. They also like to help others when they are in need. Librans would go out of their way to help a friend in dire straits, even if they have to borrow from others to do so. However, Librans are also very careful to pay back any debts they owe, and like to make sure they never have to be reminded to do so.

Career and Public Image

Publicly, Librans like to appear as nurturers. Their friends and acquaintances are their family and they wield political power in parental ways. They also like bosses who are paternal or maternal.

The sign of Cancer is on Libra's 10th career house cusp; the Moon is Libra's career planet. The Moon is by far the speediest, most changeable planet in the Horoscope. It alone among all the planets travels through the entire zodiac – all twelve signs and houses – every month. This is an important key to the way in which Librans approach their careers, and also to what they need to do to maximize their career potential. The Moon is the planet of moods and feelings – Librans need a career in which their emotions can have free expression. This is why so many Librans are involved in the creative arts. Libra's ambitions wax and wane with the Moon. They tend to wield power according to their mood.

The Moon 'rules' the masses – and that is why Libra's highest goal is to achieve a mass kind of acclaim and popularity. Librans who achieve fame cultivate the public as other people cultivate a lover or friend. Librans can be very flexible – and often fickle – in their career and ambitions. On the other hand, they can achieve their ends in a great variety of ways. They are not stuck in one attitude or with one way of doing things.

Love and Relationships

Librans express their true genius in love. In love you could not find a partner more romantic, more seductive or more fair. If there is one thing that is sure to destroy a relationship – sure to block your love from flowing – it is injustice or imbalance between lover and beloved. If one party is giving too much or taking too much, resentment is sure to surface at some time or other. Librans are careful about this. If anything, Librans might err on the side of giving more, but never giving less.

If you are in love with a Libra, make sure you keep the aura of romance alive. Do all the little things – candle-lit dinners, travel to exotic locales, flowers and small gifts. Give things that are beautiful, not necessarily expensive. Send cards. Ring regularly even if you have nothing in particular to say. The niceties are very important to a Libra. Your relationship is a work of art: make it beautiful and your Libran lover will appreciate it. If you are creative about it, he or she will appreciate it even more; for this is how your Libra will behave towards you.

Librans like their partners to be aggressive and even a bit self-willed. They know that these are qualities they sometimes lack and so they like their partners to have them. In relationships, however, Librans can be very aggressive – but always in a subtle and charming way! Librans are determined in their efforts to charm the object of their desire – and this determination can be very pleasant if you are on the receiving end.

Home and Domestic Life

Since Librans are such social creatures, they do not particularly like mundane domestic duties. They like a well-organized home – clean and neat with everything needful present – but housework is a chore and a burden, one of the unpleasant tasks in life that must be done, the quicker the better. If a Libra has enough money – and sometimes even if not – he or she will prefer to pay someone else to take care of the daily household chores. However, Librans like gardening; they love to have flowers and plants in the home.

A Libra's home is modern, and furnished in excellent taste. You will find many paintings and sculptures there. Since Librans like to be with friends and family, they enjoy entertaining at home and they make great hosts.

Capricorn is on the cusp of Libra's 4th solar house of home and family. Saturn, the planet of law, order, limits and discipline, rules Libra's domestic affairs. If Librans want their home life to be supportive and happy they need to develop some of the virtues of Saturn – order, organization and discipline. Librans, being so creative and so intensely in need of harmony, can tend to be too lax in the home and too permissive with their children. Too much of this is not always good; children need freedom but they also need limits.

Horoscope for 2016

Major Trends

When Jupiter entered Virgo, last August, you entered a multi-year prosperity cycle, which will continue for the next few years. More on this later.

On September 10, Jupiter will enter your own sign, Libra – a most happy and fortunate transit. It brings sensual pleasures and the good life, so the weight will need more watching from that date onwards. Also, Libras of childbearing age will be much more fertile than usual.

Many of the trends that we've written about in previous years are still in effect now. Long-term planets are involved, and long-term planets show long-term projects.

Saturn in your 3rd house of communication is a challenging aspect for students – especially those below college level. They will have to work harder on their studies. They need to focus more. They need to discipline themselves intellectually – which is the whole purpose of the transit. Intellectual discipline is needed for all Libras, especially students.

Pluto has been in your 4th house of home and family for many years now, and will remain there for many more. A cosmic detox is going on in the family and especially in the emotional life. Impurities in the feeling body are being brought up and purged. A great period for those involved in psychological kinds of therapy. More details on this later.

Neptune has been in your 6th house of health and work for the past few years and will be there for several more. This shows a deep interest in spiritual healing methods. You've advanced far in recent years but there's always more to learn. Again, there are more details on this later.

Volatile, explosive Uranus has been in your 7th house of love for many years. And this is a good description of your love life. Explosive. Never a dull moment. An ongoing soap opera. Learning to deal with social insecurity and instability is still the main lesson these days.

Jupiter will spend most of the year in your spiritual 12th house. So you're in a strong spiritual period these days. Growth is more internal. Although it is not visible to the eye, it is happening. When Jupiter crosses your Ascendant in September the inner growth will be more apparent and tangible.

Your most important interests in the year ahead are: the body, image and personal pleasure (from September 10 onwards); communication and intellectual interests; home and family; health and work; love and romance; and spirituality (until September 9).

Your paths of greatest fulfilment will be spirituality; and later the body, image and personal pleasure (from September 10 onwards).

Health

(Please note that this is an astrological perspective on health and not a medical one. In days of yore there was no difference, these perspectives were identical. But now there could be quite a difference. For a medical perspective, please consult your doctor or health practitioner.)

You still have two long-term planets in stressful aspect to you this year, so your health needs attending to. However, the planetary stresses this year are much, much less than they have been in previous years. Health needs watching still, but much improvement is happening.

The good news is that your 6th house of health is powerful. So, you are paying attention. This is perhaps more important than just having easy aspects.

The two stressful planets – Pluto and Uranus – are not enough by themselves to cause disease. However, when they 'gang up' on you with the short-term planets that are passing through this house, this is when you become more vulnerable. This year these periods are from January 1–20; March 21 to April 19; June 21 to July 23; and December 22–31. Be sure to rest and relax more over those periods and maintain high energy levels.

Our regular readers know that there is much that can be done to enhance the health. You should pay more attention to the following areas this year (the respective reflexology points are shown in the chart below):

• The heart. This has been important for many years now and will be important for years to come. Spiritual healers affirm that the root cause of heart problems is worry and anxiety. Avoid these like the plague. A simple faith will do much to relieve them.

Important foot reflexology points for the year ahead
Try to massage all of the foot on a regular basis – the top of the foot as well as the bottom – but pay extra attention to the points highlighted on the chart. When you massage, be aware of 'sore spots' as these need special attention. It's also a good idea to massage the ankles and below them.

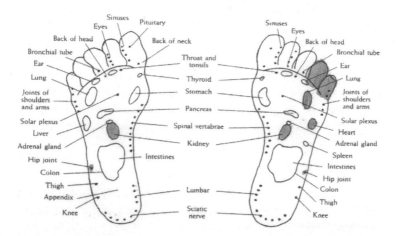

- The kidneys and hips. These areas are always important for you. Kidney action seems hyper from September 10 onwards. A herbal kidney cleanse might be a good idea if you feel under the weather. Regular hip massage is always good.
- The feet. These are also always important for you, and have become even more so ever since Neptune entered your 6th house in 2012. You respond especially well to foot reflexology – see our chart above. Foot baths and foot hydro massages are also good. There are all kinds of gadgets out on the market – some actually massage the feet, some are like foot whirlpool baths and some are just foot baths. All these things are beneficial and you might want to invest in one of them. As always, wear shoes that fit and that don't unbalance you. Shoes that pinch the toes are not so good. Comfort and correct fit are more important than fashion (from the health perspective). If you can have both, all the better.

These are the most vulnerable areas this year. Problems, if they happened (God forbid) would most likely begin here, so it is important to keep these areas healthy and fit. Most of the time problems can be prevented, and even if they can't be totally prevented they can be lessened to a great extent.

As we mentioned earlier, you respond well to spiritual healing techniques. So, if you feel under the weather, see a spiritual healer.

Neptune, your health planet, is the wateriest of the water planets and Pisces, your 6th house, is the wateriest of the water signs. Together this is a lot of water energy. The message of the Horoscope is that you have a special connection to the healing powers of the water element. You will find it very beneficial to hang out near water – oceans, rivers, lakes and springs. Water sports and boating are healthy kinds of exercise. (I also like the spiritual exercises like yoga and tai chi.) If you feel under the weather, a good long soak in the tub will do wonders for you.

Home and Family

Pluto has been in your 4th house of home and family since 2008 and he will be there for many more years. This is a dynamic transit. As we mentioned it brings a purge of family life and the family circle. Anything

impure, or anything that obstructs your ideal of family, gets removed
– exorcised. In many cases there have been actual literal deaths in the
family. In many cases there have been near-death kinds of experiences
in the lives of family members. In other cases families have broken up
and disintegrated, only to be reintegrated on a better level. The symbolism of the Horoscope is 'the death and rebirth of the family'. These
things are seldom pleasant, but the end result is good.

Pluto in your 4th house also shows many physical renovations of the
home. These are major renovations rather than cosmetic ones. They
can involve the breaking down of walls, rewiring and the ripping out of
old pipes and plumbing. Serious stuff!

Pluto is your financial planet. His position in your 4th house gives
us other messages. You're investing in the home. Spending on it.
Spending on the family. Family support should be good (especially this
year). You can also earn from the home too. With this aspect for so
many years, most of you already have home offices, but these could be
expanded this year. Family and family connections are important on a
financial level.

Saturn, your family planet, has been in Sagittarius, your 3rd house,
since late 2014. This shows a need for better communication with the
family. Lack of communication is perhaps a major source of conflict
here. It also indicates the installation of high-end communication
equipment in the home.

A parent or parent figure in your life has had surgery of late and this
trend continues in the year ahead. He or she would benefit from detox
regimes and these should be explored.

A sibling or sibling figure becomes very devoted to you later in the
year. A move is not likely this year, though. He or she has a stable,
static kind of year.

Children and children figures in your life also have a stable year.
Grandchildren (if you have them) are likely to move in the year ahead
though. (A move could have happened last year too.)

Major repairs or renovations are likely all year, but September 27 to
November 9 is an especially good time. If you're painting, redecorating
or otherwise beautifying the home, January 1 to February 17 is a good
period.

Finance and Career

As we mentioned, you have been in a strong prosperity period since August of last year. Jupiter, the planet of abundance and good fortune, is making beautiful aspects with your financial planet Pluto. Earnings increase. Financial opportunities increase. Because Jupiter is in your spiritual 12th house until September 9 this year, the financial intuition is excellent. Financial guidance will come to you in dreams and through guru or minister types. Psychics, astrologers and other spiritual channels also have important financial guidance. A millisecond of good financial intuition is worth many years of hard labour.

On September 10 Jupiter will cross your Ascendant and enter your 1st house. While this doesn't necessarily bring wealth, it does bring the high life. There will be more travel, more good food and wine and more pleasures of the senses. Generally these things happen naturally. Nothing special needs to be done. Generally, also, the supply for the high life comes too – you will find that the wherewithal needed for such a lifestyle is provided.

Family support is good all year. A parent or parent figure is not in agreement on financial matters (after September 10) but will be supportive anyway.

Pluto is your financial planet. Generally he rules inheritance. Hopefully no one has to die, but you can be named in someone's will, or be appointed to some administrative post. Sometimes this aspect indicates earnings from trust funds or insurance claims. Those of you of appropriate age are doing more estate planning these days. Taxes and estates issues are influencing your financial decision-making. Often there are earnings from tax refunds.

Your ability to borrow or pay down debt – depending on your need – is strengthened these days. If you have good ideas it is easy to attract outside money to your projects.

Pluto in your 4th house shows an affinity for real estate – both commercial and residential. It shows an affinity with the bond market – and especially the bonds of traditional blue chip companies. The creative use of debt – creative financing – is also a source of income.

The financial planet in Capricorn shows excellent financial judgement. You get value for your money. You have a long-term perspective on wealth and seem ready to undertake disciplined financial measures to achieve your aims, such as setting up savings and investment programmes. You're good at budgeting and staying within a budget at the moment (rare for you, Libra). You take a step by step, methodical approach to wealth now, building it for the long term.

This is not an especially strong career year. Your 10th house is for the most part empty. Only short-term planets will pass through here, temporarily boosting the career. But they pass rather quickly. Moreover, most of the long-term planets are below the horizon of your chart. The year ahead is more about family and getting the emotional life in right order. In general we can say that career energy will be strongest on the New and Full Moon and when the Moon is waxing. These periods are best discussed in the monthly reports.

Love and Social Life

The explosive ups and downs – stunning surprises – in the love life have been taxing even your social genius. Libras are not generally risk-takers – except when it comes to love. In love, they go where angels fear to tread. And this year more so than usual.

Many a relationship has broken up in recent years. Many a friendship has gone down the tubes. There's been many a divorce as well. Uranus in the 7th house is just not that conducive to committed kinds of relationships. It is wonderful for serial love affairs, but not for marriage or relationships that are 'like' marriage. Uranus likes change and variety. He likes freedom. A stable kind of relationship seems 'boring' and hum drum.

Also, Uranus in the 7th house indicates a penchant for unconventional types of people. Plain vanilla types are not very interesting. The attraction is to geniuses and rebels against societal norms – programmers, inventors, mathematicians, astrologers and astronomers. Media types are also interesting. The people you gravitate to are generally not serious people.

With Uranus in the 7th house it is difficult to make long-term social plans. You don't know if you're going to be with that person a few months down the road. This is so with friendships too.

Mars, your love planet, behaves rather erratically this year, adding more instability to the love life. He makes one of his rare retrogrades from April 17 to June 29. This will be a period for taking stock of things and achieving some kind of clarity about where things stand in your relationship. From August 9 to October 30 (a long time) Mars will be 'out of bounds'. This suggests that you're going way outside your social sphere in your search for love. Family members don't seem to approve.

You can mitigate problems in two ways. First, give the partner or current love as much space as possible, so long as this isn't destructive. Second, allow for change and experimentation (as much as possible) within your relationship. Do unconventional things as a couple (the more unconventional the better). Try to satisfy the partner's need for change within the relationship. You improve your odds that way.

Marriage is not advisable this year – especially for those of you looking for your first marriage. Those of you working towards the second marriage have more stability, but it looks like a status quo kind of year. The same applies to those of you working on their third marriages. Those of you working towards their fourth marriage have romance, but again it's the stability of it that is questionable.

One thing is for sure. Love will not be boring. There will never be a dull moment. You can't take anything for granted. Love can come instantly and leave just as instantly. If you're happy with these frequent but brief lightning flashes across the sky, the love life will be happy.

Self-improvement

Spiritual healing has been an important interest since 2012. We have probably discussed this in previous years, but it is still worthy of discussing again. Though it can seem like a lot of 'mumbo jumbo' there is a deep science behind it. The first thing to understand is that the body is not a 'thing' – it is not a static kind of object. It is, like the universe itself, a dynamic energy system, constantly changing. This is why astrology works. The body obeys the laws of energy. It responds to changes in energy. When the planets change the cosmic energy field, bodies respond – either positively or negatively – depending on the nature of the energy. In spiritual healing we tap into another kind of energy – the energy of spirit – the Divine. Since this energy is always perfect (so long as we don't interfere with it), it will, if allowed to act, create perfection in the physical body. Not always instantaneously, but over time. When this energy is called in – through prayer, meditation or invocation – it immediately starts a healing process on the energetic levels. Eventually this will filter down into the seemingly 'solid' physical body. Change the energy and you change the body on the subtle levels.

The second thing to understand is that healing is an 'internal activity'. It is the inflow of Divine energy into the aura and eventually into the body. If healing doesn't happen on the internal level, it won't happen on the external level either. However, if internal healing happens – and this is the focus of the spiritual healer – the external healing will happen quite naturally. Often (depending on a person's belief system) the healing will happen through seemingly external methods such as medication or supplements or the intervention of a doctor, surgeon or health professional. But these things are all 'side effects' of the internal healing that has already happened. It is just the way that spirit is working things out.

However, the Divine energy will often produce healing without any kind of human intervention or without any kind of external substance. It is not dependent on these things. It will take the easiest route to the healing.

The final thing to understand is that just because you may not see an immediate result, it doesn't mean that the power isn't acting. It is. On the subtle levels the action is instantaneous, but it can take time to filter down to the more solid material level. Keep up your procedure even if you don't feel anything. You will eventually.

The Divine energy is not just working on outer symptoms but on the root causes of the symptoms – and if these are deep-rooted things it can take time.

As you go deeper into spiritual healing you'll discover an important fact. You may think that you (or someone else) has a health problem or a financial problem. But the truth is that, underneath it all, there is a theological problem, a spiritual problem. When this is put right, the other problems clear up too.

Month-by-month Forecasts

January

Best Days Overall: 1, 2, 3, 11, 12, 19, 20, 29, 30
Most Stressful Days Overall: 9, 10, 15, 16, 21, 22, 23
Best Days for Love: 2, 3, 4, 6, 7, 8, 13, 15, 16, 21, 22, 26
Best Days for Money: 4, 5, 9, 10, 17, 18, 26, 27, 31
Best Days for Career: 9, 10, 17, 18, 21, 22, 23, 29, 30

As the year begins and the universal solar cycle waxes (grows), you're in an especially good period for starting new projects, businesses or launching new products. Your personal solar cycle is also waxing. The planetary momentum is forward. Until the 5th *all* the planets are moving forward, and from the 5th to the 25th 80 per cent of them are still forward. So there is a lot of cosmic support for your efforts. If you can schedule things from the 10th to the 24th – as the Moon waxes – you'll have even more support.

The planetary power is now moving away from you and towards others. By the 24th the shift to the Western, social sector is established. Thus your period of personal independence is over with for a while. Now personal changes are harder to make. Adapt yourself to situations as best you can. You're naturally a social person – naturally a seeker of consensus – so this situation is easier for you than for most people. You kind of enjoy it.

The lower half of the Horoscope is dominant this month. Most of the planets – at least 70 per cent of them – are below the horizon in January. Your 10th house of career is basically empty (only the Moon moves through there between the 21st and 23rd) while your 4th house of home and family is chock-full of planets. This gives a very clear message: focus on the home and family and get this in order. A stable home and domestic life – a sense of emotional wellness – is the best thing you can do for your career. You might not see the results right away, but down the road you'll see it. If the emotional life is in harmony everything else will fall into place.

The month ahead seems prosperous. Pluto, your financial planet, gets much positive stimulation, especially on the 5th and 6th. On the

4th, your love planet, Mars, moves into your money house. Both of these transits show earnings from social contacts, friends and partners. The spouse, partner or current love seems especially helpful financially. But often under this transit opportunities for business partnerships or joint ventures happen.

Jupiter, the ruler of your 3rd house of communication, spends the month on the Moon's North Node. You might be overdoing the travelling this month. It's a good idea to drive more carefully.

Health needs watching until the 20th. The most important thing is to get enough rest. Enhance the health in the ways mentioned in the yearly report.

February

Best Days Overall: 7, 8, 15, 16, 17, 25, 26
Most Stressful Days Overall: 5, 6, 11, 12, 18, 19
Best Days for Love: 1, 5, 6, 9, 10, 11, 12, 13, 14, 18, 19, 25, 28, 29
Best Days for Money: 1, 5, 6, 13, 14, 22, 23, 24, 27, 28, 29
Best Days for Career: 7, 8, 17, 18, 19, 27, 28

This is still a great month to start new projects or launch new ventures: 90 per cent of the planets are moving forward and both the personal and universal solar cycles are waxing. The Moon will wax from the 8th to the 22nd and this is a particularly good time.

Mars, your love planet, has been in your money house since January 4 and is there for the rest of the month ahead. Normally you're very much the romantic type, but these days you're more practical. Wealth is a turn-on in love. Material gifts turn you on. This is how you show love, this is how you feel loved. You seem to be meeting wealthier kinds of people these days. For singles romantic opportunities happen as you pursue your normal financial goals and with people involved in your finances. You like to socialize with people you do business with and like to do business with friends. Much of your socializing this month seems business related. Enjoy the love life for what it is, but marriage, as we mentioned, is not advisable this year.

The month ahead is basically happy. Your 5th house became strong on January 20 and is still strong until the 19th. You're in the midst of a yearly personal pleasure peak. This is a time to enjoy life and indulge in leisure and creative kinds of activities. Libras are very creative. Being in the creative flow is one of the great pleasures in life. One feels drunk even without having had anything to drink – you're on a natural high.

Health is much improved over last month. You have plenty of energy to achieve your goals. You always respond well to spiritual healing, but especially on the 28th and 29th. This is an excellent period for job seekers too. Job seekers have good fortune from the 19th onwards, but especially on the 28th and 29th.

Finances are good this month. Sudden, unexpected money can come between the 5th and the 8th. The 9th to the 11th also brings a nice payday.

Be more patient with family members – and especially a parent or parent figure – from the 1st to the 5th. They can be having some personal kinds of dramas.

The Sun enters spiritual Pisces on the 19th and Jupiter is also in your spiritual 12th house. The dream life is hyperactive and there are all kinds of supernatural type experiences happening.

March

Best Days Overall: 6, 7, 14, 15, 23, 24
Most Stressful Days Overall: 3, 4, 10, 11, 16, 17, 31
Best Days for Love: 6, 7, 10, 11, 16, 18, 19, 26, 27, 28, 29
Best Days for Money: 3, 4, 12, 13, 21, 22, 26, 27, 31
Best Days for Career: 8, 9, 16, 17, 28, 29

The month ahead is busy and eventful. With your solar cycle now entering its Full Moon phase. This (and next month) is perhaps the busiest time of your year. Two eclipses this month add more drama and turbulence to life as well.

In spite of all the drama, you're prospering. Jupiter is making beautiful aspects to your financial planet from the 12th to the 20th. This shows an expansion of earnings and financial good fortune. It shows an excellent financial intuition too.

The solar eclipse of the 9th (in America it is on the 8th) occurs in your 6th house of health and work. This brings job changes and changes in the conditions and rules of the workplace. These changes can be with your present company or with a new one. It shows dramas in the lives of co-workers. If you employ others it indicates employee turnover and instability in the workforce. There are likely to be major changes in your health regime too. This eclipse impacts on Jupiter and Saturn and brings upheavals in the affairs of life governed by these planets. Cars and communication equipment get tested. There can be many communication glitches. It will be a good idea to drive more carefully over this period. Your high tech equipment gets tested and might have to be replaced or repaired.

The impact on Saturn indicates family dramas – especially with a parent or parent figure. If there are flaws in your home, you find out about them now. Be more patient with family members during this period. They seem emotionally volatile. They should relax more and reduce their busy schedules during this period. Every solar eclipse tests friendships, and often brings life-changing dramas into the lives of friends. Be more patient with friends as well.

The lunar eclipse of the 23rd impacts most strongly on those of you born early in the sign of Libra – from October 22 to 26. All of you will feel it, but those most particularly. It occurs in your own sign and in your 1st house. It is always a good idea to reassess yourself – to redefine your image, personality and self-concept – but the eclipse forces the issue. Events happen – perhaps someone bad mouths or slanders you – that force you to define yourself for yourself. The alternative of doing nothing is unpalatable: you merely allow others to define you. This will be a six-month process. You will change your look and your image. Every lunar eclipse brings career changes, as the eclipsed planet, the Moon, is your career planet, and this eclipse is no exception. Such changes can happen in many ways. You can change careers, or there might be shake-ups in your company and industry that change the rules of the game. In the end these changes will be good, although they're not so pleasant while they're happening.

April

> Best Days Overall: 2, 3, 10, 11, 19, 20, 21, 29, 30
> Most Stressful Days Overall: 1, 6, 7, 12, 13, 27, 28
> Best Days for Love: 6, 7, 14, 15, 24, 25, 26
> Best Days for Money: 1, 8, 9, 17, 18, 22, 23, 27, 28
> Best Days for Career: 6, 7, 12, 13, 14, 15, 16, 27

Last month, on the 20th, the Sun entered your 7th house of love and you entered a yearly love and social peak. For a Libra this is saying a lot. Your love planet, Mars, also changed signs last month. So there are a lot of love changes happening.

The love life is complicated but basically happy. You're personally more popular than usual from the 5th onwards, and Venus is making nice aspects with Mars from that date onwards too. So love and romance are happening – but, as we mentioned many times before, it is the stability of these things that's questionable. On the 11th and 12th Venus is in exact trine relationship with Mars. This shows a happy romantic or social meeting. The Sun conjunct to Uranus on the 9th and 10th shows romance for children or children figures in your life (if they are of appropriate age). It also shows romance in the lives of your friends. Even parents or parent figures are enjoying social bliss on the 7th.

Mars will go retrograde on the 17th. This indicates that the love life slows down but it doesn't stop. This is a good period – from the 17th onwards – to reassess the love life and to see where you want to go in the future. However, it is not advisable during this period to make any important decisions, either positive or negative.

Mars spends the month in your 3rd house. Love is close to home, in the neighbourhood and perhaps with neighbours. Siblings and sibling figures in your life are playing cupid – they seem involved in the love life. Good mental compatibility, ease of communication and the sharing of ideas, are a major romantic turn-on. Foreplay is more verbal than physical. This transit shows that romantic opportunities can happen in educational-type settings – at lectures, seminars and even the library or bookstore.

Health is still delicate until the 19th. Make sure you get enough rest. Do your best to maintain high energy levels by dropping the inessential from your life. Keep your focus on the important things.

Pluto, your financial planet, begins a multi-month retrograde period on the 18th. Thus important purchases and financial decisions need considering carefully. Don't do a thing if you're not clear about it. In spite of Pluto's retrograde, there is prosperity from the 19th onwards. It is slower than usual, but it does happen.

May

Best Days Overall: 7, 8, 17, 18, 27, 28
Most Stressful Days Overall: 4, 5, 10, 11, 24, 25, 31
Best Days for Love: 4, 5, 6, 12, 14, 15, 21, 22, 26, 27, 30, 31
Best Days for Money: 6, 14, 15, 19, 20, 21, 24, 25
Best Days for Career: 6, 10, 11, 14, 15, 27

Last month on the 5th the planetary power shifted to the upper half of the Horoscope – the sector of career and outer goals. It is not dominant by any means, but it is at its maximum for the year. Emotional harmony, family and home concerns are still very important but so is the career. Your challenge – and it is difficult – is to be successful in both.

The month ahead is practical and down to earth. There is a Grand Trine in the Earth signs all month. People in general are not that interested in ideas or emotions – it's about the practical affairs of life. A little of this is good for you. You're a love and ideas person. You can get too lost in those things. It is good every now and then to be pulled back to 'earth'.

This practicality enhances your prosperity. This is an excellent financial period – especially until the 20th. The only complication is the retrograde of your financial planet. There will be delays and glitches in the financial life, but there's no need to make matters worse through careless mistakes or inattention. Do your best to be perfect in your financial dealings. If you're buying something make sure the store has a good returns policy. Read all the fine print in those service contracts or warranties. Make sure your cheques are signed and dated properly – and sent to the right address.

The love life is also in a state of retrogression. Mars is still retrograde and he moves back into the money house. Once again you're practical in love. Material wealth and material gifts are important to you. The good provider is more alluring than the brilliant intellectual. There is a lack of direction in love. Mars will have his 'solstice' from the 7th to the 14th. This also shows a 'pause' in the love and social life. This pause is happening because Mars is changing direction (in his latitude movement). Things will start getting clearer (but not totally clear) after the 14th.

Health is OK this month, but improves still further from the 20th onwards as the Sun moves into harmonious alignment with you. However, the job situation seems more troubled. You'll have to work harder to maintain harmony at the job. Job seekers have better aspects before the 19th than afterwards.

June

Best Days Overall: 4, 5, 13, 14, 23, 24
Most Stressful Days Overall: 1, 6, 7, 20, 21, 22, 27, 28
Best Days for Love: 1, 4, 5, 7, 14, 16, 17, 25, 26, 27, 28
Best Days for Money: 2, 3, 10, 11, 15, 16, 17, 20, 21, 29, 30
Best Days for Career: 4, 5, 6, 7, 13, 14, 25

You've had much stronger career periods in your life, but this month you enter a yearly career peak. This begins on the 18th as Venus crosses the Mid-heaven and enters your 10th house. The Sun follows suit on the 21st. So there is career success and advancement happening now. Whatever is achieved happens simultaneously with strong family demands, so the achievements are perhaps greater than in other years.

The eclipses of March are long over with, but these eclipse points are being re-stimulated this month. It is as if we have 'mini eclipses' happening. From the 8th to the 9th both the Sun and Venus are on eclipse points. So take it easy during that period and re-schedule stressful kinds of activities. This advice holds true for friends as well. Computers and high tech equipment are likely to be more temperamental than usual on those days. Venus moves over an eclipse point again on the 20th and 21st, as does the Sun on the 23rd and 24th. Mercury moves over an eclipse point on the 23rd and 24th. Avoid foreign travel (if possible) those days. College level students make important changes to their educational plans.

Jupiter spends the month on the Moon's North Node. You might be overdoing the travelling urge this month (your 9th house of foreign travel was very strong last month, and you could be feeling a residual effect). Travel is wonderful, but there's no need to be compulsive about it.

Finances are more challenging from the 18th onwards. Sure, you will earn and have what you need, but you'll have to work harder for it. You seem 'distant' from financial affairs and from the money people in your life from the 18th onwards. Friends are less supportive than usual. Technological glitches can hamper earnings. You're more interested in status and prestige than in mere money. You're willing to sacrifice earnings for status. In addition, your financial planet, Pluto, is still retrograde. Try not to judge your financial future from the events of the month – these are short-term issues. The good news here is that the spouse, partner or current love seems financially supportive.

Health needs more attention being paid to it from the 18th onwards as well. At least half of the planets are in stressful aspect with you. So, make sure you get enough rest. Things that we normally do without thinking when the energy level is normal might not be so easy to do at this time. Listen to the body. If you feel discomfort, pause and rest. Enhance the health in the ways mentioned in the yearly report.

July

Best Days Overall: 1, 2, 10, 11, 12, 20, 21, 29, 30
Most Stressful Days Overall: 3, 4, 18, 19, 24, 25, 31
Best Days for Love: 3, 4, 13, 14, 15, 22, 23, 24, 25, 31
Best Days for Money: 8, 9, 13, 14, 18, 19, 27, 28
Best Days for Career: 3, 4, 13, 14, 24, 31

Last month, from the 19th to the 23rd, Venus, the ruler of your Horoscope, was having one of her solstices. She paused in the heavens and changed direction (in latitude). So there was a pause in your life and a change of direction too. Around this time the planetary power shifted from the social Western sector to the independent Eastern one. You're becoming more independent (less Libra-like) day by day. Personal power is increasing. You don't need to do things by consensus. If something needs to be changed – something that concerns you – take action. Make the change. Now there is less need to adapt to situations. If conditions are uncomfortable, create new ones that are more comfortable for you.

Health still needs attention until the 22nd. The good news is that you're on the case and focusing on it. You should feel physically stronger and have more energy from the 22nd onwards. In the meantime, get as much rest as practical. Spend time in a health spa or book yourself more massages. See a spiritual healer.

You're still very much in a yearly career peak until the 22nd. You're succeeding, though you might not see the bottom-line results of your success for a while. This will happen later. You still need to work hard to achieve your financial goals this month, but you'll see improvements after the 22nd. You're still in a prosperous year and these problems are just bumps on the road. Family support and the support of the spouse, partner or current love is still strong. Your financial planet is still retrograde this month, so keep in mind our previous discussions of this.

The job situation seems unstable this month. You're performing well, but you could feel a sense of deficiency. Job seekers have better aspects before the 22nd than afterwards.

Love is still practical this month. Love opportunities happen as you pursue your normal financial goals and with people involved in your finances. Your social contacts and social skills are important for earnings. Much of your socializing seems business related. The problem in love is pretty much what it has been for some years now – you don't seem to be attracting serious people. They mostly just want to play.

Avoid unnecessary travel on the 1st, 2nd, 7th, 10th and 11th. Necessary travel is another story. Only you can decide what is or is not necessary.

August

Best Days Overall: 7, 8, 16, 17, 18, 25, 26
Most Stressful Days Overall: 1, 14, 15, 21, 22, 27, 28
Best Days for Love: 1, 2, 3, 12, 14, 15, 21, 22, 23, 24, 29, 30
Best Days for Money: 4, 5, 9, 10, 14, 15, 23, 24, 31
Best Days for Career: 1, 2, 3, 12, 13, 23, 27, 28, 31

Venus, the ruler of your Horoscope, moves unusually fast this month and will journey through three signs and houses of your Horoscope. This indicates that you cover a lot of territory, that you make rapid progress and have good confidence and self-esteem this August.

The love planet Mars leaves your money house on the 2nd and enters the 3rd house of communication and intellectual interests. This gives us many messages. Love is close to home, in the neighbourhood, and there is no need to travel far and wide in search of it. You are probably seeing people outside your normal social sphere this month – but the action is in your neighbourhood. Mars is 'out of bounds' from the 9th onwards. Once again you're attracted by intellectuals – teachers, writers, journalists, sales and marketing people. Ease of communication and mental compatibility are important turn-ons in love. Love and social opportunities happen in educational-type settings – at a lecture, a school function, the library or the bookstore. Foreigners are also catching your eye. Love is good all month but especially on the 30th and 31st. The personal appearance shines then.

The love life is good for friends and for children and children figures in your life. The 15th and 16th seem especially good.

The month ahead is prosperous and this is just the beginning. Prosperity will happen for the rest of the year ahead – and well into next year. The financial intuition is excellent. Financial opportunities come as you get involved in charities and altruistic causes. It happens when you're not thinking too much about yourself. The 16th, 17th, 26th and 28th are nice paydays. A spiritual breakthrough will change your financial outlook (as well as other outlooks in your life). Your 12th house of spirituality is strong all month, but especially after the 22nd. Much of your growth and development will be internal this month, but it will become manifest externally in due course.

Your spiritual interests are stronger than your work interests and this could create some problems at the job. You'll have to force yourself to pay more attention to work. It is very important that you have work that is in harmony with your spiritual ideals and interests. Job seekers have to work harder this month.

Health is good right now, and it will get even better next month. Take it a bit easier on the 20th and 21st, though.

September

Best Days Overall: 3, 4, 13, 14, 21, 22, 30
Most Stressful Days Overall: 10, 11, 12, 17, 18, 23, 24
Best Days for Love: 3, 4, 8, 9, 13, 14, 17, 18, 23, 27, 28
Best Days for Money: 1, 2, 5, 6, 7, 10, 11, 12, 13, 19, 20, 21, 28, 29
Best Days for Career: 1, 2, 11, 12, 20, 23, 24, 30

An eventful month ahead, Libra. There will be much turbulence, but also many good things. Jupiter enters your sign on the 10th and initiates a long-term cycle of prosperity and optimism. When the Sun enters on the 22nd you begin a yearly personal pleasure peak. So the month ahead should be happy.

Two eclipses are creating much turbulence in the world and in your environment this month. However, their effect is not too strong on you personally.

The solar eclipse of the 1st occurs in your 12th house of spirituality. This announces spiritual changes – changes in practice, attitude and teachings. Generally this comes from new revelation received. (You're still in the midst of a very spiritual period, until the 22nd.) There are dramas and shake-ups in spiritual or charitable organizations you belong to and in the lives of the leaders of these organizations. The dream life will be hyperactive and perhaps troubling, but don't give it too much weight. These dream images are most likely psychic flotsam and jetsam stirred up by the eclipse. Mars and Saturn are impacted here. Thus love is being tested. Good relationships survive, but mediocre ones are in trouble. There are dramas in the lives of family members and especially a parent or parent figure. Sometimes repairs are needed in the home. Friendships, not just romantic relationships, are also getting tested. This is often through dramas in the lives of friends.

The lunar eclipse of the 16th occurs in your 6th house and shows job changes and changes in the work environment and conditions of work. This can be with your present situation or with a new one. There are life-changing dramas in the lives of co-workers. If you employ others there is likely to be more employee turnover than normal. Every lunar eclipse brings career changes. Sometimes this is a literal change – you change your actual career. But most of the time such an eclipse indicates changes in the 'rules of the game' – policy changes, changes in the leadership of your company, changes in your industry and so forth. There are more dramas in the lives of parents or parent figures. Sometimes this kind of eclipse produces a health scare and changes in the health regime. These changes have probably been needed for a long time now, but the eclipse forces the issue.

Health is basically good this month, so most likely the eclipse will produce only a scare.

October

Best Days Overall: 1, 2, 10, 11, 19, 27, 28, 29
Most Stressful Days Overall: 8, 9, 15, 21, 22
Best Days For Love: 3, 4, 8, 9, 12, 13, 14, 15, 17, 23, 24, 25, 26
Best Days For Money: 1, 3, 4, 8, 9, 10, 17, 18, 19, 25, 26, 27, 28, 30, 31
Best Days For Career: 1, 2, 10, 11, 20, 21, 22, 30

Last month, on the 22nd, the planetary power reached its maximum Eastern position. Thus you're in the period of your maximum personal power right now, which continues until the 23rd. Make the changes that need to be made. Create conditions as you desire them to be. You have the power now. Take responsibility for your own happiness. Have things your way. Knowing you, Libra, you're unlikely to ride roughshod over others; you'll do these things with grace and charm.

Those of you involved in the intellectual arena – writers or teachers – are having a great month. There is success in all these endeavours. There is success for sales, marketing, advertising and PR people too.

This is a great month – and it will be a great year ahead – for taking courses in subjects that interest you. The mind is sharp and absorbs knowledge well. If you're already an expert in a certain field this is a great time to share that knowledge with others.

A new car or new communication equipment is coming to you (it could have happened last month too.)

Libras of childbearing age are extremely fertile now.

The month ahead is also prosperous. Not only is Jupiter in your sign, but on the 23rd the Sun enters the money house. You begin a yearly financial peak. You're living at a higher standard and the wherewithal to support this is forthcoming.

You look great – though you need to watch the weight. You have energy, charisma and star quality. But love is complicated. Most likely you're too independent and this doesn't sit well with the current relationship. This problem will pass by the 23rd. The love planet, Mars, spends the month in the sign of Capricorn. Thus you're more practical and serious about love. The problem is that the people you attract are not as serious as you. Now you're attracted by emotional intimacy, to those you can share your feelings with. Mars spends the month 'out of bounds' and you're probably going outside your normal social sphere in search for love. But this doesn't seem necessary. Love is still close to home. Family and family connections are important. There is more socializing at home and with the family this month – and this can lead to romantic meetings. With Mars sitting in Capricorn it is more difficult for you to express feelings of love and warmth. You can be perceived as cold or unfeeling these days – even though you're not like that. Make it a point to project love and warmth to others.

November

Best Days Overall: 6, 7, 8, 15, 16, 24, 25
Most Stressful Days Overall: 4, 5, 11, 12, 17, 18
Best Days for Love: 2, 3, 4, 5, 11, 12, 13, 15, 21, 22, 24, 25
Best Days for Money: 1, 4, 5, 6, 7, 13, 14, 15, 16, 21, 22, 23, 24, 25, 26, 27, 28
Best Days for Career: 9, 10, 17, 18, 29

The planetary power is now mostly below the horizon. Your 10th house of career is basically empty (only the Moon moves through there on the 17th and 18th), while your 4th house of home and family is very strong. A very clear message is being sent here: let go of career issues for a while and focus on the home, family and your emotional well-ness. The lower half of the Horoscope is not just stronger than the upper half – it is completely dominant. At least 80 per cent (and it is sometimes 90 per cent) of the planets are below the horizon this month. You're in the night time of your year, soon to approach the midnight hour. Achieve your goals through the powers of night, rather than the ways of the day. Get into the 'mood, feeling' of what you want – whether it be things or conditions – and allow the mood to work out as it will. Before things happen on the external level they must happen first internally.

Prosperity is still strong this month. You're still at a yearly financial peak until the 22nd. The Moon spends an unusual amount of time in the money house this month – four days instead of the usual two days. This shows the financial support of elders, bosses, parents and parent figures. You also have the favour of friends. It's beneficial to spend on high tech equipment and gadgets to keep up to date – this is important financially. Venus conjuncts your financial planet Pluto on the 24th and 25th and brings a nice payday or financial opportunity. You're in harmony with the 'money people' in your life.

Your 3rd house of communication and intellectual interests is strong all month. The ruler of the 3rd house is in your own sign and the ruler of your Horoscope, Venus, is in the 3rd house until the 12th. This shows success in intellectual pursuits – success for students, writers and teachers. Sales and marketing people also have a good month. There are good – cooperative – relations with siblings, sibling figures and neighbours this month.

Neptune, your health and work planet, spends the month camped out on an eclipse point – re-stimulating the old eclipse. Thus there are dramas at the workplace and in the lives of co-workers. The job situation seems unstable. If you employ others, there is instability in the work-force. Health is good, but there can be changes in the health regime.

The winter solstice happens next month, but Venus has one of her solstices this month – from the 13th to the 16th. She pauses in the heavens. She doesn't budge in her latitude. This shows a pause and change of direction for you. It is as if life stops for a few days and then it resumes in a different direction.

December

>   Best Days Overall: 4, 5, 12, 13, 21, 22, 31
>   Most Stressful Days Overall: 1, 2, 3, 8, 9, 14, 15, 29, 30
>   Best Days for Love: 2, 3, 4, 5, 8, 9, 12, 13, 21, 22, 24
>   Best Days for Money: 1, 2, 4, 5, 10, 11, 12, 13, 19, 20, 21, 22, 24, 25, 29, 30, 31
>   Best Days for Career: 8, 9, 14, 15, 17, 18, 29

The lower half of the chart is overwhelmingly dominant this month; 80 per cent (sometimes 90 per cent) of the planets are below the horizon – a huge percentage. Your 4th house of home and family is even more powerful than last month, while your 10th house of career is basically empty (except on the 14th and 15th when the Moon passes through). So this is not a career period. The month ahead is about home, family and emotional wellness.

This is a month for psychological breakthroughs. Those of you involved in formal therapies will make good progress. Even if you're not in formal therapy, you'll have psychological insight and progress now. Nature will do the job. The nostalgia you feel is part of nature's therapy. You find yourself thinking of the past, of old experiences – the good and the bad. Somehow or other, the memories come up. Someone questions you about a past event, or wants to know your story. Dreams of past experiences happen. Nature forces you to confront these things from your present perspective and, through this, healing happens.

The message of the chart this month is 'get the emotional life right and everything else falls into place'. Right feeling is more important than 'right doing' – right feeling will lead to right actions.

When the 4th house is strong we are emotionally more powerful. This is a double-edged sword. If the emotions are in harmony, desires manifest quickly. If the emotions become negative it's like dropping a nuclear bomb on your dreams. This is especially important in finance these days. Pluto is in your 4th house. In the right mood, money comes quickly and easily. In a bad mood, you feel poor.

Finances do tend to be good right now, however – especially after the 21st. Pluto is moving forward and receiving helpful aspects.

Health needs attention paying to it from the 21st onwards. As always, the important thing is to get enough rest. High energy will repel most problems. On the 20th Mars moves into your 6th house. Thus it is good to enhance the health through physical exercise and scalp and face massage. It's also important to stay in harmony with the current love. Love problems can impact on the health. Love seems basically happy and this is a good health signal. Until the 20th you're not too serious about love; you just want fun and this is what you're attracting. After the 20th you gravitate to spiritual types and to health professionals. There is more socializing at the workplace.

Scorpio

m,

THE SCORPION

Birthdays from
23rd October to
22nd November

Personality Profile

SCORPIO AT A GLANCE

Element – Water

Ruling Planet – Pluto
   Co-ruling Planet – Mars
   Career Planet – Sun
   Love Planet – Venus
   Money Planet – Jupiter
   Planet of Health and Work – Mars
   Planet of Home and Family Life – Uranus

Colour – red-violet

Colour that promotes love, romance and social harmony – green

Colour that promotes earning power – blue

Gems – bloodstone, malachite, topaz

Metals – iron, radium, steel

Scents – cherry blossom, coconut, sandalwood, watermelon

Quality – fixed (= stability)

Quality most needed for balance – a wider view of things

Strongest virtues – loyalty, concentration, determination, courage, depth

Deepest needs – to penetrate and transform

Characteristics to avoid – jealousy, vindictiveness, fanaticism

Signs of greatest overall compatibility – Cancer, Pisces

Signs of greatest overall incompatibility – Taurus, Leo, Aquarius

Sign most helpful to career – Leo

Sign most helpful for emotional support – Aquarius

Sign most helpful financially – Sagittarius

Sign best for marriage and/or partnerships – Taurus

Sign most helpful for creative projects – Pisces

Best Sign to have fun with – Pisces

Signs most helpful in spiritual matters – Cancer, Libra

Best day of the week – Tuesday

Understanding a Scorpio

One symbol of the sign of Scorpio is the phoenix. If you meditate upon the legend of the phoenix you will begin to understand the Scorpio character – his or her powers and abilities, interests and deepest urges.

The phoenix of mythology was a bird that could recreate and reproduce itself. It did so in a most intriguing way: it would seek a fire – usually in a religious temple – fly into it, consume itself in the flames and then emerge a new bird. If this is not the ultimate, most profound transformation, then what is?

Transformation is what Scorpios are all about – in their minds, bodies, affairs and relationships (Scorpios are also society's transformers). To change something in a natural, not an artificial way, involves a transformation from within. This type of change is radical change as opposed to a mere cosmetic make-over. Some people think that change means altering just their appearance, but this is not the kind of thing that interests a Scorpio. Scorpios seek deep, fundamental change. Since real change always proceeds from within, a Scorpio is very interested in – and usually accustomed to – the inner, intimate and philosophical side of life.

Scorpios are people of depth and intellect. If you want to interest them you must present them with more than just a superficial image. You and your interests, projects or business deals must have real substance to them in order to stimulate a Scorpio. If they haven't, he or she will find you out – and that will be the end of the story.

If we observe life – the processes of growth and decay – we see the transformational powers of Scorpio at work all the time. The caterpillar changes itself into a butterfly; the infant grows into a child and then an adult. To Scorpios this definite and perpetual transformation is not something to be feared. They see it as a normal part of life. This acceptance of transformation gives Scorpios the key to understanding the true meaning of life.

Scorpios' understanding of life (including life's weaknesses) makes them powerful warriors – in all senses of the word. Add to this their depth, patience and endurance and you have a powerful personality. Scorpios have good, long memories and can at times be quite vindictive – they can wait years to get their revenge. As a friend, though, there is no one more loyal and true than a Scorpio. Few are willing to make the sacrifices that a Scorpio will make for a true friend.

The results of a transformation are quite obvious, although the process of transformation is invisible and secret. This is why Scorpios are considered secretive in nature. A seed will not grow properly if you keep digging it up and exposing it to the light of day. It must stay buried – invisible – until it starts to grow. In the same manner, Scorpios fear revealing too much about themselves or their hopes to other people. However, they will be more than happy to let you see the finished product – but only when it is completely unwrapped. On the other hand, Scorpios like knowing everyone else's secrets as much as they dislike anyone knowing theirs.

Finance

Love, birth, life as well as death are Nature's most potent transformations; Scorpios are interested in all of these. In our society, money is a transforming power, too, and a Scorpio is interested in money for that reason. To a Scorpio money is power, money causes change, money controls. It is the power of money that fascinates them. But Scorpios can be too materialistic if they are not careful. They can be overly awed by the power of money, to a point where they think that money rules the world.

Even the term 'plutocrat' comes from Pluto, the ruler of the sign of Scorpio. Scorpios will – in one way or another – achieve the financial status they strive for. When they do so they are careful in the way they handle their wealth. Part of this financial carefulness is really a kind of honesty, for Scorpios are usually involved with other people's money – as accountants, lawyers, stockbrokers or corporate managers – and when you handle other people's money you have to be more cautious than when you handle your own.

In order to fulfil their financial goals, Scorpios have important lessons to learn. They need to develop qualities that do not come naturally to them, such as breadth of vision, optimism, faith, trust and, above all, generosity. They need to see the wealth in Nature and in life, as well as in its more obvious forms of money and power. When they develop generosity their financial potential reaches great heights, for Jupiter, the Lord of Opulence and Good Fortune, is Scorpio's money planet.

Career and Public Image

Scorpio's greatest aspiration in life is to be considered by society as a source of light and life. They want to be leaders, to be stars. But they follow a very different road from Leos, the other stars of the zodiac. A Scorpio arrives at the goal secretly, without ostentation; a Leo pursues it openly. Scorpios seek the glamour and fun of the rich and famous in a restrained, discreet way.

Scorpios are by nature introverted and tend to avoid the limelight. But if they want to attain their highest career goals they need to open up a bit and to express themselves more. They need to stop hiding their light under a bushel and let it shine. Above all, they need to let go of any vindictiveness and small-mindedness. All their gifts and insights were given to them for one important reason – to serve life and to increase the joy of living for others.

Love and Relationships

Scorpio is another zodiac sign that likes committed, clearly defined, structured relationships. They are cautious about marriage, but when they do commit to a relationship they tend to be faithful – and heaven help the mate caught or even suspected of infidelity! The jealousy of the Scorpio is legendary. They can be so intense in their jealousy that even the thought or intention of infidelity will be detected and is likely to cause as much of a storm as if the deed had actually been done.

Scorpios tend to settle down with those who are wealthier than they are. They usually have enough intensity for two, so in their partners they seek someone pleasant, hard-working, amiable, stable and easy-going. They want someone they can lean on, someone loyal behind them as they fight the battles of life. To a Scorpio a partner, be it a lover or a friend, is a real partner – not an adversary. Most of all a Scorpio is looking for an ally, not a competitor.

If you are in love with a Scorpio you will need a lot of patience. It takes a long time to get to know Scorpios, because they do not reveal themselves readily. But if you persist and your motives are honourable, you will gradually be allowed into a Scorpio's inner chambers of the mind and heart.

Home and Domestic Life

Uranus is ruler of Scorpio's 4th solar house of home and family, and is the planet of science, technology, changes and democracy. This tells us a lot about a Scorpio's conduct in the home and what he or she needs in order to have a happy, harmonious home life.

Scorpios can sometimes bring their passion, intensity and wilfulness into the home and family, which is not always the place for these qualities. These traits are good for the warrior and the transformer, but not so good for the nurturer and family member. Because of this (and also because of their need for change and transformation) the Scorpio may be prone to sudden changes of residence. If not carefully constrained, the sometimes inflexible Scorpio can produce turmoil and sudden upheavals within the family.

Scorpios need to develop some of the virtues of Aquarius in order to cope better with domestic matters. There is a need to build a team spirit at home, to treat family activities as truly group activities – family members should all have a say in what does and does not get done. For at times a Scorpio can be most dictatorial. When a Scorpio gets dictatorial it is much worse than if a Leo or Capricorn (the two other power signs in the zodiac) does. For the dictatorship of a Scorpio is applied with more zeal, passion, intensity and concentration than is true of either a Leo or Capricorn. Obviously this can be unbearable to family members – especially if they are sensitive types.

In order for a Scorpio to get the full benefit of the emotional support that a family can give, he or she needs to let go of conservatism and be a bit more experimental, to explore new techniques in childrearing, be more democratic with family members and to try to manage things by consensus rather than by autocratic edict.

Horoscope for 2016

Major Trends

Many of the trends that we have written of in past years are still in effect. Long-term planets are involved, and long-term planets indicate long-term projects.

Saturn has been in your money house since December 2014. Though prosperity is happening, you could feel tight. Often this is a result of an extra financial responsibility that you can't avoid. All that's needed is a reorganization and this is what's happening. There's more on this later.

Pluto, the ruler of your Horoscope, has been in your 3rd house of communication for many years now, and will remain there for many more years to come. This is a wonderful position for students, writers, teachers, sales and marketing people. There is a strong focus on the mind and communication.

Neptune has been in your 5th house of fun and creativity for many years. This shows an affinity for spiritual-type entertainment. You might prefer a Full Moon ceremony or the Kirtan to a night out on the town. It also shows inspired creativity. Those of you involved in the creative or performing arts are unusually inspired these days.

Uranus has been in your 6th house for many years. Thus there have been many, many job changes. Not only literal job changes, but changes in the conditions of work. This transit also shows dramatic changes in the health regime.

Your financial planet Jupiter spends most of the year in Virgo and in wonderful aspect to the ruler of your chart, Pluto. This shows prosperity. Jupiter will leave Virgo on September 10 and enter in Libra, which indicates important financial changes – changes in thinking and strategy. Again, there's more on this later.

Your most important interests this year are: finance; communication and intellectual interests; children, fun and creativity; health and work; friends, groups and group activities (until September 9); and spirituality (from September 10 onwards).

Your paths of greatest fulfilment this year are: friends, groups and group activities; and spirituality (from September 10 onwards).

Health

(Please note that this is an astrological perspective on health and not a medical one. In days of yore there was no difference, these perspectives were identical. But now there could be quite a difference. For a medical perspective, please consult your doctor or health practitioner.)

Saturn left your sign at the end of December 2014, which brought a great improvement in your overall health and energy. This year there are no long-term planets in stressful aspect to you; they are either making nice aspects or leaving you alone. Health should be good therefore. If there have been any pre-existing conditions, you should see improvement in them too.

There will be periods in the year when health and energy are less easy than usual, but these come from the short-term planetary transits and are not trends for the year ahead. When they pass, normal good health and energy return.

Health is good, yet your 6th house of health is very strong this year. There are two ways to read this. One, perhaps you are over-zealous about your health and are magnifying little things into big things. The other way to read this is that you're involved in healthy lifestyles and health regimes, even though you basically feel OK. You want to make sure that you keep feeling OK. Often both readings are true.

Good though your health is, you can make it even better. Give special attention to the following areas – the vulnerable areas in your chart (the reflexology points are shown in the following chart):

- The colon, bladder and sexual organs. These are always important for you, Scorpio. It's a good idea to have regular colonics. Many natural healers affirm that all disease – without exception – begins in the colon. This is debatable, but in your case it could be true. Safe sex and sexual moderation are also always important for you.
- The head, face and scalp. Head and face massage tends always to be powerful for you, craniosacral therapy likewise.
- The adrenals. These are also always important for Scorpio. The important thing is to avoid anger and fear, the two emotions that stress the adrenals.

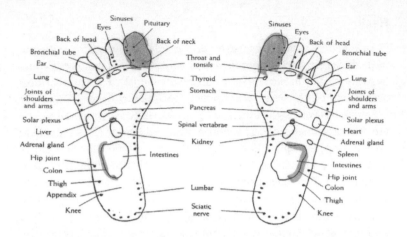

Important foot reflexology points for the year ahead

Try to massage all of the foot on a regular basis – the top of the foot as well as the bottom – but pay extra attention to the points highlighted on the chart. When you massage, be aware of 'sore spots' as these need special attention. It's also a good idea to massage the ankles and below them.

- The musculature. It is always important for Scorpio to maintain good muscle tone. A weak or flabby muscle can knock the spine or skeleton out of alignment, and misaligned vertebrae can cause all kinds of other problems. Vigorous physical exercise (in accordance with your age and stage in life) is very beneficial.
- The ankles and calves. These have only become important in recent years – ever since Uranus entered your 6th house. Both should be regularly massaged. Give the ankles more support when exercising.

Uranus is your family planet. His position in your 6th house of health shows the importance of keeping harmony in the family. Health problems, if they happen (God forbid) could stem from family disharmony, and so the first step to recover good health is to restore harmony as quickly as possible.

It is also important to keep moods positive and constructive. This is easier than it has been in recent years, but is still a challenge. Good health for you means good emotional health. Meditation will be a big help here.

The good thing about Uranus in your 6th house is that you're throwing out all the rule books. You're learning how your body functions through trial, error and experimentation. Each one of us is wired up differently. Things that work for one person will not necessarily work for another. So, it is every person's responsibility to learn what works for them. This is happening for you.

Home and Family

This has been a very turbulent area for some years now. To say it was unstable is an understatement. Things are getting easier now, but there is still turbulence.

The main problem is that you seem in disagreement – out of harmony – with the family. There have been conflicts with a parent or parent figure. There is still disagreement, but less so. It's a matter of intensity.

Moves, break-ups and shake-ups in the family unit have been happening. Family members seem hot under the collar – ready to erupt at any little thing. If you can bridge your differences things will go much easier. There is a need for more patience with them.

Keeping the harmony with the family is a challenge, but if you can do it, you'll see improvement in your health and energy.

Your family planet Uranus in your 6th house shows that you are working to improve the health of the physical home. This has been a long-term trend. Make sure air conditioning ducts are clean. Sometimes paint or furniture contain toxic materials – these should be removed. You've been installing health gadgets and health equipment in the home and this trend continues in the year ahead.

Your 6th house is also your house of work. Thus you're working more from home, installing a home office or expanding the existing one. The home is as much a place of work as a home.

Moves could happen for you, but they aren't advisable this year.

One of the parents or parent figures in your life could move this year. (It could have happened last year too.) There is more harmony with this parent figure than with the other one we discussed earlier. This one is prospering and seems generous with you.

Siblings and sibling figures could have had multiple moves in recent years. There is much restlessness and this trend continues in the year ahead. Children and children figures have a stable kind of year. Grandchildren (if you have them) could move from September 10 onwards.

Major repairs, renovations or construction in the home could happen any time, but if you have choice in the matter, November 9 to December 19 is the best period for this. August 26 to September 27 is a good second choice.

If you're beautifying the home – repainting, redecorating, or buying objects of beauty – January 20 to March 12 is a good time.

Finance and Career

When Jupiter, your financial planet, moved into Virgo in August of last year, he started to make wonderful aspects to Pluto, the ruler of your chart. This shows prosperity. The trend continues strongly until September 9 and shows not only prosperity, but a kind of happy prosperity. You're enjoying how you earn. You seem comfortable with it.

Jupiter in Virgo is in your 11th house. Thus earnings come from online activities and perhaps an online business. Your innovations and, in some cases, inventions, are profitable. You spend on technology but earn from it as well. It is good to stay up to date with the latest developments.

The financial planet in the 11th house also shows rich friends, and they seem supportive of you. They can support you directly or indirectly through providing opportunity. The 11th house is the house of 'fondest hopes and wishes'. The message is that you're attaining many of your financial 'fondest hopes and wishes' this year.

The financial planet in Virgo indicates a sound financial judgement. Scorpio has this naturally, but now even more so. You get value for your money. You have no problem analysing the health of any investment or purchase. You're in synch with all the details of these things.

From an investment perspective, you have a special feeling for the technology sector of the market. You are always good with bonds, but technology sector bonds seem most favourable.

After September 10 finances get more complicated, and you'll have to work harder to attain your goals. Jupiter moves into your spiritual 12th house. From here on in it is the financial intuition that's important. But following the intuition doesn't seem that simple. For a start, it causes more disagreements with the family and a parent or parent figure (adding to the already existing family disharmony). Also sometimes intuition will lead you in a way that is outside your comfort zone. Intuition is always right (if it is a true intuition) but not necessarily comfortable. You have to be willing to follow it and let the chips fall where they may. And that's easier said than done!

The financial planet in the 12th house shows that you'll be in a period for exploring the spiritual dimensions of wealth. This is a time for 'miracle money' rather than natural money. Your challenge is to access the supernatural sources of supply rather than the natural ones. Many of you already have much knowledge of this, but if not, read up as much as you can about it. The works of Ernest Holmes and Emmet Fox are good starting points.

It will be very good to be involved in charities and altruistic causes from September 10 onwards. This will help the bottom line. You may be asked to contribute time or money, but these donations will bring interesting financial opportunities – and important contacts.

Saturn (as we mentioned) is in your money house all year. There's a need to reorganize and restructure the financial life. You have all the resources you need, you just have to rearrange things in a different way.

The last two years were banner career years. There was much elevation and recognition for your professional achievements. Many of you received awards and honours. There should have been promotions and pay rises too. This year, though, career is less important. It is more or less stable. I read this as good. You're basically content with the career as it is and have no need to make major changes, or give it undue attention.

Love and Social Life

The 7th house of love and social activities is not prominent this year and is not a house of power. Aside from the movement of short-term planets through it, it is basically empty. There is nothing in the cosmos against romance, but nothing especially supportive of it either. This tends to the status quo. Married couples will most likely stay married. Singles will most likely stay single. You seem content with things as they are.

Jupiter's move into Libra on September 10 will expand the social life, but this social activity seems business related and not really of the romantic kind. The same is true with friendships. Jupiter in your 11th house until that date brings new friends into the picture, but again it seems business related.

Venus, your love planet, moves unusually quickly this year. Generally she moves through twelve signs and houses in a given year, but this year she will move through fifteen. She will visit three signs more than once. This indicates social confidence. It shows someone who covers a lot of social territory. For singles it suggests revisiting old loves or relationships.

Venus will spend a long time (two months) 'out of bounds' this year – from October 17 to December 17. This shows that you're going way out of your normal social sphere in search of love. It also shows a relationship that could be 'out of bounds' for you.

Because Venus is moving so fast there are many short-term trends in love, depending on where she is and the kind of aspects she receives. These are best discussed in the monthly reports.

Siblings and sibling figures in your life are having a stable love year. Likewise parents or parent figures. Children or children figures have romance (if they are of appropriate age). Marriage could easily happen there. Even younger children will be making new friends and socializing more.

On a general level your most active social period will be from April 19 to May 24.

Self-improvement

Saturn in the money house creates a feeling of constriction – a feeling of limitation – in finance. But this is not punishment, it's educational. His goal is to plug the holes in the financial consciousness and make you financially healthier. Do you have redundant bank accounts or brokerage accounts? Now is the time to streamline them. Are you paying too much for your cable TV or mobile phone? Are you paying for services that you don't use? This is a good year to correct this. If a person has been irresponsible in finance – over-spending, running up debts for frivolous things – a Saturn transit through this house can be quite a trauma. The debts come due and need to be repaid. The price for bad financial habits has to be paid. But if a person has been responsible in their financial dealings, Saturn will actually enrich them – and in a healthy kind of way. Saturn in the money house for these people means 'enduring wealth'.

Saturn in the money house favours practical steps to enhance wealth. It favours savings and investment plans – and it takes some discipline to stick with these things. It favours building wealth over the long term, step by step.

The financial planet in your 12th house from September 10 onwards doesn't deny Saturn's actions but adds a spiritual dimension to them. Much of this has been discussed. This is a time when many of you will learn that wealth is an 'interior activity'. Things have to happen 'through you' before they can happen 'to you'. This is the spiritual perspective on wealth. If there are financial problems, we don't try to fix them from outside, but work to get our mind aligned with the spiritual principle of 'affluence'. This is counter-intuitive to worldly thought and takes some meditation to grasp. It is OK (and even good) to have a budget and an investment plan. It is good to have long-term financial goals. But the real work should be on the spiritual level.

Spirit is constantly pouring out its affluence upon us. From its perspective, there is no limit whatsoever. The only limitations are individual – how much a person can receive and accept. The person who can receive more (and we're talking on the interior level) will have more.

I have discussed this issue with very wealthy people. Though they don't use spiritual terminology, they do say that wealth is a state of mind; an astrologer would say it is 'a state of consciousness'. So if there are financial worries or problems, get into the 'wealth state of mind' as quickly as possible. The problems will start to dissolve of their own weight. Getting the hang of this – and it will take some work and meditation – is well worth the effort.

Month-by-month Forecasts

January

Best Days Overall: 4, 5, 13, 14, 21, 22, 23, 31
Most Stressful Days Overall: 11, 12, 17, 18, 24, 25
Best Days for Love: 6, 7, 8, 15, 16, 17, 18, 26
Best Days for Money: 6, 7, 9, 10, 17, 18, 26, 27
Best Days for Career: 9, 10, 17, 18, 24, 25, 29, 30

You begin your year with the lower half of the Horoscope dominant. After the 4th, at least 80 per cent of the planets (and sometimes more) are below the horizon. You're in the midnight of your year (especially after the 20th) and the activities of night are more important than the activities of the day. Night is for building up the forces for the next day. Outwardly we seem inactive, but inwardly there is much dynamic activity happening. Night sets the stage for the next day. Night sets the stage for future career success. This is the time for handling the issues that make future career success possible – building a harmonious home and family life and getting into emotional harmony. If these are in order everything else will fall into place.

Mars, your planet of health and work, moves into your sign on the 4th and spends the rest of the month there. This gives many messages. You have energy and independence. You get things done quickly. You excel in athletics and exercise regimes (each according to their level). Job seekers have job opportunities come to them – they don't have to do much to hunt them out, they just appear. The same is true for those of you who employ others. Employees seek you out rather than vice versa. But there is a downside here. You can be impatient, in a rush, wanting things to happen 'yesterday'. Rush can lead to accidents and injury if you're not careful. You need to watch your temper as you can overreact to the smallest things. You could be attracting belligerent people into your life. You're more prone to violent solutions to problems. The challenge for you is to use this Mars energy constructively.

Saturn has been in your money house for over a year now, so the finances are being reorganized. Generally this happens because of feelings of 'lack'. You're bumping up against your financial limitations.

This is the situation for the rest of the year. However, the current month is a prosperous one. You might still have that feeling of 'lack' or 'deficiency' but the reality is different. Your financial planet is receiving nice aspects – the 13th to the 16th looks especially good. Jupiter, however, is retrograde at the moment so earnings might come more slowly and with delays – but they will come. This is a time to strive for financial clarity. When this happens, you will be able to move forward when Jupiter starts moving forward in May. Best to avoid major financial commitments – large purchases or investments – until May. But if you can't wait, make sure you do your homework.

The Sun had his solstice last month, Venus, your love planet, will have one of her solstices from the 25th to the 30th. She pauses in the heavens. She starts to change direction. A social pause and change of direction is happening for you too.

February

Best Days Overall: 1, 9, 10, 18, 19, 27, 28, 29
Most Stressful Days Overall: 7, 8, 13, 14, 20, 21
Best Days for Love: 5, 6, 13, 14, 25
Best Days for Money: 2, 3, 4, 5, 6, 13, 14, 22, 23, 24
Best Days for Career: 7, 8, 17, 20, 21, 27, 28

The universal solar cycle started to wax (grow) on December 21. Your personal solar cycle started to wax on your last birthday. The planetary power is in forward motion this month – almost all of the planets are moving forward. So, this is an excellent month for starting a new business, a new project or for launching a new product. There is much cosmic support – and we need all the help we can get! If you can schedule this from the 8th to the 22nd, as the Moon is also waxing, you have the best period of the month – and the year – for this. (Last month was also very good, but the current month is even better.)

Mars is still in your sign all this month and you should review our discussion of this last month. However, this month things seem more complicated. This month the planetary power shifts from the independent East to the social West. It is time to focus more on others and their needs, time to tone down self-will, time to placate others and achieve goals by consensus. But Mars in your own sign produces oppo-site urges. Mars is always for direct action, not consensus. So it is a bit of a struggle.

Your 4th house is still very strong until the 19th. Home and family is the real career, the real mission now. You have to be there for the family. You have to find your emotional comfort zone and function from there. You're still building the infrastructure for future career success.

This is a great month for psychological therapies. A great month for resolving old traumas – closing the book on them. Past mistakes need to be confessed and corrected. The pain needs to be released. The past has no real power over us when understanding comes. We need not be victims of it.

Love looks happy this month. Love is close to home, in the neigh-bourhood and perhaps with neighbours, until the 17th. A very nice romantic meeting happens between the 9th and the 11th. However, Venus in Capricorn can make you seem cold – even though you're not like that. It is important to project love and warmth to others this month – make it a project. On the 17th Venus moves into Aquarius, your 4th house. Love is still close to home. A romantic evening at home is more enjoyable than a night out on the town. There is more socializing at home and with the family. Family members like to play cupid. Old flames from the past can come into the picture. There is a tendency to want to re-live happy love experiences from the past. The problem with this is that you lose the 'here and now' moment. You could be losing an experience that is better than what you once had.

March

Best Days Overall: 8, 9, 16, 17, 26, 27
Most Stressful Days Overall: 6, 7, 12, 13, 18, 19
Best Days for Love: 6, 7, 12, 13, 16, 26, 27
Best Days for Money: 1, 2, 3, 4, 12, 13, 21, 22, 28, 29, 31
Best Days for Career: 8, 9, 16, 17, 18, 19, 28, 29

Mars leaves your sign on the 6th and the planetary power is still in the Western, social sector. The conflicts of last month are over with. It is easier now to develop the social skills and to put others first. It is easier to take a vacation from yourself. Let others have their way so long as it isn't destructive.

The main headline of the month are two eclipses: a solar eclipse on the 9th and a lunar eclipse on the 23rd. Though you will feel the impact in various areas of life, these are basically benign to you.

The solar eclipse of the 9th (in America it occurs on the 8th) happens in your 5th house. It affects children and children figures in your life. They go through some life-changing dramas. Some of these are quite normal – puberty or graduation, things of this nature – but other dramas could also happen, so it is best to keep them out of harm's way during this period. They don't need to be doing daredevil-type stunts.

This eclipse impacts on Jupiter and Saturn. The impact on Jupiter, your financial planet, shows important financial changes happening. You've been making financial changes for over a year, but now even more so. Generally this happens as the result of some unexpected expense or some new revelation about the financial condition or status. (That stock you thought was a long-term winner turns out to be a dog; that fund with the great track record is revealed to be not so great after all.) The impact on Saturn shows that cars and communication equipment will be tested. They might need repair or replacement. It would be sensible to drive more carefully over this period. Siblings or sibling figures in your life have personal dramas.

Every solar eclipse affects the career and this one is no different. Twice a year you get a chance to redefine your goals and plans thanks to solar eclipses. Often such an eclipse indicates shake-ups in your company or industry. The rules of the game change and you must adapt to them. There are personal dramas in the lives of bosses, parents or parent figures.

The lunar eclipse of the 23rd occurs in your 12th house of spirituality. This shows dramatic changes in your spiritual life – in your practice, attitudes and teachings. There are shake-ups in a spiritual or charitable organization you're involved with and dramas in the lives of gurus and guru figures. This eclipse impacts on Mercury, testing friendships and technology equipment. Make sure your important files are backed up and your anti-virus software is up to date. There are dramas in the lives of friends. This eclipse often brings encounters with death (although not usually literal death). Perhaps you have a close call – or a friend has a close call. Perhaps you have dreams of it. You're forced to confront your own mortality. This is educational, not punitive. It indicates that it is time to get more serious about life. It is not advisable to travel during this eclipse period; try to schedule any trips around it.

April

Best Days Overall: 4, 5, 12, 13, 22, 23
Most Stressful Days Overall: 2, 3, 8, 9, 14, 15, 16, 29, 30
Best Days for Love: 6, 8, 9, 14, 15, 25, 26
Best Days for Money: 1, 8, 9, 17, 18, 24, 25, 26, 27, 28
Best Days for Career: 6, 7, 14, 15, 16, 27

Your 6th house of health and work became strong on March 20 and is still very strong until the 19th. Job seekers have many, many opportunities now. Even those already employed have opportunities for more work – overtime or second jobs. The only problem is the retrograde of Mars, ruler of this house, which begins on the 17th. This means that these opportunities need more study and research doing on them – they might not be what they seem. Do the homework, resolve the doubts, before accepting.

Health is good this month and you're very focused here. This focus will help later on in the month when health becomes more delicate (from the 19th onwards). Enhance the health in the ways mentioned in the yearly report, but also give more attention to the liver and thighs. Be cautious about major changes to the health regime or diet from the 17th onwards. Get as much knowledge and information as you can.

On the 19th the Sun enters your 7th house of love and you begin a yearly love and social peak. The social life looks very successful. It is almost like your career this month. It is important to you and this tends to success. Sexual magnetism is always important for a Scorpio, but now you're also turned on by power and status. You gravitate to people above you in status. You meet people who can help you career-wise. A lot of your socializing involves the career after the 19th and it will be beneficial to enhance the career by social means.

Before the 19th, the career is enhanced through work and productivity. Your good work ethic is noted by superiors. But after the 19th it is important to attend or host the right kinds of parties or gatherings.

On the 5th your love planet Venus enters Aries and stays there for the rest of the month. This makes you – temporarily – a 'love at first sight' kind of person. You can jump into things too quickly. You have the aspects for the office romance all month.

Retrograde activity among the planets is greatly increased this month, with at least 40 per cent, and sometimes 50 per cent of the planets retrograde. Things slow down in the world. Progress is slower. These are times to learn patience. Time and time alone will resolve most issues.

Earnings are much stronger from the 19th onwards. But Jupiter is still retrograde. Review our discussion of this from earlier months.

May

Best Days Overall: 1, 2, 3, 10, 11, 19, 20, 21, 29, 30
Most Stressful Days Overall: 6, 12, 13, 27, 28
Best Days for Love: 6, 14, 15, 26, 27
Best Days for Money: 6, 14, 15, 22, 23, 24, 25
Best Days for Career: 6, 12, 13, 14, 15, 27

Love is the main headline of the month ahead. You're still in the midst of a yearly love and social peak. Social activity is at a yearly high. Romance is on your mind. You're in the mood for it and there are plenty of opportunities to indulge. The 10th to the 14th seem exceptionally good for love.

The message of the Horoscope is 'if the love and social life is in order, everything else will fall into place'. So, if there have been discords with friends or the current love, now is the time to restore the harmony. Good social relations will enhance the bottom line and the career as well.

Finances are improving this month. Jupiter moves forward on the 9th after many months of retrograde motion. This brings financial clarity and confidence. The financial judgement is good now. Hopefully you've used the past few months to make solid plans, as you can now start putting those plans into motion. The 2nd to the 4th and the 10th and 11th bring financial windfalls and opportunity. A business partnership or joint venture could happen on the 10th and 11th – the opportunity comes.

On the 20th the spouse, partner or current love has a yearly financial peak. You seem very involved in this. He or she will tend to be more generous.

The Sun had its solstice on December 21. Venus had one of hers from January 25 to 30. Mars will have his from the 7th to the 14th. He pauses in the heavens as he gets ready to change direction. This shows a pause in your work and health routine. If you have days off owing to you, this might be a good time to take a brief vacation. Take a pause in your health regimes too. This is a pause that refreshes. The pause will bring clarity and renewed enthusiasm later.

Health needs watching until the 20th. The most important thing is to get as much rest as practical. Avoid getting overtired. Don't try to run the car on an empty gas tank. In many cases what seems like a serious health problem on the surface is cured by a good night's sleep or a brief vacation. It was never a real health problem, though there might have been symptoms – it was a low energy problem.

June

Best Days Overall: 6, 7, 15, 16, 17, 25, 26
Most Stressful Days Overall: 2, 3, 8, 9, 23, 24, 29, 30
Best Days for Love: 2, 3, 4, 5, 14, 25, 26, 29, 30
Best Days for Money: 2, 3, 10, 11, 18, 19, 20, 21, 29, 30
Best Days for Career: 4, 5, 8, 9, 13, 14, 25

Last month the planetary power started to shift to the upper half of your chart, although it is not yet dominant by any means. Home, family and emotional wellness are still the most important things in your life, but you're at the sunrise of your year. You've just woken up from a good night's sleep (hopefully) and are ready to partake of the activities of the day. Time to focus more on the career and your outer goals. Since the bottom half of the chart is still very powerful, your challenge is to be successful in your domestic life and in the career. You're performing a balancing act now.

Your 8th house – your favourite house – became powerful on May 20 and is still powerful until the 21st. Scorpio by nature is sexually active, but this month even more so. But there's more to the 8th house than just sex. The 8th house is about the deeper things in life. It is about death and resurrection, personal transformation and reinvention, and giving birth to your own ideal of self. These activities require a purging of old effete material – whether they be physical things, or mental or emotional patterns. To give birth to your ideal of self requires a kind of 'ego death' – one dies to the old self and its patterns and takes on the patterns of the new and desired self. Scorpio is very much involved in these kinds of projects, both personally and for other people. And these projects go well.

There are many things in our lives in need of resurrection. It can be one's business, or relationship, or some project of the heart. This is a month to make it happen. The how and the why will be revealed as you go along.

Personal finances are stressful early in the month. You have to work harder – much harder – to achieve your financial goals. However, you have help. The spouse, partner or current love is still having a banner financial month and is likely to pick up the slack. This is a month (until the 21st) where you have to focus on the financial interest of others – to put their financial interest ahead of your own. This is not so easy to do and you're feeling the stress. However, as you persist in this, your own prosperity will happen in due course, by karmic law. Jupiter, your financial planet, spends the month on the Moon's North Node. Thus you might be over-emphasizing your personal financial interest and it could be hurting you.

Health is much improved now and it gets even better after the 21st. Mars is back in your sign all this month. Avoid hurry, impatience and temper tantrums. These can lead to accident or injury or violent confrontations.

July

Best Days Overall: 3, 4, 13, 14, 22, 23, 31
Most Stressful Days Overall: 6, 7, 20, 21, 27, 28
Best Days for Love: 3, 4, 15, 24, 25, 27, 28
Best Days for Money: 8, 9, 15, 16, 18, 19, 27, 28
Best Days for Career: 3, 4, 6, 7, 13, 14, 24

The month ahead looks happy and successful, with a few challenges thrown in to keep things interesting and to keep you on your toes.

You begin the month full of energy and with the wind at your back. Things basically run smoothly. Health is good. You have the energy of ten people. There is great optimism and a 'can do' spirit. On the 22nd, the Sun crosses your Mid-heaven and enters your 10th house of career; you begin a yearly career peak. There is much success happening.

Love is a bit complicated until the 12th. You and the beloved seem very distant from each other. Sometimes this shows a physical condition – a physical separation – but most of the time it shows a 'psychic condition'. You can be in the same place physically, but worlds apart psychologically. Your challenge will be to bridge the separation, bridge your differences. If this can be done, your relationship will become more powerful.

Love will become more harmonious after the 12th as Venus moves away from her opposition to Pluto. She will be in your 10th house of career from that date onwards. This shows that love is high on your agenda and that you're willing to put in the work necessary to keep love alive. For singles this shows romantic opportunity as they pursue their career goals or with people involved in the career. Singles are attracted to the powerful during this period, and often this indicates romantic opportunity with bosses or superiors. Sometimes bosses like to play cupid under this transit. Parent figures too. In general there is more socializing with powerful people – with authority figures in your life. Much of the socializing after the 12th seems business or career related. Your social skills are playing a huge role in your career during this period.

Your financial life is still being reorganized but the month ahead seems OK. Jupiter still makes nice aspects to Pluto and is not being stressed by other planets. You will have all the resources you need.

Mars in your 1st house all month gives physical strength, energy and passion. You excel in exercise regimes and in athletics. You have more sex appeal. The only problem is rush and haste. Get things done, but do them mindfully.

August

Best Days Overall: 1, 9, 10, 19, 20, 27, 28
Most Stressful Days Overall: 2, 3, 16, 17, 18, 23, 24, 29, 30
Best Days for Love: 3, 14, 15, 23, 24
Best Days for Money: 4, 5, 12, 13, 14, 15, 23, 24, 31
Best Days for Career: 2, 3, 12, 13, 23, 29, 30, 31

Last month, on the 22nd, the planetary power started to shift into the Eastern sector of your chart. This means that from here on in, personal power and independence will get stronger and stronger. The cosmic energy is flowing towards you rather than away from you. You have the power to make changes that need to be made. You have the power to have things your way. If others don't go along with you, go it alone. Your personal initiative matters now. Don't compromise. Create the conditions that make for your happiness.

You're still in a very successful period. A yearly career peak. This goes on until the 22nd.

Last month, on the 22nd, the health became more delicate, and remains so until the 22nd of this month. The most important thing is to rest and relax more to maintain high energy levels. One way to do this is to keep the focus on the essentials in your life and to let go of the trivia. Enhance the health through thigh massage and liver detoxes from the 2nd onwards, as well as in the ways mentioned in the yearly report. Health is much improved after the 22nd. Your health planet Mars goes 'out of bounds' from the 9th to the 31st. This shows that you're experimenting with new techniques and new therapies. You're going outside your natural sphere when it comes to health.

Job seekers too are going outside their normal sphere looking for work.

The month ahead will be prosperous – a mini yearly financial peak. Jupiter, your financial planet, receives positive stimulation from the short-term planets – the Sun, Venus and Mercury. Mercury will exactly conjunct Jupiter from the 20th to the 24th. This suggests the ability to pay down debt or to borrow – depending on your need. It shows that money can come from insurance claims, tax refunds or estates. From the 26th to the 28th Venus will conjunct Jupiter. This not only increases earnings, but brings partnership or joint venture opportunities. Financial increase and opportunity can come at a party or gathering – or through the current love.

Mars enters the money house on the 2nd and stays there for the rest of the month. This shows earnings from work – from the job. If you are already employed there are opportunities for overtime or for jobs on the side. If you're unemployed, job opportunities can come.

On the 22nd your 11th house becomes very powerful. This house has been strong all year – Jupiter is there – but now even more so. It will be a strong social period. New and happy friendships are being made. Fondest hopes and wishes are coming to pass. Singles will find love opportunities as they get involved with groups and group activities.

September

Best Days Overall: 5, 6, 7, 15, 16, 23, 24
Most Stressful Days Overall: 13, 14, 19, 20, 25, 26, 27
Best Days for Love: 3, 4, 13, 14, 19, 20, 23
Best Days for Money: 1, 2, 8, 9, 12, 13, 21
Best Days for Career: 1, 2, 11, 12, 20, 25, 26, 27, 30

A lot of changes are happening this month, Scorpio. The universal energies are now shifting in a new way. On the 10th Jupiter enters your 12th house of spirituality. From here on in – for the next year – you're in a more spiritual period. Your spiritual understanding is not going to be 'abstract and philosophical', however; in fact it will have concrete bottom-line results. You are naturally very intuitive, and now the financial intuition comes into play in a big way. You need to trust it.

Two eclipses this month shake things up. This is their purpose. There is a cosmic plan for the world and for your life. If people are on a divergent path, due to human free will, the eclipse brings them back to the plan.

The solar eclipse of the 1st occurs in your 11th house. This will test friendships, computers and high tech equipment. There can be life-changing dramas in the lives of friends. Make sure your important files are backed up and that your anti-virus, anti-phishing software is up to date. There are dramas in your place of worship and in the lives of worship leaders. Students at college level make important educational changes. (Sometimes this happens because the school makes changes.) This eclipse impacts on Mars, the health and work planet. Job changes are happening. There can be changes in the conditions of work too. Sometimes this produces a health scare or health drama. However, your overall health looks good, and most likely it will be nothing more than a scare. There will be important changes to the health regime over the next six months, though. Every solar eclipse brings career change and this one is no different. There are changes in your company and industry – and often dramas in the lives of bosses and parent figures.

The lunar eclipse of the 16th occurs in your 5th house, impacting on the children or children figures in your life. Do your best to keep them out of harm's way during this period. They don't need to be engaged in stressful, risky activities. Children and children figures will be redefin-ing themselves over the next six months. They will change their self-concept and self-image. They will change the way they want others to see them. They will adopt a 'new look'. It will not be a good idea to travel during this period; if you must travel, try to schedule your trip around the eclipse. Your religious and philosophical beliefs get tested by events. Some of them will have to change or be modified.

Venus moves into your own sign on the 22nd. This brings love into the life. If you're single, just go about your daily business and love will find you. If you are in a relationship, the spouse, partner or current love is very devoted to you.

October

Best Days Overall: 3, 4, 12, 13, 21, 22, 30, 31
Most Stressful Days Overall: 10, 11, 17, 23, 24
Best Days for Love: 3, 4, 12, 13, 16, 17, 23, 24
Best Days for Money: 1, 5, 6, 7, 10, 18, 19, 27, 28
Best Days for Career: 1, 2, 10, 11, 20, 23, 24, 30

A happy and successful month, Scorpio. Enjoy.

The planetary power is now in its most Easterly position. You are in the place of maximum personal power and independence of your year. You can – and should – have things your way. If conditions irk you, change them to something happier. Some people might call you self-ish, but your happiness will help all around you. When you're feeling good and in good personal conditions, you're better able to help others.

You're still in a very spiritual period until the 23rd. This is a wonderful time for the study of scripture or sacred literature. Wonderful for meditation and other spiritual studies. It will be very good to get involved in charitable kinds of activities. You'll find that as you get involved in these things, your career is boosted as a side effect. Career guidance will come in dreams or through psychics, ministers or spiritual channels. Your career is not just about you – the whole world is affected by it and the spiritual beings are highly concerned with it.

Health is excellent all month – but especially from the 23rd onwards. With energy all kinds of things are possible, things you never thought possible when energy was low. All kinds of doors open for you. Happy career opportunities are also coming. You look successful – others see you this way. Venus is still in your sign until the 18th. This gives beauty and grace to the image. In a man's chart it indicates young and beautiful women coming into the picture. In a woman's chart it shows that her own beauty is magnified. Love still seeks you out until the 18th. There's nothing much that you need to do – just show up.

Venus moves into your money house on the 18th. This shows good financial support from the spouse, partner or current love and that much of your socializing is business related. Singles find love opportunities as they pursue their financial goals and with people involved in their finances. Wealth is a great romantic turn-on from the 18th onwards.

Children and children figures in your life are going through all kinds of changes and dramas. They lack a sense of direction. Neptune will be on an old eclipse point all month. They don't need to be involved in risky kinds of activities.

A job opportunity – off the beaten path – comes from the 18th to the 20th. Job changes or disturbances at the job come from the 27th to the 29th.

November

Best Days Overall: 1, 9, 10, 17, 18, 26, 27, 28
Most Stressful Days Overall: 6, 7, 8, 13, 14, 19, 20
Best Days for Love: 2, 3, 13, 14, 21, 22
Best Days for Money: 2, 3, 6, 7, 15, 16, 24, 25, 29, 30
Best Days for Career: 9, 10, 18, 19, 20, 29

When the Sun entered your sign on October 23, you began one of your yearly personal pleasure peaks. This continues until the 22nd. This is a wonderful period for getting the body and image the way you want it. Good for sprucing up the image and pampering the body. On the 22nd the Sun enters your money house and you begin a yearly financial peak. Finances may have felt tight this year, but this month there is prosperity. You have the financial favour of parents, parent figures, bosses and elders. Your good career reputation helps the bottom line. Often this transit shows pay rises – either monetary or in kind. Venus is still in the money house until the 12th and is in mutual reception with Jupiter, your financial planet. This shows great cooperation between the two planets. Thus the current love, and friends, are cooperating in your financial life and are supportive, providing financial opportunity. This alignment favours business partnerships and joint ventures. You like to do business with friends and to socialize with the people you do business with.

Venus will spend the month 'out of bounds'. This shows that in love matters you're moving outside your normal social circle. You're exploring new frontiers. The Sun will have its solstice next month, but Venus has one of hers from the 13th to the 16th. She is stationary in her latitude motion. She pauses and gets ready to change direction. This is what is happening socially. There is a pause in the love life and then a new direction. A happy love opportunity comes on the 24th and 25th. Be more patient with the beloved on the 29th and 30th – he or she doesn't need to be involved in risky activities and seems temperamental during that period.

There is still much instability in the lives of the children or children figures in your life. Many personal dramas going on. The 8th and the 9th and the 18th and 19th bring love dramas – perhaps a crisis. Happily this is short term.

Though your finances are good, speculations are best avoided this month. The cosmos has many ways it can prosper you. Be careful of overspending from the 19th to the 25th.

Last month, on the 25th, as Mercury entered your sign, the planetary power shifted from the upper to the lower half of your Horoscope. It is time to rest a bit from career activities and focus on the home, family and your sense of emotional wellness. Night is falling in your year and you should be about the activities of night.

The Sun reactivates an old eclipse point on the 30th. Be more patient with parents and parent figures then. They are apt to be more temperamental.

December

Best Days Overall: 6, 7, 14, 15, 24, 25
Most Stressful Days Overall: 4, 5, 10, 11, 16, 17, 31
Best Days for Love: 2, 3, 10, 11, 12, 13, 21, 22
Best Days for Money: 4, 5, 12, 13, 21, 22, 26, 27, 31
Best Days for Career: 8, 9, 16, 17, 18, 29

Most of the planets are moving forward this month; 90 per cent are in forward motion until the 19th and after the 29th, while 80 per cent of them are forward from the 19th to the 29th. Your personal solar cycle is waxing and on the 21st the universal solar cycle will start to wax. You're in an excellent time – from the 21st onwards – for starting a new project, venture or launching a new product. The only problem is

Mercury's retrograde between the 19th and the 29th. The best time for starting new things is from the 29th to the end of the month. Next month will also be excellent.

You're still in a yearly financial peak until the 21st. So though there are still financial challenges, prosperity is happening. From the 19th onwards the challenge will be to come into financial harmony with the family. Family expenses seem unusually high and are forcing financial changes.

The month ahead is more about home, family and emotional wellness than it is about the career. Yet a happy career opportunity comes on the 7th or 8th. There is career success during that period.

The Winter Solstice on the 21st is a time when the Sun pauses in the heavens – he pauses in his latitudinal motion. Then after the pause he will change direction. So a pause in the career and outer activities is called for this period. (This happens anyway in most of the world as the holiday season is in full sway.) Then will come a change in your career direction.

On the 21st the Sun enters your 3rd house of communication, inaugurating a period for pursuing these interests. Now is a great time to read the books you've always wanted to read or catch up on your emails, texts and letter-writing. It is an excellent period for students and they should do well in their studies.

Health is good this month. Emotional health is the most important thing – especially until the 20th. If you feel under the weather, chances are that there is some family discord or emotional issue behind it. Restore the harmony as quickly as possible. After the 20th you can enhance the health by paying more attention to the feet. Foot massage is extremely beneficial. You also respond well to spiritual therapies – meditation, the laying on of hands, reiki and the manipulation of subtle energies.

Venus moves into your 4th house on the 7th. This indicates socializing at home and with the family – which is hardly surprising as this is the holiday season. The chart just shows what is. Love is close to home this month.

Sagittarius

THE ARCHER

Birthdays from
23rd November to
20th December

Personality Profile

SAGITTARIUS AT A GLANCE

Element – Fire

Ruling Planet – Jupiter
  Career Planet – Mercury
  Love Planet – Mercury
  Money Planet – Saturn
  Planet of Health and Work – Venus
  Planet of Home and Family Life – Neptune
  Planet of Spirituality – Pluto

Colours – blue, dark blue

Colours that promote love, romance and social harmony – yellow,
  yellow-orange

Colours that promote earning power – black, indigo

Gems – carbuncle, turquoise

Metal – tin

Scents – carnation, jasmine, myrrh

Quality – mutable (= flexibility)

Qualities most needed for balance – attention to detail, administrative and organizational skills

Strongest virtues – generosity, honesty, broad-mindedness, tremendous vision

Deepest need – to expand mentally

Characteristics to avoid – over-optimism, exaggeration, being too generous with other people's money

Signs of greatest overall compatibility – Aries, Leo

Signs of greatest overall incompatibility – Gemini, Virgo, Pisces

Sign most helpful to career – Virgo

Sign most helpful for emotional support – Pisces

Sign most helpful financially – Capricorn

Sign best for marriage and/or partnerships – Gemini

Sign most helpful for creative projects – Aries

Best Sign to have fun with – Aries

Signs most helpful in spiritual matters – Leo, Scorpio

Best day of the week – Thursday

Understanding a Sagittarius

If you look at the symbol of the archer you will gain a good, intuitive understanding of a person born under this astrological sign. The development of archery was humanity's first refinement of the power to hunt and wage war. The ability to shoot an arrow far beyond the ordinary range of a spear extended humanity's horizons, wealth, personal will and power.

Today, instead of using bows and arrows we project our power with fuels and mighty engines, but the essential reason for using these new powers remains the same. These powers represent our ability to extend our personal sphere of influence – and this is what Sagittarius is all about. Sagittarians are always seeking to expand their horizons, to cover more territory and increase their range and scope. This applies to all aspects of their lives: economic, social and intellectual.

Sagittarians are noted for the development of the mind – the higher intellect – which understands philosophical and spiritual concepts. This mind represents the higher part of the psychic nature and is motivated not by self-centred considerations but by the light and grace of a Higher Power. Thus, Sagittarians love higher education of all kinds. They might be bored with formal schooling but they love to study on their own and in their own way. A love of foreign travel and interest in places far away from home are also noteworthy characteristics of the Sagittarian type.

If you give some thought to all these Sagittarian attributes you will see that they spring from the inner Sagittarian desire to develop. To travel more is to know more, to know more is to be more, to cultivate the higher mind is to grow and to reach more. All these traits tend to broaden the intellectual – and indirectly, the economic and material – horizons of the Sagittarian.

The generosity of the Sagittarian is legendary. There are many reasons for this. One is that Sagittarians seem to have an inborn consciousness of wealth. They feel that they are rich, that they are lucky, that they can attain any financial goal – and so they feel that they can afford to be generous. Sagittarians do not carry the burdens of want and limitation which stop most other people from giving generously. Another reason for their generosity is their religious and philo-sophical idealism, derived from the higher mind. This higher mind is by nature generous because it is unaffected by material circumstances. Still another reason is that the act of giving tends to enhance their emotional nature. Every act of giving seems to be enriching, and this is reward enough for the Sagittarian.

Finance

Sagittarians generally entice wealth. They either attract it or create it. They have the ideas, energy and talent to make their vision of paradise on Earth a reality. However, mere wealth is not enough. Sagittarians want luxury – earning a comfortable living seems small and insignifi-cant to them.

In order for Sagittarians to attain their true earning potential they must develop better managerial and organizational skills. They must learn to set limits, to arrive at their goals through a series of attainable sub-goals or objectives. It is very rare that a person goes from rags to riches overnight. But a long, drawn-out process is difficult for Sagittarians. Like Leos, they want to achieve wealth and success quickly and impressively. They must be aware, however, that this over-optimism can lead to unrealistic financial ventures and disappointing losses. Of course, no zodiac sign can bounce back as quickly as Sagittarius, but only needless heartache will be caused by this attitude. Sagittarians need to maintain their vision – never letting it go – but they must also work towards it in practical and efficient ways.

Career and Public Image

Sagittarians are big thinkers. They want it all: money, fame, glamour, prestige, public acclaim and a place in history. They often go after all these goals. Some attain them, some do not – much depends on each individual's personal Horoscope. But if Sagittarians want to attain public and professional status they must understand that these things are not conferred to enhance one's ego but as rewards for the amount of service that one does for the whole of humanity. If and when they figure out ways to serve more, Sagittarians can rise to the top.

The ego of the Sagittarian is gigantic – and perhaps rightly so. They have much to be proud of. If they want public acclaim, however, they will have to learn to tone down the ego a bit, to become more humble and self-effacing, without falling into the trap of self-denial and self-abasement. They must also learn to master the details of life, which can sometimes elude them.

At their jobs Sagittarians are hard workers who like to please their bosses and co-workers. They are dependable, trustworthy and enjoy a challenge. Sagittarians are friendly to work with and helpful to their colleagues. They usually contribute intelligent ideas or new methods that improve the work environment for everyone. Sagittarians always look for challenging positions and careers that develop their intellect, even if they have to work very hard in order to succeed. They also work well under the supervision of others, although by nature they would rather be the supervisors and increase their sphere of influence. Sagittarians excel at professions that allow them to be in contact with many different people and to travel to new and exciting locations.

Love and Relationships

Sagittarians love freedom for themselves and will readily grant it to their partners. They like their relationships to be fluid and ever-changing. Sagittarians tend to be fickle in love and to change their minds about their partners quite frequently.

Sagittarians feel threatened by a clearly defined, well-structured relationship, as they feel this limits their freedom. The Sagittarian tends to marry more than once in life.

Sagittarians in love are passionate, generous, open, benevolent and very active. They demonstrate their affections very openly. However, just like an Aries they tend to be egocentric in the way they relate to their partners. Sagittarians should develop the ability to see others' points of view, not just their own. They need to develop some objectivity and cool intellectual clarity in their relationships so that they can develop better two-way communication with their partners. Sagittarians tend to be overly idealistic about their partners and about love in general. A cool and rational attitude will help them to perceive reality more clearly and enable them to avoid disappointment.

Home and Domestic Life

Sagittarians tend to grant a lot of freedom to their family. They like big homes and many children and are one of the most fertile signs of the zodiac. However, when it comes to their children Sagittarians generally err on the side of allowing them too much freedom. Sometimes their children get the idea that there are no limits. However, allowing freedom in the home is basically a positive thing – so long as a measure of balance is maintained – for it enables all family members to develop as they should.

Horoscope for 2016

Major Trends

Saturn in your 1st house is a mixed blessing. On the one hand it shows prosperity. Financial opportunities are seeking you out. On the other it can unduly dampen your natural optimism and enthusiasm for life. With this kind of transit one feels older than one's years. Even young people find themselves thinking of old age. However, it does make a person more serious about life. It gives a good work ethic and tends to success.

Pluto has been in your money house for many years. He will remain there for many more years too. Thus – and this is a long-term project – there is a financial detox happening in your life. Impurities are being purged so that only what is healthy remains. This often produces financial near-death experiences. More on this later.

Neptune has been in your 4th house of home and family since 2012 and will be there for many more years to come. The emotional life is becoming more refined. The emotional sensitivities are stronger. Even family members are becoming more spiritual.

Uranus has been in your 5th house for many years. This shows that children and children figures in your life are more difficult to handle. They are more rebellious. You can't take an authoritarian approach with them. They need to understand the 'whys' of what you want from them. It also shows a very unique and original creativity.

Jupiter, the ruler of your Horoscope, has been in your 10th house of career since August of last year. Thus you're in a banner career year. You seem on top of your game and above everyone in your world. A very successful year.

Jupiter will move into your 11th house on September 10. This will expand your social life and bring new and important friends into the picture.

Your most important interests this year are: the body, image and personal pleasure; finance; home and family; children, fun and creativity; career (until September 9); and friends, groups and group activities (from September 10).

Your paths of greatest fulfilment this year will be career; and friends, groups and group activities (from September 10 onwards).

Health

(Please note that this is an astrological perspective on health and not a medical one. In days of yore there was no difference, these perspectives were identical. But now there could be quite a difference. For a medical perspective, please consult your doctor or health practitioner.)

Health needs more attention paying to it this year. Three long-term planets are in stressful aspect with you. This is challenging enough, but when they are joined by the short-term planets, the vulnerability is increased. The times to be most careful, to make sure that you get enough rest and maintain high energy, are from February 18 to March 20, May 21 to June 20 and August 23 to September 22.

Your 6th house of health is not strong this year and this can be an additional problem. You might not be paying enough attention here. This is the kind of year where you need to force yourself to pay attention – even when you don't feel like it.

Since the body is a dynamic energy system, the first line of defence is to maintain high energy levels. The spiritual immune system – the aura – must be strong. This will repel microbes and other opportunistic invaders. But health can also be enhanced by giving more attention to the following – the vulnerable areas in the Horoscope (the respective reflexology points are shown in the following chart):

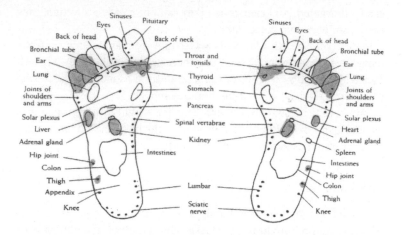

Important foot reflexology points for the year ahead

Try to massage all of the foot on a regular basis – the top of the foot as well as the bottom – but pay extra attention to the points highlighted on the chart. When you massage, be aware of 'sore spots' as these need special attention. It's also a good idea to massage the ankles and below them.

- The heart. This has only become important to you since last year as Saturn entered your sign. You are normally not a worrier, but this year the tendency is greater. Replace worry with faith.
- The liver and thighs. These are always important for you. Liver action is more sluggish this year and needs more energy. A herbal liver detox might be good if you feel under the weather. Thighs should be regularly massaged.
- The throat and neck. Another important area for you. Tension tends to collect in the neck and needs release. Regular neck massage – and craniosacral therapy – would be good.
- The kidneys and hips. These too are always important for you. Hips should be regularly massaged, and a herbal kidney cleanse might be good if you feel under the weather.

Since these are the areas where problems would most likely begin, it is a good idea to keep them healthy and fit. Most of the time problems can be prevented. And even when they can't be totally prevented, they can be softened to a great extent.

Venus, your health planet, is a fast-moving planet. This year she moves even faster than usual. Thus there are many short-term health trends depending on where Venus is and the aspects she receives. These are best dealt with in the monthly reports.

Saturn in your own sign is excellent for weight loss regimes. It is wonderful for disciplined regimes to keep the body and image in right shape. It is not especially good for fertility.

Home and Family

Your 4th house of home and family is strong, but so is your 10th house of career. You're caught in the classic conundrum of trying to balance a successful home life with a successful career. Your focus on the career seems to put you at odds with the family and especially with a parent or parent figure. You seem 'distant' from the family this year – even though you consider them important. You seem distant from this parent figure as well. It will take conscious effort to maintain harmony here.

Your distance from the family and the parent figure can make you unaware of many behind the scenes manoeuvres. Things are not what they seem to be. These things will come out in due course and are probably not pleasant. You're successful and above everyone and this contributes to the problem. The person at the top is the natural target.

You have the aspects of someone who would enjoy living near water – near the beach, a lake or river. Many of you have moved to these kinds of places in recent years. Some of you would relish living on a boat too. This year, however, a move is not seen. The aspects are better for this a few years down the road.

Family members seem deeply into spirituality these days. There are probably spiritual meetings of some type in the home. I could envision the home decorated with spiritual symbols: icons, altars, incense burners and other such paraphernalia. The smell of sage or other burning herbs permeates the home.

Neptune in the 4th house indicates great emotional sensitivity. This is true for you and for family members. This is a double-edged sword.

On the one hand it gives empathy and compassion for others. But on the other it can make a person easily hurt by the slightest thing – tone of voice, body language, some minor error of omission. Be more careful in this department – it will save much heartache down the road.

Both of the parent figures in your life are prospering this year. In the case of one of them, you seem very personally involved. Moves are not likely for them this year.

Children and children figures in your life need as much space as possible. It would be a mistake to over-control or micro-manage them. If they are of appropriate age, there is romance in the year ahead, although marriage wouldn't be advisable just yet. But even young children will have an expanded social life – especially from September 10 onwards. Moves could happen, but they are not likely. Grandchildren (if you have them) are likely to move this year. Sometimes it's not a literal move but their room is enlarged or they have the use of more living space.

If you're planning any construction work or major repairs on the home, December 19 to the end of the year would be a good time. If you're redecorating or beautifying the home, February 19 to April 5 is a good time for this.

Finance and Career

You are, as we mentioned, in a prosperous period these days. The money house is strong and has been for many years now. Your financial planet, Saturn, is in a prominent position in your 1st house. There is great focus here and this tends to success.

The financial planet in your 1st house shows that financial opportunity comes to you. And not just opportunity but money itself. There's not much you need to do, by the way; it seeks you out. Just go about your normal daily routine.

There are some challenges, but you have the drive and the focus to overcome them.

One of the challenges is that you seem in a dilemma about career success and finance. Generally they go together, but not always. Should I focus on status and perhaps earn less? Should I focus on money, though perhaps it brings less prestige? It will take some work, but in the end you'll be able to combine the two urges into something work-able for you. Both are important – status and money. There are no rules as to how you will do this. Each person finds their own solution.

By September 10, as Jupiter moves away from his stressful aspect with your financial planet, you become more comfortable with finance. Earnings should become even stronger. You're enjoying finance more too.

Pluto has been in your money house for many years. Aside from the financial detox going on, it shows that you're going deeper into the spiritual – supernatural – sources of supply. Now, Sagittarius has a natural, inborn understanding of this. But these days you're under-standing more. The financial intuition is extremely good this year, especially until September 9; you just have to trust it. The Beings of the Spirit world seem very concerned about your financial life and are active on your behalf. They tend to work on the internal levels, through dreams, visions, ideas and sometimes hunches. Sometimes they will work through spiritual types of people such as astrologers, ministers, psychics and spiritual channels. If you feel you need guidance, it will be good to consult with these people.

Sometimes they will work through the animals and insects in your environment. Birds might fly in a particular formation or over a partic-ular place; an animal that you don't usually see could appear; or you might see animals or birds doing unusual things. These are all messages, once you learn to decode them.

Saturn as your financial planet favours a business or corporate kind of job. Your managerial abilities are important in finance. It favours real estate (commercial) and traditional blue chip companies. If these are involved in travel, higher education or publishing, all the better. Foreign investments are more interesting this year and you will have opportunities there. Foreigners or foreign companies seem important in the financial life.

Favourable financial numbers are 3, 8, 10, 13, 15, 20 and 21.

Career, as we mentioned, is super right now. There is much success and elevation happening. You seem honoured, appreciated and raised in status. You are honoured as much for who you are as for your professional achievements. Personal appearance and overall demean-our play a huge role in your success. You have the aspects that models, athletes and celebrities have. Your body and image are part of the career.

Love and Social Life

This is not an especially strong love and social year. Your 7th house of love and social activities is for the most part empty (only short-term planets will move through there – and briefly). Your 1st house of self, is strong. Most of the long-term planets are in the Eastern sector of your chart. This tends to more self-involvement rather than involvement with others. Some years are like that. The cosmos emphasizes a balanced development. So, some years, romance takes a back seat to other things.

The empty 7th house tends to show a stable kind of year. If you were satisfied with the love life last year you'll be satisfied in the year ahead. Married couples tend to stay married and singles tend to stay single.

The social life becomes more active from September 10 onwards as Jupiter enters your 11th house of friends. You become more popular. You go out of your way for friends. But this transit is not a romantic one. It's more about friendship and group activities.

There are a few complications in love – happily these are very correctable. The first complication is Saturn in your 1st house. We may have discussed this last year, but it applies now too. This can make you seem cold, aloof, distant and uncaring. Now, Sagittarius is not at all like this, but the Saturn energy can give this impression. This can inhibit the love life and limit opportunity. So, like last year, you need to make a conscious effort to project love and warmth to others. Do this every night and watch how the love life changes.

Mercury, your love planet, will go into retrograde motion four times in the year ahead – usually it only happens three times. Thus he will spend more than usual time in retrograde motion. This tends to weaken the social confidence and judgement. Current relationships seem to go backwards instead of forward and there are more delays and glitches in social matters than usual. The best way to deal with this is to use the retrograde periods to review the love life and see where improvements can be made. Then when Mercury goes forward again you can act on these plans.

Your love planet is a fast-moving planet. During the course of the year he will move through all the signs and houses of your Horoscope. So love and social opportunities can happen in many ways and with many kinds of people – depending on where Mercury is and the aspects he receives. These short-term trends are best dealt with in the monthly reports.

In general we can say that your most active love period will be from May 20 to June 30.

Self-improvement

Secular psychological therapy has its good points. It gives emotional release to people and often insights into present emotional issues. Often medication gives helpful relief too. But for you, with Neptune in your 4th house of home and family, you need a spiritual approach to emotional issues. Many of your issues have to do with things in previous lives, and with your spiritual mission and job. Without this kind of perspective, you'll only go up to a certain point in your therapy – and no further.

If you're a believer in the Divine, a very good psychological exercise is to 'surrender' the emotional body – the feeling nature – to the Divine and let it have its way. If this is done sincerely – not just with the lips, but with the heart and with full intent – a great peace will come over you. Little by little the Divine peace, joy and harmony – the natural state of the feeling body – will assert itself. We don't create this. It's about allowing it to happen.

Saturn in your 1st house shows that your ego nature, your self-esteem and confidence, is getting 'reality therapy' this year (it was happening last year as well). Is self-esteem too high? Is there overconfidence? Saturn will adjust it. But the same is true in reverse. Is self-esteem too low? Do you feel like a 'worm of the dust'? Saturn will adjust this too. Saturn is going to build a healthy, realistic self-confidence in you. Your confidence will not be based on mere feeling or bravado but on reality. Saturn will arrange all these things.

Pluto in your money house is revealing the deeper spiritual secrets of wealth and supply. This we have mentioned above, and it has been the financial agenda for many years now. Many of you are beginning to see (and for some it will be in future years) that wealth – supply – is essentially spiritual. It is a spiritual force and a spiritual substance. This is what produces the outer, tangible objects of wealth – the money, the cars, the homes. This spiritual substance exists in unlimited quantities. The only limitations are personal – how much a person can receive and accept. Outer wealth is only the side effect of this inflow of spiritual substance. Perhaps the most difficult thing is to withdraw attention from the 'outer' objects and place it on the source. One releases this supply by recognition and acknowledgement. It is an internal activity. By the spiritual law, this internal activity is made manifest externally – in very natural kinds of ways.

Though the activity of wealth is internal and happens in quiet meditative times, this doesn't mean that you just sit around idly and get rich. The inflow of spiritual wealth will lead to the right actions that are necessary. You might find yourselves busier than you ever were. But this 'busy-ness' is also a side effect of the internal spiritual substance.

Month-by-month Forecasts

January

Best Days Overall: 6, 7, 15, 16, 24, 25
Most Stressful Days Overall: 13, 14, 19, 20, 26, 27
Best Days for Love: 6, 7, 8, 10, 15, 16, 17, 18, 19, 20, 26, 27
Best Days for Money: 6, 7, 9, 10, 15, 16, 17, 18, 24, 25, 26, 27
Best Days for Career: 10, 17, 18, 26, 27

There is a very strong cosmic window for the next two months for starting a new business or project. Many forces are supporting this. Your personal solar cycle is waxing (growing) and so is the universal solar cycle. The planetary momentum is forward too – *all* the planets are forward until the 5th, and from then on in between 80 and 90 per cent are still going forward. If you can start this project as the Moon also waxes (from the 10th to the 24th) you have the most auspicious start time of the period.

You begin your year with the planetary power in the bottom half of your chart. Career is still very important – and successful – but it is good to shift your energy to the home, family and your emotional well-ness. You have to balance the career with your family and emotional life. The two planets associated with the career – Mercury and Jupiter – are both retrograde most of the month so career problems need time to resolve. It is safe to shift more attention to the family.

Last month, on the 21st, you entered a yearly financial peak. This continues until the 20th of this month. So you're still in a period of peak earnings. Half the planets are either in the money house or moving through there this month. This is a lot of financial energy. The Sun in the money house shows earnings from foreigners, foreign companies or in foreign lands. It shows business-related travel too. Pluto in the money house (and he will be there all year) shows that you have good financial intuition. Venus and Mercury in the money house shows the support of friends and partners. The social connections are important.

Health is good this month too. Your health planet Venus is in your sign until the 24th. You are focused here. Good health is not only good for its own sake, but from a cosmetic perspective too. You look good. Your sense of style is excellent and this is a good period – until the 24th – to buy clothing or accessories. Your choices will be good. You can enhance the health further by giving more attention to the liver and thighs, which are always important areas for you. After the 24th enhance the health by giving more attention to the spine, knees, teeth and bones. Back massage will be powerful.

Love is complicated this month. The problem is not about conflict or compatibility, but lack of direction. Neither you nor the beloved know where you want to go. It is a time for gaining clarity about things. Singles will date, but it is not advisable to get too serious about things. Romantic opportunity happens as you pursue your financial goals.

February

Best Days Overall: 2, 3, 4, 11, 12, 20, 21
Most Stressful Days Overall: 9, 10, 15, 16, 17, 22, 23, 24
Best Days for Love: 5, 6, 13, 14, 15, 16, 17, 25, 26
Best Days for Money: 2, 3, 5, 6, 11, 12, 13, 14, 20, 21, 22, 23, 24
Best Days for Career: 5, 6, 15, 16, 22, 23, 24, 25, 26

The planetary power is mostly in the Eastern sector of your chart, and has been since the beginning of the year. You're still in a period of strong personal power and independence (while this is good, it hasn't helped the love life). Thus it is a time to take personal responsibility for your own happiness and the conditions of your life. If they are unpleasant you have the power to change them. You don't need the approval of others right now. It might seem selfish, but your happiness helps everyone around you. Your interests are no less important than anyone else's. Later on, it will be more difficult to make the changes. Now is the time.

As we mentioned last month, you're still a wonderful period for starting a business, project or launching a new product. The major cycles are supporting you. The planetary power is strongly forward – 90 per cent of the planets are moving forward all this month. From the 8th to the 22nd is the best period to start such projects this month.

The love life is much improved. Mercury went forward on January 25 and will be forward all month. The 5th to the 7th looks exceptionally good for the love life, there is a happy romantic experience. Until the 14th love opportunities come as you pursue your financial goals and with people involved in your finances. Wealth seems the major romantic turn-on at this time. After the 14th you're attracted to intellectual brilliance – the genius type. You like the beloved to be unconventional. You like doing unconventional things – unconventional dates. Love is in the neighbourhood and at educational-type functions from the 14th onwards.

Health is basically good this month, but after the 19th make sure you get enough rest. Pace yourself. Don't allow yourself to get overtired. Until the 17th enhance the health by giving more attention to the spine, knees, teeth and bones. Back massage is a wonderful therapy. After the 17th give more attention to the ankles and calves. Massage them if you feel under the weather. You respond well to new and unconventional types of therapies after the 17th.

Finances are good, but there is some disturbance from the 1st to the 5th. You might have to make some changes. Job seekers have an excellent opportunity between the 9th and 11th. After the 19th you have to work harder to attain your financial goals. It's nothing serious, just more work involved. Overall prosperity is good.

March

Best Days Overall: 1, 2, 10, 11, 18, 19, 28, 29
Most Stressful Days Overall: 8, 9, 14, 15, 21, 22
Best Days for Love: 6, 7, 8, 14, 15, 16, 17, 26, 27, 28, 29
Best Days for Money: 1, 2, 3, 4, 10, 11, 12, 13, 18, 19, 21, 22, 28, 29, 31
Best Days for Career: 8, 16, 17, 21, 22, 28, 29

On the 19th of last month, the planetary power reached the lowest point in your chart. You're in the midnight hour of your year. The magical hour. Things seem dormant on the outside, but inside many wonderful things are happening. The new day, the new cycle, is being born. Emotional wellness and domestic harmony should be your main concern now.

We have two eclipses this month and these are guaranteed to bring change – both personal and in the world at large. The solar eclipse of the 9th (in America it is on the 8th) occurs in your 4th house of home and family and affects you strongly. So take a nice, easy relaxed schedule over this period. It brings personal and family dramas. Family members have dramatic kinds of experiences. Flaws in the home tend to be discovered under this kind of eclipse and repairs have to be made. Emotions run high at home. The dream life will be very disturbed (up to ten days before the actual eclipse) and shouldn't be taken too seriously. You are forced to redefine yourself for yourself. If you don't do this others will, and it won't be so pleasant. Over the next six or so months you will present a new image – a new look – to the world. This eclipse impacts on Saturn, your financial planet, so there are important financial changes happening. All in all, it is a pretty dynamic period.

The lunar eclipse of the 23rd is milder on you, but it is still not advisable to indulge in risky, daredevil type stunts this period. The eclipsed planet, the Moon, is ruler of your 8th house of transformation, and it can bring near-death kinds of experiences, encounters with death and dreams or visions of death. The Dark Angel pays a visit, not to punish you, but just to let you know that he's around. It is time to be more serious about life and be about the business that you were

born to do. This eclipse is stronger on the current love, spouse or partner than on you. He or she is making important financial changes –
usually due to some upheaval or drama. He or she can be having
dramatic personal experiences too. The relationship will get tested.

Health needs watching this month – especially until the 20th (and
especially around the period of the solar eclipse). As always, the most
important thing is to get enough rest. High energy will repel most
problems. Until the 12th enhance the health through calf and ankle
massage. Be alert for new therapies. After the 12th, foot massage is
powerful. The feet contain reflexes to the whole body. You will also
respond well to spiritual therapies. If you feel under the weather, see a
spiritual healer.

April

Best Days Overall: 6, 7, 14, 15, 16, 24, 25, 26
Most Stressful Days Overall: 4, 5, 10, 11, 17, 18
Best Days for Love: 6, 8, 9, 10, 11, 14, 15, 17, 18, 25, 26, 27, 28
Best Days for Money: 1, 6, 7, 8, 9, 14, 15, 16, 17, 18, 24, 25, 26,
    27, 28
Best Days for Career: 8, 9, 17, 18, 27, 28

Last month the planetary power began to shift from the Eastern sector
towards the social West. This means that the planetary power is
moving away from you rather than towards you – it moves towards
others. So should you. There was nothing wrong with your previous
independence, and there's nothing especially noble about your concern
for others – it's just the cycle you're in. This is a time to take a vacation
from your self – many problems in life have their origin in excessive
self-concern – and be there for others. Your good comes through
others and not necessarily from your personal abilities or personal
initiative. Likeability – your social grace – is the dominant factor for
your good. So, it's time to cultivate the social skills.

Last month on the 20th you entered one of your yearly personal
pleasure peaks. This goes on until April 19. There are opportunities for
leisure travel, sporting and theatre events. Your personal creativity is
much stronger than usual. You'll find that it is more marketable than

you thought. Many planets in your 5th house make beautiful aspects to your financial planet, Saturn.

It is a good financial month too. The only rub is that Saturn went retrograde on the 25th of last month and will be retrograde for many more months. Earnings are happening – more than usual – but they happen with delays and complications. You can reduce problems by being more mindful in your financial affairs. If you're online be careful of how you click the mouse – you might be duplicating your order. When you write a cheque make sure it's dated and signed properly. Take care over the little things – it could save much heartache later on.

Many planets in the 5th house make people more speculative and risk taking – especially in finance. But with Saturn retrograde (and Mars going retrograde on the 17th) this is not advisable.

Health is excellent this month. Most of the planets are in harmonious aspect with you. You can enhance it further through foot massage until the 5th and through scalp and face massage afterwards. Mars moved into your sign on March 5 and will be there for the entire month. This too is good for health. It gives courage and the 'can do' spirit. You excel in sports and exercise regimes. You have a happier demeanour (Saturn in your sign has made you very serious). This happy-go-lucky spirit is good for the love life. There is a happy romantic meeting between the 15th and 16th. But love is good from the 6th onwards. There are love opportunities at work or as you pursue your health goals.

May

Best Days Overall: 4, 5, 12, 13, 22, 23, 31
Most Stressful Days Overall: 1, 2, 3, 7, 8, 14, 15, 29, 30
Best Days for Love: 6, 7, 8, 14, 15, 24, 25, 26, 27
Best Days for Money: 4, 5, 6, 12, 13, 14, 15, 22, 23, 24, 25, 31
Best Days for Career: 6, 14, 15, 24, 25

Mars, still in your own sign until the 27th, complicates the social life – which is becoming ever stronger (most of the planets are in the social Western sector). Mars can make a person too self-willed, too impatient and prone to anger. What is needed are the social skills and Mars is not noted for that. Use your extra energy to be helpful to others. If someone angers you, take a few deep breaths before answering.

Last month on the 19th your 6th house of health and work became powerful and this is the case until the 20th of this month. If you're a job seeker, this is an excellent month – especially on the 10th and 11th. Sagittarians are not detail oriented. They hate the minutiae of life. They like looking at the 'big picture' and doing the important things. Yet, drab detail has to be handled, and this is a good month for it. Not only is your 6th house of work strong, but we will have a Grand Trine in the Earth signs all month. This too fosters more practicality.

The focus on health until the 20th will stand you in good stead after that date, when health becomes more delicate. Enhance the health through throat and neck massage until the 24th and through arm and shoulder massage afterwards. Spiritual healing is very effective on the 13th and 14th.

Sometimes we are at the gym or spa and romance happens – these are the kinds of aspects you have this month. You could be doing some mundane job, and someone beautiful is there. Office romances are also seen here. But Mercury is retrograde until the 20th so there can be delays and complications in love. The social judgement is not up to par either. Things improve after the 20th, however, when the love planet moves forward again and the Sun enters your 7th house of love. You begin a yearly love and social peak. The 22nd to the 25th is especially good for romance.

Mars has one of his solstices from the 7th to the 14th. He pauses in the heavens during that period and then changes direction. This is the story of children and children figures in your life. They pause for a while and change their direction in life. It also shows what happens in your creative life.

Jupiter, the ruler of your Horoscope, has been in retrograde motion since January 9. This month on the 9th he starts moving forward again. You have direction. There is more self-confidence and self-esteem. You're starting to move forward in life. Your goals are clear.

June

Best Days Overall: 1, 8, 9, 18, 19, 27, 28
Most Stressful Days Overall: 4, 5, 10, 11, 12, 25, 26
Best Days for Love: 2, 3, 4, 5, 12, 13, 14, 23, 24, 25, 26
Best Days for Money: 1, 2, 3, 8, 9, 10, 11, 18, 19, 20, 21, 22, 27, 28, 29, 30
Best Days for Career: 2, 3, 10, 11, 12, 13, 23, 24

Now that Mars is out of your sign for a while, the love and social life should go much better. You're still in a yearly love and social peak until the 21st. Mercury, your love planet, is moving forward as well. You have good social confidence and many social opportunities. Singles have many romantic opportunities – perhaps too many. Saturn in your sign is still a complication. You may be coming over as cold, distant and too business-like in your relationships. Make it a point to project love and warmth to others.

The planetary power shifts this month, and this represents a psychological shift for you. Now, from the 3rd onwards, the upper half of your Horoscope starts to become stronger. It is morning in your year. Time to be up and about and handling the affairs of the outer world. Time to let go of home and family issues for a while and focus on your career. You won't be able to completely ignore domestic responsibilities, but you can shift more attention to the career. You're still in a very successful year.

This is a month where we have many 'mini-eclipses' happening. Transiting planets are re-activating eclipse points. The Sun re-activates eclipse points on the 8th, 9th, 23rd and 24th. If you're travelling, try to schedule your trips around those days. There could be dramas in your place of worship or school. On the 8th and 9th Venus also re-activates an eclipse point. This can bring health scares or turbulence in your job, signalling a new direction at work and in your health regime. Venus has one of her solstices at the same time that the Sun is having his – from the 19th to the 23rd. So pause from work – do what's required but no extra. A change of direction is about to happen.

Mercury re-activates an eclipse point on the 23rd and 24th. This can complicate the love life. The spouse, partner or current love can be more temperamental. More patience is required.

The Summer Solstice of the 21st is another good time to pause and reflect. This is especially true for students. A change of direction in their studies is happening. It is also good to review your religious and philosophical beliefs. A change of direction is happening here too.

Health improves after the 21st. In the meantime you can enhance the health through arm and shoulder massage until the 18th, and through right diet afterwards. Until the 18th health problems are probably coming from social discord. Restore harmony here as quickly as you can.

July

Best Days Overall: 6, 7, 15, 16, 24, 25
Most Stressful Days Overall: 1, 2, 8, 9, 22, 23, 29, 30
Best Days for Love: 1, 2, 3, 4, 14, 15, 24, 25, 29, 30
Best Days for Money: 6, 7, 8, 9, 15, 16, 18, 19, 24, 25, 27, 28
Best Days for Career: 3, 4, 8, 9, 14, 15, 24, 25

The career is going very well and will get even better next month. Many of you are at lifetime career highs. Your personal appearance and overall demeanour are extremely important here. Family might feel a lack of your attention, but career should be the focus now. A family member – it looks like a parent or parent figure – feels this sense of lack or of deprivation. He or she lacks direction at the moment and this is not helping matters.

Your financial planet Saturn has been retrograde for many months and this continues this month. There is much prosperity happening in July, but it comes with glitches and delays. You just need more patience. The spouse, partner or current love is also prospering this month – he or she is in a yearly financial peak. The beloved is likely to be more generous and supportive.

Your 8th house of transformation became powerful on the 21st of last month and is still powerful until July 22. Thus you're in a very good period for weight loss or detox regimes. This is an excellent time to get rid of the needless – the effete – things in your life, whether they be possessions, or mental or emotional patterns. This is a time to reinvent yourself, to resurrect yourself, to give birth to the person you want to be. But before new birth can happen, the old you has to die.

Health is good this month and will get even better after the 22nd. Detox regimes enhance the health until the 12th. After the 12th give more attention to the heart.

Mercury, your love planet, re-stimulates an eclipse point on the 1st and 2nd. This can produce some crisis or drama in love. And perhaps this is the reason why you're moving outside your normal sphere socially – from the 1st to the 9th. Mercury is 'out of bounds' during that period.

On the 22nd the Sun enters your 9th house – your favourite house. The cosmos impels you to do what you most love – to travel, expand your mind and deepen your theological and philosophical understanding. A good, juicy theological discussion can be more interesting than a night out on the town just now. And the visit of a guru or spiritual teacher more of an event than that of a rock star.

This is a wonderful time for college or post-graduate level students. The chart shows success in their studies. They are highly motivated.

August

Best Days Overall: 2, 3, 12, 13, 21, 22, 29, 30
Most Stressful Days Overall: 4, 5, 19, 20, 25, 26, 31
Best Days for Love: 3, 4, 5, 14, 15, 23, 24, 25, 26, 31
Best Days for Money: 2, 3, 4, 5, 12, 13, 14, 15, 21, 22, 23, 24, 29, 30, 31
Best Days for Career: 4, 5, 14, 15, 23, 24, 31

An active, frenetic, but very successful month, Sagittarius. Your main challenge will be to maintain high energy levels in the midst of all the activity – especially from the 22nd onwards. It's great to succeed – and this is happening – but not at the expense of your health. You can manage to have both if you keep your focus on the essentials and let go of trivia. You can also enhance the health by paying more attention to the heart until the 5th, and to the small intestine afterwards. Eating right is important after the 5th.

You are still in travel mode this month. Until the 22nd there is pleasure travel, although afterwards it seems related to the career.

The career is enhanced by your willingness to travel, and also by your willingness to mentor others. Your good work ethic is important from the 5th onwards. Your social contacts and likeability are also important this month. It is not enough to be competent in what you do, you must also be able to get on with others.

Mars moves back into your sign on the 2nd. On the one hand this gives you more energy and drive – something you need this month. You get things done in a hurry. However, as our regular readers undoubtedly know, Mars is not noted for his social skills. This can create problems if you're not careful. Watch the temper as well.

Neptune, your family planet, is, like last month, still conjunct to the Moon's South Node. There is a feeling of deficiency in the home and in family members. Perhaps they feel neglected. A parent or parent figure feels this especially – and feels low self-esteem.

Finances are still excellent until the 23rd. There is a lot of financial help available and a lot of support. Perhaps the most important development this month is that Saturn finally moves forward after many months of retrograde motion. This happens on the 13th. There is more financial clarity and direction now. The financial judgement is sharper. After the 23rd, finances are more stressful. It seems that your focus on the career is distracting you from money issues. Basically you just have to work harder to achieve your financial goals than usual. The stresses are short term.

Your love planet, Mercury, spends the month in your 10th house of career. This shows many things. Love is high on your agenda and you're paying attention. Singles have romantic opportunities as they pursue their career goals and with people involved in the career. Much of the socializing this month is career related (office, company or industry events). And, you're attracted to people of high status and prestige.

September

Best Days Overall: 8, 9, 17, 18, 25, 26, 27
Most Stressful Days Overall: 1, 2, 15, 16, 21, 22, 28, 29
Best Days for Love: 1, 2, 3, 4, 10, 11, 12, 13, 14, 19, 20, 21, 22, 23, 28, 29
Best Days for Money: 1, 2, 8, 9, 10, 11, 12, 13, 19, 20, 21, 25, 26, 27
Best Days for Career: 1, 2, 10, 11, 12, 19, 20, 28, 29

Another busy and hectic kind of month, with two eclipses just to add to the stress. Make sure you get enough rest this month. Try to spend more time at a health spa or schedule more massages. Keep the focus on the essentials in your life and let trivial matters go.

You can enhance the health through hip massage until the 22nd and through detoxes after that date. You respond well to spiritual healing after the 22nd too.

The solar eclipse on the 1st occurs in your 10th house of career. Career is in full bloom right now but this eclipse indicates changes in your industry, company or profession. You will in all probability take a new approach to the career. There are dramatic events too in the lives of parents, parent figures and bosses. Students make important changes to educational plans – often they change schools or courses. There are dramas in your place of worship and in the lives of worship leaders. This eclipse – a strong one – also impacts on Mars and Saturn. Thus there are financial dramas, disturbance and important changes. Children and children figures should take it easy over this period, as life-changing dramas in their lives are indicated for them too.

The lunar eclipse of the 16th also affects you strongly. Spend more quiet time at home over this period. This eclipse occurs in your 4th house of home and family and brings family dramas and upheavals. Be more patient with family members and especially with a parent or parent figure. If there are still flaws in the home not dealt with by the eclipses of March you find out about them now. The dream life is not very reliable this period, and it is probably disturbing. This happens because the emotional plane of the planets is all disturbed and all kinds of negative images and feelings abound. Every lunar eclipse impacts on the finances of the spouse, partner or current love and this one is no different. A financial crisis or disturbance forces a re-evaluation of the financial strategy and planning.

Aside from the eclipses there's another major event this month. Jupiter, the ruler of your Horoscope, changes signs, moving from your 10th house into your 11th. This shows a new direction in your personal life and goals. Career has been important – and successful – all year (and it is still successful this month). But your interest is waning. By the 22nd, your major career goals have largely been achieved, and even if they have not been completely achieved good progress towards them has been made. Now you want to enjoy the fruits of career success – the fellowship and friendships of those you meet at the top.

October

> Best Days Overall: 5, 6, 7, 15, 23, 24
> Most Stressful Days Overall: 12, 13, 19, 25, 26
> Best Days for Love: 3, 4, 10, 12, 13, 18, 19, 20, 23, 24, 30
> Best Days for Money: 1, 5, 6, 8, 9, 10, 15, 18, 19, 23, 24, 27, 28
> Best Days for Career: 10, 19, 20, 25, 26, 30

In late August the planetary power began to shift to the East. This means that the planetary power is flowing towards you rather than away from you. Very soon – in the next two months – the planets will approach their maximum Eastern position. Thus personal power and personal independence are approaching their maximum. This should be used to your advantage. Now it is much easier to make the changes you need to make in your life, to change conditions to the way you want them to be. You have the power and the direction, now that Jupiter is moving forward. Now is time to create your personal nirvana. There's no need to adapt or compromise now. The world will adapt to you rather than vice versa.

Your 11th house of friends became very strong last month on the 22nd. It is still strong until the 23rd. So this is a social kind of month. New and important friendships are being made. Rather than being a boss – which you have been all year – you are a friend. You project this image. People see you this way and it makes you more popular. This is a great period for being involved with groups and organizations. There are even romantic opportunities that happen in group settings. (The 11th and 12th seem especially good.) This is a month where fondest hopes and wishes come to pass. The rest of the year – and well into next year – will also be like this. This is also a very good period for expanding your knowledge of science, computers, technology and astrology. Many people have their first introduction to astrology when their 11th house is strong.

If you have children of marriageable age, there is romance happening for them. Marriage could happen in the coming year.

A parent or parent figure is prospering now. You seem very involved with it.

Health is much improved over last month. You can enhance it further through spiritual healing techniques until the 18th. Detoxing is also effective. After the 18th Venus moves into your own sign. You look healthy and others see you this way. There is beauty and glamour to the image. You're warmer to others, more approachable too. The love life should be better.

Finances are also much improved this month. Jupiter and other short-term planets have moved away from their stressful aspect to your finance planet, Saturn. Earnings are increasing and happening in much easier ways. You seem personally more comfortable with the way you earn.

Though career is less important now, there are happy career successes and opportunities on the 11th and 12th.

November

Best Days Overall: 2, 3, 11, 12, 19, 20, 29, 30
Most Stressful Days Overall: 9, 10, 15, 16, 21, 22, 23
Best Days for Love: 1, 2, 3, 10, 13, 15, 16, 19, 20, 21, 22, 29, 30
Best Days for Money: 2, 3, 4, 5, 6, 7, 11, 12, 15, 16, 19, 20, 24, 25, 29, 30
Best Days for Career: 1, 10, 19, 20, 21, 22, 23, 29, 30

Last month on the 23rd your 12th house of spirituality became powerful and remains so until the 22nd. This is a time for spiritual breakthroughs. It is a time for spiritual studies and spiritual practice. Most of the problems that people face, though they might think of them as social, financial or health issues, are in reality spiritual and theological problems. Thus when understanding comes – when a breakthrough happens – all these other things tend to fall into place. This is your situation now. Get right spiritually – get in good connection with the Divine within you – and everything else will just straighten out. You understand this instinctively, Sagittarius, but this is a time to put it into practice.

When the 12th house is strong the urge is to transcend the world, to transcend the body and to rise above physical conditions and circumstances. It is through this 'rising above' that problems get solved. It gives a higher perspective on things. It is like looking at the world from the air rather than from the ground. This requires a kind of 'withdrawal' from the world and it becomes normal to desire more solitude and seclusion. Have no fear; you're not becoming a hermit or a recluse. By the 22nd you will be back in your body, back in the world and enjoying yourself fully. The insights you've gained will be incorporated into your physical condition.

On the 22nd the planetary power will be at its maximum Eastern position. Your personal power and independence are at their maximum. Keep in mind our discussion of this last month.

On the 22nd you enter a yearly personal pleasure peak. Life is fun and you're enjoying it to the fullest. All the pleasures of the body are open to you. You look good. There is much confidence and great self-esteem. Most likely you'll be travelling. There are happy educational opportunities, and college students get good news at school. Those seeking entry to college have wonderful opportunities.

The love life is sweet this month too. On the 12th your love planet enters your sign. Love pursues you. You have love on your terms. If you are in a relationship the beloved puts you first. It is a harmonious kind of month.

Venus has been in your sign since October 18 and will be there until the 12th. This not only enhances the personal appearance but brings happy job opportunities. And, there's not much you need to do – they find you. Happy career opportunities are also coming.

December

Best Days Overall: 8, 9, 16, 17, 26, 27
Most Stressful Days Overall: 6, 7, 12, 13, 19, 20
Best Days for Love: 2, 3, 10, 11, 12, 13, 19, 20, 21, 22, 29, 30
Best Days for Money: 1, 2, 3, 4, 5, 8, 9, 12, 13, 16, 17, 21, 22, 26,
    27, 29, 30, 31
Best Days for Career: 10, 11, 19, 20, 29, 30

You're still very much in a happy period, still in a yearly personal pleasure peak. The body and personal appearance shine. You exude star quality and unbridled optimism. There is prosperity happening too as Saturn receives much positive stimulation. (This was the case last month as well.) Earnings are increasing and financial windfalls happen. On the 21st, as the Sun enters your money house, you begin a yearly financial peak. But you will feel the effects of this even before that date.

Your love planet, Mercury, is 'out of bounds' from the 1st to the 17th. This shows that you're looking for love outside your normal sphere. For those of you in relationships it indicates socializing – attending parties or events – outside your normal sphere. (Venus is also 'out of bounds' from the 1st to the 3rd and this reinforces what we are saying.)

Mercury's 'out of bounds' condition also impacts on the career. Opportunities come from 'out of the way' places and 'out of the way' people. Bosses can make demands that are outside the norm. A parent or parent figure is outside his or her natural sphere.

Health is excellent this month (and last month too). You have all the energy you need to achieve whatever you want to achieve. If you like, you can enhance the health further through back and knee massage until the 7th and through ankle and calf massage afterwards. Until the 7th you're pretty conservative in health matters and you gravitate to orthodox kinds of therapies. However, after the 7th you become more experimental.

Last month on the 22nd the planetary power began to shift to the lower half of your Horoscope. Career goals have been mostly attained – the short-term ones anyway – and now it is time to begin to focus on the family, the home and your emotional wellness. Your busy outer life could have pulled you away from your point of emotional harmony and now it's time to get back to it. When the lower half of the Horoscope is dominant we are in the night time of our year. We don't ignore career or outer objectives but we approach them in a different way – an inner kind of way; we dream, we visualize, we get into the mood and feeling of what we want to achieve. We are acting, but in an interior rather than exterior way.

Jupiter, the ruler of your Horoscope, opposes Uranus from the 19th onwards. Drive more carefully then. Be more patient with neighbours and siblings (there seems to be some conflict here). Try to avoid arguments.

Capricorn

♑

THE GOAT

Birthdays from
21st December to
19th January

Personality Profile

CAPRICORN AT A GLANCE

Element – Earth

Ruling Planet – Saturn
  Career Planet – Venus
  Love Planet – Moon
  Money Planet – Uranus
  Planet of Communications – Neptune
  Planet of Health and Work – Mercury
  Planet of Home and Family Life – Mars
  Planet of Spirituality – Jupiter

Colours – black, indigo

Colours that promote love, romance and social harmony – puce, silver

Colour that promotes earning power – ultramarine blue

Gem – black onyx

Metal – lead

Scents – magnolia, pine, sweet pea, wintergreen

Quality – cardinal (= activity)

Qualities most needed for balance – warmth, spontaneity, a sense of fun

Strongest virtues – sense of duty, organization, perseverance, patience, ability to take the long-term view

Deepest needs – to manage, take charge and administrate

Characteristics to avoid – pessimism, depression, undue materialism and undue conservatism

Signs of greatest overall compatibility – Taurus, Virgo

Signs of greatest overall incompatibility – Aries, Cancer, Libra

Sign most helpful to career – Libra

Sign most helpful for emotional support – Aries

Sign most helpful financially – Aquarius

Sign best for marriage and/or partnerships – Cancer

Sign most helpful for creative projects – Taurus

Best Sign to have fun with – Taurus

Signs most helpful in spiritual matters – Virgo, Sagittarius

Best day of the week – Saturday

Understanding a Capricorn

The virtues of Capricorns are such that there will always be people for and against them. Many admire them, many dislike them. Why? It seems to be because of Capricorn's power urges. A well-developed Capricorn has his or her eyes set on the heights of power, prestige and authority. In the sign of Capricorn, ambition is not a fatal flaw, but rather the highest virtue.

Capricorns are not frightened by the resentment their authority may sometimes breed. In Capricorn's cool, calculated, organized mind all the dangers are already factored into the equation – the unpopularity, the animosity, the misunderstandings, even the outright slander – and a plan is always in place for dealing with these things in the most effi-cient way. To the Capricorn, situations that would terrify an ordinary mind are merely problems to be managed, bumps on the road to ever-growing power, effectiveness and prestige.

Some people attribute pessimism to the Capricorn sign, but this is a bit deceptive. It is true that Capricorns like to take into account the negative side of things. It is also true that they love to imagine the worst possible scenario in every undertaking. Other people might find such analyses depressing, but Capricorns only do these things so that they can formulate a way out – an escape route.

Capricorns will argue with success. They will show you that you are not doing as well as you think you are. Capricorns do this to them-selves as well as to others. They do not mean to discourage you but rather to root out any impediments to your greater success. A Capricorn boss or supervisor feels that no matter how good the performance there is always room for improvement. This explains why Capricorn supervisors are difficult to handle and even infuriating at times. Their actions are, however, quite often effective – they can get their subordi-nates to improve and become better at their jobs.

Capricorn is a born manager and administrator. Leo is better at being king or queen, but Capricorn is better at being prime minister – the person actually wielding power.

Capricorn is interested in the virtues that last, in the things that will stand the test of time and trials of circumstance. Temporary fads and fashions mean little to a Capricorn – except as things to be used for profit or power. Capricorns apply this attitude to business, love, to their thinking and even to their philosophy and religion.

Finance

Capricorns generally attain wealth and they usually earn it. They are willing to work long and hard for what they want. They are quite amenable to forgoing a short-term gain in favour of long-term benefits. Financially, they come into their own later in life.

However, if Capricorns are to attain their financial goals they must shed some of their strong conservatism. Perhaps this is the least desirable trait of the Capricorn. They can resist anything new merely because it is new and untried. They are afraid of experimentation. Capricorns need to be willing to take a few risks. They should be more eager to market new products or explore different managerial techniques. Otherwise, progress will leave them behind. If necessary, Capricorns must be ready to change with the times, to discard old methods that no longer work.

Very often this experimentation will mean that Capricorns have to break with existing authority. They might even consider changing their present position or starting their own ventures. If so, they should be willing to accept all the risks and just get on with it. Only then will a Capricorn be on the road to the highest financial gains.

Career and Public Image

A Capricorn's ambition and quest for power are evident. It is perhaps the most ambitious sign of the zodiac – and usually the most successful in a worldly sense. However, there are lessons Capricorns need to learn in order to fulfil their highest aspirations.

Intelligence, hard work, cool efficiency and organization will take them a certain distance, but will not carry them to the very top. Capricorns need to cultivate their social graces, to develop a social style, along with charm and an ability to get along with people. They need to bring beauty into their lives and to cultivate the right social contacts. They must learn to wield power gracefully, so that people love them for it – a very delicate art. They also need to learn how to bring people together in order to fulfil certain objectives. In short, Capricorns require some of the gifts – the social graces – of Libra to get to the top.

Once they have learned this, Capricorns will be successful in their careers. They are ambitious, hard workers who are not afraid of putting in the required time and effort. Capricorns take their time in getting the job done – in order to do it well – and they like moving up the corporate ladder slowly but surely. Being so driven by success, Capricorns are generally liked by their bosses, who respect and trust them.

Love and Relationships

Like Scorpio and Pisces, Capricorn is a difficult sign to get to know. They are deep, introverted and like to keep their own counsel. Capricorns do not like to reveal their innermost thoughts. If you are in love with a Capricorn, be patient and take your time. Little by little you will get to understand him or her.

Capricorns have a deep romantic nature, but they do not show it straightaway. They are cool, matter of fact and not especially emotional. They will often show their love in practical ways.

It takes time for a Capricorn – male or female – to fall in love. They are not the love-at-first-sight kind. If a Capricorn is involved with a Leo or Aries, these Fire types will be totally mystified – to them the Capricorn will seem cold, unfeeling, unaffectionate and not very spontaneous. Of course none of this is true; it is just that Capricorn likes to take things slowly. They like to be sure of their ground before making any demonstrations of love or commitment.

Even in love affairs Capricorns are deliberate. They need more time to make decisions than is true of the other signs of the zodiac, but given this time they become just as passionate. Capricorns like a relationship to be structured, committed, well regulated, well defined, predictable and even routine. They prefer partners who are nurturers, and they in turn like to nurture their partners. This is their basic psychology. Whether such a relationship is good for them is another issue altogether. Capricorns have enough routine in their lives as it is. They might be better off in relationships that are a bit more stimulating, changeable and fluctuating.

Home and Domestic Life

The home of a Capricorn – as with a Virgo – is going to be tidy and well organized. Capricorns tend to manage their families in the same way they manage their businesses. Capricorns are often so career-driven that they find little time for the home and family. They should try to get more actively involved in their family and domestic life. Capricorns do, however, take their children very seriously and are very proud parents – particularly should their children grow up to become respected members of society.

Horoscope for 2016

Major Trends

When Saturn, the ruler of your Horoscope, entered your 12th house late in 2014 you entered a highly spiritual period in your life. Capricorn, by nature, is outer oriented, down to earth and practical. The inner life is not that appealing to them. Yet last year and this year, you're more involved with this. You're becoming much deeper as a person.

Pluto has been in your sign for many years now and will be here for many years to come. This shows a detoxification of the body, the image and the self-concept. Your old ways of thinking of yourself – your old ego structure – is crumbling, getting purified, and being reborn into something better. You're giving birth to the ideal body and image. More on this later.

Neptune, the most spiritual of the planets, has been in your 3rd house of communication since 2012, refining and spiritualizing the mental faculties. Your taste in reading is becoming more elevated. You gravitate to spiritual-type books and magazines, to poetry and inspired kinds of writing. This is a long-term trend.

Uranus has been in your 4th house for many years too – the long-term planets are pretty much where they have been for the last few years. This indicates drama and turmoil in the family circle. Perhaps break-ups. The emotional life tends to be unstable. Your challenge is to maintain some semblance of emotional harmony in the midst of all the turmoil. Meditation will be a big help here.

Jupiter has been in your 9th house since August of last year, and will stay there until September 9. This shows many things. There is more foreign travel in your life. Students, either at college level or about to enter college, have a successful year. There is good news and good fortune in these matters.

Jupiter will cross your Mid-heaven and enter your 10th house on September 10, inaugurating the beginning of a very strong career cycle. There is much success, elevation and recognition happening in the career.

Your areas of greatest interest are: the body, image and personal pleasure; communication and intellectual interests; home and family; religion, philosophy, higher education and travel (until September 9); and career (from September 10 onwards).

Your paths of greatest fulfilment this year will be religion, philosophy, higher education and travel; and career.

Health

(Please note that this is an astrological perspective on health and not a medical one. In days of yore there was no difference, these perspectives were identical. But now there could be quite a difference. For a medical perspective, please consult your doctor or health practitioner.)

Two long-term planets (strong ones too) are in stressful alignment with you at the start of the year, and after September 10, it will be three long-term planets stressing you. So health needs more watching this year. By themselves these planets are stressful enough, but when the short-term planets join the picture, the vulnerability is increased. This year the most vulnerable periods are from March 21 to April 19, June 21 to July 23 and September 23 to October 23 (this last period will be when you're at your most vulnerable during the year).

Your 6th house of health is not powerful this year. This can lead to a lack of attention here, and this is a problem. You may have to force yourself to pay attention even when you don't feel like it. It will not be a good idea to ignore the health this year or to take it for granted.

The good news is that there's much you can do to enhance health and prevent problems from developing. The first line of defence is always to maintain high energy levels. The spiritual immune system, the aura, weakens when energy is too low. So, a simple solution is to rest and relax more. Pace yourself. Focus on the essentials in your life and let frivolities go.

Also give more attention to the following areas – the vulnerable areas of your chart. Their reflexology points are shown in the following chart.

- The heart. This has only become important in recent years. Worry and anxiety are said (by spiritual healers) to be the root cause of heart problems. Avoid this. Learn to relax under stress.
- The spine, knees, teeth, bones, skin and overall skeletal alignment. These areas are always important for a Capricorn. Regular back and knee massage is always beneficial, as are regular visits to a chiropractor or osteopath. Make sure the vertebrae are in proper alignment. Regular dental cleanings and check-ups are good. If you're out in the sun use a good sun screen.

Important foot reflexology points for the year ahead
Try to massage all of the foot on a regular basis – the top of the foot as well as the bottom – but pay extra attention to the points highlighted on the chart. When you massage, be aware of 'sore spots' as these need special attention. It's also a good idea to massage the ankles and below them.

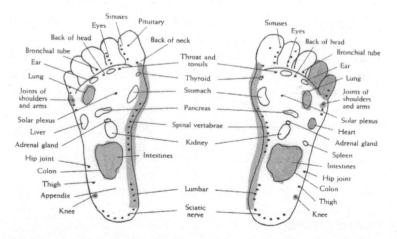

- The lungs, small intestine, arms, shoulders and respiratory system. These areas too are always important for a Capricorn. Regular arm and shoulder massage is always good.

Most of the time, this special attention will prevent problems from developing. But even in cases where problems can't be totally prevented (due to strong karmic momentum) they can be eased to a great extent.

Mercury, your health planet, is a fast-moving planet, as our regular readers know. During the course of a year he will move through all the signs and houses of your Horoscope. Thus there are many short-term trends in health that depend on where he is and the aspects he receives. These are best dealt with in the monthly reports.

Mercury will go into retrograde motion four times this year – usually it is only three. Thus there tends to be more uncertainty about health matters than usual. Major changes to the health regime will need more research and homework than usual.

Home and Family

Home and family has been turbulent for some years now. Never a dull moment. Always some kind of surprising drama unfolding. There have been many break-ups in the family unit in recent years, many shake-ups and many moves. There have also been many renovations of the home.

The good news here is that things are less turbulent than they have been. This area still requires your attention, but the intensity of the strife and turmoil is much reduced.

With Uranus in the 4th house you never know where you stand with family members or with a parent or parent figure. You can be in total harmony with each other one minute and at each other's throat the next. Mood changes, both personal and in family members, are swift, extreme and bewildering.

Family has been called a 'womb and a tomb'* – it is both at the same time. It is a womb in that it's a protective mechanism, a survival mechanism of nature. A foetus will not survive without the womb.

---

* *Isidore Friedman*

However, when it is time to emerge from the womb, the foetus *must* come out. This coming out involves much pain. Childbirth is painful and disruptive. But if the foetus doesn't emerge, the previous womb becomes a tomb. Many of you are facing this 'womb-tomb' dilemma these days with the family. If you don't emerge, it is death (a psychological kind of death), but emerging is painful and disruptive.

Uranus is your financial planet. His position in the 4th house shows much spending on the home and family. The needs of the family are good financial motivators. But it also shows someone who earns money from home – perhaps through a home office or home-based business. It shows that family and family connections are important financially.

Uranus in the 4th house shows a constant upgrading of the home. In a sense we could compare it to upgrading your computer and software. It is done with regularity. As soon as you finish one upgrade, another more alluring one appears. Every time you think that the home is perfect, a new idea comes, and you make it more perfect. This is why there are often multiple moves under this aspect. No sooner do you find your dream home than another more alluring dream home is seen.

This transit also shows that you're making the home more 'high tech' – you're installing all kinds of new gadgetry in the home.

The marriage of the parents or parent figures has been tested for some years now and this continues in the year ahead. Divorce and separations here wouldn't be a surprise. One of them has a passion for personal freedom these days and this will stress a marriage. He or she seems very rebellious and difficult to handle. The other parent figure begins to prosper from September 10 onwards. He or she has also been making major repairs in the home.

Siblings and sibling figures have a static, stable kind of year. Likewise, children and children figures. Grandchildren (if you have them) shouldn't move this year.

Construction and renovations to the home could happen any time this year, but if you have free will in the matter, September 10–27 would be a good time. If you're redecorating or otherwise beautifying the home, March 20 to April 30 seems a good time (this too could happen at any time, but if you have some free will, this period is best).

Finance and Career

Practical Capricorn is always interested in finance, but this year less so than usual. Career will be more important than mere money. And there's logic to this. Career success tends to lead to more money, although not always right away.

Your money house is empty for the most part this year, with only short-term, fast-moving planets transiting through here. This shows a stable kind of financial year. You seem content with things as they are and want to continue along the same lines. However, it does also show a tendency to take earnings for granted. It shows a lack of attention. If financial problems arise, this is probably the reason. Give finance the attention it deserves.

Many of the financial trends that we've written about in previous years are still very much in effect.

Uranus, your financial planet, has been in Aries, your 4th house, for many years. This shows a desire to be financially independent, a need to be in control of your own financial destiny. This aspect is not so good for partnerships or joint ventures. It also shows an affinity for 'start-ups' – new businesses. If you work for others, you gravitate to start-ups. But it also shows that you are starting your own new venture – or are involved in a new venture.

Uranus favours the high tech field – the online world, online businesses or online activities. You spend on technology, but it's a good investment. You earn more than you spend. Those of you who invest will have a special affinity for the technology sector of the market, and especially for technology start-ups.

Uranus is also associated with new inventions. This often suggests that you're involved with your own new invention or with the invention of another.

The financial life is certainly more exciting with Uranus as your financial planet, Capricorn. There's never a dull moment. Earnings and earnings opportunities can happen at any time and in any place, and often when you least expect it. A family member who a minute ago was at your throat can suddenly open the wallet or bring you a financial opportunity.

Uranus in your 4th house shows that you're earning money from home, as we have mentioned. But it also shows earning money from real estate (residential or commercial), restaurants, the food business, hotels or motels. Industries that cater to the home are good too, either for jobs, or businesses or investments.

Jupiter crosses your Mid-heaven on September 10, as we mentioned. This indicates career success. It shows promotions (but not necessarily pay rises), honours and the expansion of your career horizons. It is interesting that you could receive more honour and recognition because of your charitable and philanthropic activities than because of your professional achievements.

Being involved with charities and good causes will enhance the career and be noticed by the powers that be. In addition, important career contacts or other opportunities can come via these things.

Love and Social Life

The year ahead is an excellent social year, but it is not a romantic kind of year. Your 7th house of love is empty for the most part (only short-term, fast-moving planets will move through there), while your 1st house of self is powerful. Most of the long-term planets are in the independent, Eastern sector of your chart (and this trend will get even more pronounced after September 10). So partnerships and love relationships are not a big issue. The year ahead is more about personal independence than about romance.

Generally this shows a love year that tends to the status quo. Married couples tend to stay married and singles tend to stay single. There is nothing against love, if you want it, but nothing that especially supports it. You'll have to work harder this year to attain romantic goals.

Socially, the headline is about friendships. This is a happy area. Jupiter is making beautiful aspects to Pluto, your planet of friends. This shows that new and important friends are made. Also that friends – good ones – are seeking you out. You don't have to run after them. These friends seem very devoted to you as well. They are there for you.

The area of friendship has been turbulent in recent years. Many friends have had life-altering experiences and major dramas. But life seems quieter in the year ahead.

Jupiter, your spiritual planet, is involved in your friendships. This indicates spiritual-type friends (which makes sense as you're in a spiritual kind of year) and the meeting of new and significant people at charity, altruistic or spiritual kinds of events and functions.

The Moon is your love planet. She is the fastest-moving of all the planets and in any given month she will move through the entire Horoscope – all the signs and all the houses. Thus love and social opportunities can come in a variety of ways and in a variety of places. It all depends on where the Moon is and the kinds of aspects she receives. These short-term trends are best discussed in the monthly reports.

In general we can say that your love and social magnetism are strongest on the New and Full Moons and when the Moon is waxing.

The marriage of parents and parent figures is stressed, as we have mentioned. Siblings or sibling figures in your life who are single have love this year – and it seems happy. Marriage or a relationship that is like a marriage is likely. Children and children figures in your life have a good romantic year – if they are of appropriate age. A serious relationship and perhaps even marriage is likely. Even younger children will be having a happy social life.

Self-improvement

Pluto in your 1st house is wonderful for weight loss and detox regimes, as we have mentioned. It also tends to cosmetic surgeries. Saturn in your 12th house gives us other messages. Since last year, you have been receiving revelation on spiritual methods to change the body and the appearance, through meditation, visualization and diet. These methods, though slower, might be better than cosmetic surgery. (But sometimes the cosmetic surgery is the side effect of these methods.)

The body was designed to be subservient to the mind and the spirit. It doesn't really have a will of its own. It often seems that way to us because of mis-identity. But when one puts the focus of attention in the right place – the Divine – the body will naturally reflect the health, beauty and radiance that it was originally designed to reflect.

Remaking and remoulding the physical body is a valid spiritual path this year. Much new knowledge and insight will be gained in the process. Much worldly-oriented rubbish will be removed as well.

You're giving birth to your ideal body and image these days. This is a long-term project that has been going on for many years and will continue for many more to come. Be patient. It won't happen overnight. But as you persist you'll see steady progress.

The emotional life, as we mentioned, has been turbulent and unstable. The cosmic energy has an agenda here. You're being forced to move to a place that is above the emotional level. The emotional level is only one aspect of who you are, you're much more than that. As you're able to view these things from a higher perspective, they will have less and less power over you. You will no longer be the victim of moods – high or low – but the observer and (eventually) the master of them.

Emotional stability will not only help in your family life, but also in your finances. Capricorns are basically practical people with sound financial judgement. But ever since your financial planet has moved into your 4th house, moods have been playing an undue role in your finances. In a good mood you feel rich. In a bad mood, the world is coming to an end. These moods can affect the financial judgement and lead to mistakes. In a good mood, you'll tend to overspend; in a low mood, however, you might pass up a good financial or investment opportunity. Strive for emotional stability.

Month-by-month Forecasts

January

Best Days Overall: 9, 10, 17, 18, 26, 27
Most Stressful Days Overall: 1, 2, 3, 15, 16, 21, 22, 23, 29, 30
Best Days for Love: 6, 7, 8, 9, 10, 15, 16, 18, 21, 22, 23, 26, 29, 30
Best Days for Money: 6, 7, 9, 10, 11, 12, 15, 16, 17, 18, 26, 27
Best Days for Career: 1, 2, 3, 6, 7, 8, 15, 16, 26, 29, 30

Usually spring is considered the best time to start new businesses or ventures, but for you I like the next two months even better – from your birthday onwards. Many of you have already had your birthday. Thus many cosmic cycles are at play here supporting you. Your personal solar cycle is waxing (growing) from your birthday onwards. The universal solar cycle is waxing (since December 21). Perhaps most importantly, the planetary momentum is forward this month. All of this adds 'oomph' to your project. If you can also start your venture between the 10th to the 24th – as the Moon waxes – you'll have the optimum time for launching a new venture.

You begin your year with the planets in their most Eastern position. The planetary power is on you rather than on others, and you are at your maximum level of personal power and independence. You don't need to rely on others that much. You can go it alone if they don't approve. This is a time to create conditions that please you and to have life on your terms. Later on, this will be more difficult to do. Of course, others are always to be treated with respect. But so long as you're not harming anyone, by all means have things your own way.

You are in the midst of a yearly personal pleasure peak this month. It began last month on the 21st and continues until the 20th. A happy period. This is a time to enjoy all the pleasures of the body, to pamper yourself, to buy the clothing and accessories you need and to get the body and image in right shape.

Finances are stressful early in the month, until the 20th. You have to work harder for earnings. There are more challenges to deal with. But these things are of short duration. On the 20th, as the Sun enters your 2nd money house, you enter a yearly financial peak. There is prosperity and it will happen much more easily than before.

Though your 7th house of love is basically empty this month (only the Moon moves through there on the 21st, 22nd and 23rd) love looks good. For a start, you look good, and there is much personal dynamism and charisma. The opposite sex takes notice. Venus travels with Saturn on the 8th and 9th, bringing happy romantic opportunities – though they do not seem particularly serious. They probably won't lead to marriage, just fun. On the 24th Venus enters your own sign, further adding to your physical appeal.

Health is excellent all month.

February

Best Days Overall: 5, 6, 13, 14, 22, 23, 24
Most Stressful Days Overall: 11, 12, 18, 19, 25, 26
Best Days for Love: 5, 6, 7, 8, 13, 14, 17, 18, 19, 25, 27, 28
Best Days for Money: 2, 3, 5, 6, 7, 8, 11, 12, 13, 14, 20, 21, 22, 23, 24
Best Days for Career: 5, 6, 13, 14, 25, 26

As we mentioned last month, February is also an excellent month for starting a new business or venture. Ninety per cent of the planets are moving forward this month (many more than in the spring) and your personal and universal solar cycles are still in their growing phases. From the 8th to the 22nd would be the best time to kick start a new project, as this is when the Moon will also be waxing.

Capricorns are always ambitious, but now with most of the planets below the horizon the planetary power is moving away from your career and towards the home and family. Finance is still very important – you're still in the midst of a yearly financial peak – but career takes a back seat. In fact this is the kind of month – from the 17th onwards – where you measure career success in monetary terms. By this measure, the career is successful this month. This is a time for a low career profile. Focus on the things that make career success possible – emotional wellness, a stable home and family life.

The money rolls in this month. Happy job opportunities have been coming to you since the beginning of the year. There is another nice opportunity happening from the 5th to the 7th. (You could be travelling during that period too.) The Sun in your money house shows the financial support of the spouse, partner or current love. You're in a good period for paying down or making debt – depending on your need. Money can come from insurance claims, estates or tax refunds. Those of the appropriate age are doing estate planning now. Estate and tax issues are governing your financial decision-making. Even those of you not involved in estate planning or tax claims are being affected – the estate and tax planning of others is affecting your finances.

On the 17th Venus enters the money house. This shows 'happy money' – money that is earned in pleasurable ways. It also shows the financial favour of bosses, elders, parents or parent figures. They seem helpful this period. If you have issues with the government, this might be a good time to deal with them.

Health and energy are good this month. You can enhance it further by paying more attention to the spine, knees, teeth and bones until the 14th, and to the ankles and calves after the 14th. If you feel tired or under the weather after the 14th a new, experimental kind of therapy might just do the trick.

Love is more or less stable this month. Nothing special one way or another. It doesn't seem a major priority. Most of you are satisfied with the status quo.

March

Best Days Overall: 3, 4, 12, 13, 21, 22, 31
Most Stressful Days Overall: 10, 11, 16, 17, 23, 24
Best Days for Love: 6, 7, 8, 9, 16, 17, 26, 27, 28, 29
Best Days for Money: 1, 2, 3, 4, 6, 7, 10, 11, 12, 13, 18, 19, 21, 22, 28, 29, 31
Best Days for Career: 6, 7, 16, 23, 24, 26, 27

By now most short-term financial goals have been achieved and your interest shifts to the intellectual realm. The whole point of wealth is to give us the time and wherewithal to develop the mind. So the month ahead is good for taking courses (or teaching courses in your area of expertise), reading and catching up on all the letters, texts, emails and calls that you owe. Students do well in their studies. Sales and marketing people are better at what they do.

We have two eclipses this month. These are guaranteed to shake up the world and your environment. This is their function.

The solar eclipse of the 9th (in America it happens on the 8th) occurs in your 3rd house of communication. This is a strong eclipse so take it nice and easy over this period. There is no need for daredevil-type stunts. More quiet time at home is recommended. The eclipse will test cars and communication equipment. There can be communication glitches. Siblings and sibling figures in your life experience life-changing dramas, as perhaps do neighbours as well. You could be having 'encounters' with death. The Dark Angel lets you know that he's around. He works in all sorts of ways. You can have a close call – a brush with death – or you could hear of the death of someone close to you or known to you. Often people have dreams about death. This is all to remind you to get more serious about life. To get on with the work that you were born to do. This eclipse impacts on Saturn, your planetary ruler – reinforcing the above. It also impacts on Mars, your family planet. Thus there can be near-death kinds of experiences in the lives of a parent or parent figure or family member. Repairs might be needed in the home.

The lunar eclipse of the 23rd also affects you strongly, especially those of you born between December 21 and December 25. The eclipse occurs in your 10th house of career, indicating career changes and upheavals. There are many scenarios as to what happens – sometimes people change the actual career, sometimes they change their approach, sometimes there are shake-ups in the company, industry or in government regulations that change the rules of the game. Sometimes there are management shake-ups and dramas in the lives of bosses. There are dramatic kinds of events in the lives of parents and parent figures too. Be more patient with them. Every lunar eclipse tests the love life and the current relationship. Good relationships survive and get even better, once the dirty laundry is washed clean. Flawed ones can end.

April

Best Days Overall: 1, 8, 9, 17, 18, 27, 28
Most Stressful Days Overall: 6, 7, 12, 13, 19, 20, 21
Best Days for Love: 6, 7, 12, 13, 14, 15, 16, 25, 26, 27
Best Days for Money: 1, 2, 3, 6, 7, 8, 9, 14, 15, 16, 17, 18, 24, 25, 26, 27, 28, 29, 30
Best Days for Career: 6, 14, 15, 19, 20, 25, 26

Health and energy became more delicate on March 20, and they still need watching this month until the 19th. The most important thing, as our regular readers know, is to maintain high energy levels. Don't allow yourself to get overtired. Enhance the health through head and face massage until the 6th and with neck massage afterwards. Craniosacral therapy will be beneficial if you feel under the weather. Health and energy will improve after the 19th.

The planetary power is now at its nadir (lowest point) in your chart this month. The main activities are internal rather than external. Even your career planet, Venus, spends most of the month in your 4th house. Home and family are the real career – the real mission – this month. On a more mundane level this indicates pursuing the career from home, rather than the office. Many career changes are happening now, but behind the scenes. Venus re-activates an eclipse point on the 7th and 8th. On the 22nd and 23rd she conjuncts Uranus, your financial planet, bringing sudden changes. (These can be profitable ones, by the way.)

This is a time to work on the career in internal rather than external ways – through dreaming, meditation and getting in the mood of where you want to be. In the winter the sages say that the earth dreams. In the spring she makes the dreams manifest. First comes the vision, then the manifestation. So it is with you.

The month ahead will be prosperous. Uranus receives much positive stimulation. He is energized. Earnings should increase. The New Moon of the 7th occurs right on Uranus. Debts can be paid down on the 9th and 10th or made – depending on your need. There is financial favour from bosses, parents and parent figures on the 22nd and 23rd. Job seekers have good fortune on the 15th and 16th.

Mars entered your 12th house on March 6 and will be there for the month ahead. This shows a spiritual type of activism. A need to act on spiritual ideals and principles. Often it shows secret conflicts going on.

Normally spring is a good time to start new projects, but as mentioned earlier, the first two months of the year were much better for this. This month at least 40 per cent (and sometimes 50 per cent) of the planets are going backwards.

May

Best Days Overall: 6, 14, 15, 24, 25
Most Stressful Days Overall: 4, 5, 10, 11, 17, 18, 31
Best Days for Love: 6, 10, 11, 14, 15, 26, 27
Best Days for Money: 4, 5, 6, 12, 13, 14, 15, 22, 23, 24, 25, 27, 28, 31
Best Days for Career: 6, 14, 15, 17, 18, 26, 27

On April 19, as the Sun entered your 5th house, you began one of your yearly personal pleasure peaks. This is a time to enjoy life, to schedule in leisure activities and entertainments and to be involved with children. It is said that children are the best teachers of joy. Being around them can make us more joyous.

Capricorn being a serious sign, with a serious outlook on life, can often downplay leisure. You feel it is a waste of time. But the cosmos thinks otherwise. The 5th house of fun and creativity is equal in importance with every other house – even the 10th career house. There is logic in leisure – and luck too. One comes out of it refreshed and with new and practical ideas.

We have a Grand Trine in the Earth signs this month, which is a pleasant configuration for you as one of those Earth signs. This alignment tends to emphasize the practical virtues. Your abilities are more recognized and appreciated now. Many of your ideas which may have been rejected in the past are now accepted – now that people around you are more practical and down to earth. Enjoy the party while it lasts; on the 20th work calls to you – and you'll be working hard.

This Grand Trine in Earth tends to prosperity – even though your financial planet is not especially active. The only issue right now is the many retrogrades happening – half the planets are retrograde until the 9th, and from the 9th to the 22nd 40 per cent are retrograde. So things are moving more slowly this month and much of the good that we see can happen with a 'delayed' reaction.

Health is much improved this month. Health and energy are especially good until the 20th and are not bad after that. You can enhance things further through neck massage this month – especially if you feel tired or under the weather. After the 20th there is great focus on health – most likely on healthy lifestyles and diet.

Most of the planets are now in the Western, social sector of your chart. (They began moving to the West last month.) This means that the planetary power is moving away from you rather than towards you. It moves towards others and so should you. It is time to focus on others' needs. Time to take a vacation from self and let others have their way, so long as it isn't destructive. Your good will come from others and their good graces and not from your initiative or personal abilities.

There is a happy travel opportunity from the 22nd to the 25th.

June

Best Days Overall: 2, 3, 10, 11, 12, 20, 21, 22, 29, 30
Most Stressful Days Overall: 1, 6, 7, 13, 14, 27, 28
Best Days for Love: 4, 5, 6, 7, 13, 14, 25, 26
Best Days for Money: 1, 2, 3, 8, 9, 10, 11, 18, 19, 20, 21, 23, 24, 27, 28, 29, 30
Best Days for Career: 4, 5, 13, 14, 25, 26

Your 7th house of love, romance and social activities hasn't been powerful this year so far. Every now and then the Moon moves through there, but that's about it. Love has been basically stable and not a priority. Things change this month as the Sun (and two other planets) enter the 7th house. You begin a yearly love and social peak. There are more parties and gatherings to attend. You're more in the mood for romance – whether you are single or in a relationship. Singles have many romantic opportunities from the 18th onwards with a wide variety of people: foreign types, highly educated types, minister types, fun and game types and people with strong sexual magnetism. Probably you will sample them all.

This much power in the 7th house also shows that you get along with all kinds of different people. Love can happen in a variety of ways and in a variety of different settings – in school, at your place of worship, at your workplace or as you pursue your health goals.

Financially you are good until the 21st, but afterwards there is more stress and challenge involved. There are more obstacles to deal with. You have to work harder for earnings than usual. The good news is that the spouse, partner or current love is prospering – he or she is having financial windfalls – and is likely to be more generous with you. He or she will prosper over the next two months as well.

The planetary power is now at its most distant point from you. So self-confidence and self-esteem are not at their highest. Perhaps this is a good thing. Self-assertion is not called for now. Let others have their way so long as it isn't destructive. With so much power in the West try to adapt to situations as best you can. Later, when the planetary power moves towards the East again, you'll be able to make the changes that need to be made.

There's a lot of water in the Horoscope from the 13th onwards – a Grand Trine in the Water signs. This shows an era of good feeling and emotional sensitivity. Capricorn is a hard-headed practical type – this much water can be uncomfortable. People are easily hurt by seeming trifles – some careless body language or the wrong tone of voice – so you'll have to be more careful about this.

Health needs some attention from the 21st onwards. As always make sure you get enough rest. Enhance the health through neck massage until the 13th and through arm and shoulder massage after that date. Right diet is important from the 13th onwards; the stomach seems more sensitive then. Do your best to keep your moods positive and constructive too.

July

Best Days Overall: 8, 9, 18, 19, 27, 28
Most Stressful Days Overall: 3, 4, 10, 11, 12, 24, 25, 31
Best Days for Love: 3, 4, 13, 14, 15, 24, 25, 31
Best Days for Money: 6, 7, 8, 9, 15, 16, 18, 19, 20, 21, 24, 25, 27, 28
Best Days for Career: 3, 4, 10, 11, 12, 15, 24, 25

You and the spouse, partner or current love are not in financial agreement and this stresses the finances. This will resolve itself after the 22nd, but in the meantime, patience.

The beloved is still prospering, but your personal finances are stressed. You just have to work harder to achieve your financial goals. You have to go the extra mile. Your personal finances will improve greatly after the 22nd.

Health still needs watching until the 22nd – review our discussion of this last month. There will, however, be big improvements after the 22nd. In the meantime, eat right and keep your mood as positive as possible. Meditation will be a big help. With so much water in the chart (until the 22nd) it is easy to fall into depression without realizing it. After the 14th health is enhanced by giving more attention to the heart.

Last month, on the 21st, the planetary power began to shift from the lower half to the upper half of the Horoscope. This continues this month and for a few more months to come. It is morning in your year and it is time to get up and be about the affairs of the day – the career and outer affairs of life. Family is still important, but now focus more attention on the career. Approach the career by the methods of day – by overt, physical actions.

You're still in the midst of a yearly love and social peak until the 22nd. It is doubtful that marriage will happen but there is more dating and party going. The New Moon of the 4th is exceptionally good for love – and it seems like a high libido kind of day.

Capricorns tend to be slim – this is their natural pattern. If you see an overweight Capricorn they're off their pattern and we must look closer at the causes. Should there be a need to lose weight, the month ahead – from the 22nd onwards – is an excellent time for this.

Neptune spends the month conjunct to the Moon's South Node. This affects siblings and sibling figures in your life. They feel deficient – lacking – especially in regards to self-esteem and confidence.

Your financial planet Uranus starts to retrograde at the end of the month, on the 29th. He will be moving backwards for many months. Earnings are good this period but after the 29th they will probably happen with more delays.

August

Best Days Overall: 4, 5, 14, 15, 23, 24, 31
Most Stressful Days Overall: 1, 7, 8, 21, 22, 27, 28
Best Days for Love: 1, 2, 3, 12, 13, 14, 15, 23, 24, 27, 28, 31
Best Days for Money: 2, 3, 4, 5, 12, 13, 14, 15, 16, 17, 18, 21, 22, 23, 24, 29, 30, 31
Best Days for Career: 3, 7, 8, 14, 15, 23, 24

Earnings are still good this month – especially until the 22nd – but most likely there are delays and glitches involved, thanks to Uranus's retrograde motion. Try not to make matters worse by being sloppy in your financial transactions. Online payments can be tricky as each website has different procedures. Sometimes computer glitches will register duplicate payments, sometimes no payment. Care should be taken when writing cheques too. All the little details of finance need to be handled 'just so'. Your financial planet will be retrograde for many more months, so this is a time to review the financial life. See where improvements can be made and get ready to put your plans into action when Uranus goes forward again.

You're in a great period for paying down debt or for making it – depending on your need. If you have a viable business idea this is a good time to approach outside investors for backing.

Your 8th house of transformation has been strong since July 22 and remains so until the 22nd. Generally this shows higher libido and more sexual activity. Age is not really an issue – whatever your age, libido will be stronger than usual. You have been involved in personal transformation for some years now – Pluto is in your sign. But this month, until the 22nd, is especially good for these kinds of projects. Time to give birth to the person that you want to be.

The spouse, partner or current love is still in the midst of a yearly financial peak. Happily you and the beloved are in better financial harmony and are cooperating. He or she is likely to be more generous with you.

This is an excellent month for weight loss and detox regimes – more so than usual. It is a great month to take stock of your possessions and get rid of the things that you don't need or use. A good house cleaning is in order. It would be good too to get rid of emotional and mental patterns that are no longer useful to you. Clear the decks so that the new and the better can come in.

Health is good this month and gets even better after the 22nd. You can enhance it further by eating right and giving more attention to the small intestine.

There is a happy travel or educational opportunity from the 20th to the 24th. Job seekers have good opportunities over that period too.

September

Best Days Overall: 1, 2, 10, 11, 12, 19, 20, 28, 29
Most Stressful Days Overall: 3, 4, 17, 18, 23, 24, 30
Best Days for Love: 1, 2, 3, 4, 11, 12, 13, 14, 20, 23, 24, 30
Best Days for Money: 1, 2, 8, 9, 12, 13, 14, 17, 18, 21, 25, 26, 27
Best Days for Career: 3, 4, 13, 14, 23, 30

Relations with siblings, sibling figures and neighbours have been tense all year. This month even more so. You need to work harder to maintain harmony. It will also be a good idea to drive more defensively this month.

We have two eclipses this month and these are always guaranteed to produce change and drama – both personally and in the world. It makes the month more hectic.

The solar eclipse of the 1st occurs in your 9th house. Best to avoid foreign travel during that period. Students at college level (or who are about to enter college) make dramatic changes to their educational plans. Often they change schools or courses, or change direction in their educational planning. There are upheavals in your place of worship and in the lives of worship leaders and members of your congregation. Often this kind of eclipse tests your personal philosophy and your outlook on life. Your belief systems get challenged by events and often they will have to be modified or dropped. A change in the belief system is a powerful thing. It will bring change to almost every area of life – eventually. Saturn, the ruler of your Horoscope, is impacted by this eclipse, so take a nice easy schedule during this period. You will be redefining yourself in the coming months and adopting a whole new look and image. Family dramas are happening too – Mars, your family planet, is also affected by the eclipse. Be patient with family members now; most likely there are life-changing events happening. Often repairs are needed in the home.

The lunar eclipse of the 16th occurs in your already troubled 3rd house of communication. So be more patient with siblings, sibling figures and neighbours as they are probably more temperamental than usual now. Sometimes this kind of eclipse brings major changes in the neighbourhood – major construction, road closures, etc. Communications are affected. Phones can drop calls or not work properly. Emails are not received. Letters get lost. Every lunar eclipse tests love and partnerships and this one is no different. Sometimes the problem is in the relationship itself – long-suppressed feelings and grievances surface to be dealt with. But sometimes the testing is due to some drama in the life of the spouse, partner or current love. Good relationships survive but the flawed ones can dissolve.

The other major headline this month is Jupiter's move into your 10th house of career on the 10th. This is bringing huge career success to you. The Sun will enter your 10th house on the 22nd, putting you into a yearly (and for many a lifetime) career peak.

October

Best Days Overall: 8, 9, 17, 25, 26
Most Stressful Days Overall: 1, 2, 15, 21, 22, 27, 28, 29
Best Days for Love: 1, 2, 3, 4, 10, 11, 12, 13, 20, 21, 22, 23, 24, 30
Best Days for Money: 1, 5, 6, 10, 11, 15, 16, 18, 19, 23, 24, 27, 28
Best Days for Career: 1, 2, 3, 4, 12, 13, 23, 24, 27, 28, 29

The planetary power is now at its zenith (highest point) in your Horoscope. It is upward and onward for you. The planets are lifting you higher and higher. There are pay rises (overt or covert), promotions and elevation in your professional status, and more recognition for your achievements. In many cases honours come.

Jupiter is your spiritual planet. His position in your 10th house shows that you are honoured and recognized as much for your charitable and spiritual activities as for your professional achievements. Being involved with charities and good causes is a valid way to advance your career. Your good work ethic is also important. Superiors take notice.

Venus, your career planet, goes out of bounds from the 27th to the 31st – it might be good to be a little unconventional in your career approach too. Going off the beaten track can enhance things. Don't be afraid to be original.

Health became more delicate on September 22 and is still delicate this month until the 23rd. So make sure you get as much rest as possible. Don't allow yourself to get overtired. Often we think we're achieving more when we work in spite of fatigue. But generally this is illusion; there is a tendency to make mistakes and the work needs to be redone. So you're actually increasing your workload when you do this. Enhance the health through right diet and through paying attention to the small intestine until the 7th. From the 7th to the 25th pay more attention to the kidneys and hips. Hip massage will be good. After the 25th attend to the colon, bladder and sexual organs.

For many months the Western, social sector of your chart has been dominant. You have needed to adapt yourself to others and to situations. This is changing now. On the 7th Mercury crosses from the West to the East and the Eastern sector of your chart becomes more powerful. Day by day (you haven't yet reached the peak) personal power and independence increases. By now you know what conditions are irksome, and you now have the power to change them to your liking.

Finances are a bit stressful this month. Your financial planet is still retrograde and receiving stressful aspects. You just need to work harder than usual to achieve your goals. Career – status and professional prestige – seems more important than money right now. Patience. Patience. Patience. Things get easier after the 23rd.

November

Best Days Overall: 4, 5, 13, 14, 21, 22, 23
Most Stressful Days Overall: 11, 12, 17, 18, 24, 25
Best Days for Love: 1, 2, 3, 10, 13, 17, 18, 19, 20, 21, 22, 29, 30
Best Days for Money: 2, 3, 6, 7, 8, 11, 12, 15, 16, 19, 20, 24, 25,
   29, 30
Best Days for Career: 2, 3, 13, 21, 22, 24, 25

Career is still going great guns. Your career planet, Venus, will spend the entire month 'out of bounds'. As we mentioned last month, don't be afraid to be original or go off the beaten track in career matters – it probably helps you.

The Sun will have his solstice next month, but Venus is having one of hers from the 13th to the 16th. She pauses in the heavens (in her latitudinal motion) and then reverses direction. And this is most likely what's happening in the career. A pause, then a change of direction. This pause and change will be good.

It is still very beneficial to enhance the career through charitable work and through non-profit kinds of projects – especially until the 12th. Venus is in mutual reception with Jupiter. Each is a guest in the house of the other and this shows good cooperation between them. A friend – a social connection – is very helpful in the career from the 24th to the 25th. After the 12th career opportunities seek you out. You are seen as successful by others and you dress and act the part.

Finance is much improved over last month, but still major purchases or financial decisions should be delayed, if possible. Uranus, your financial planet, is still retrograde. The best thing you can do financially is to gain mental clarity on things. Then proper plans can be made. Earnings will increase after the 22nd, but still there are delays and glitches with this increase.

Health is also much improved over last month. You can enhance it even more by giving more attention to the colon, bladder and sexual organs until the 12th. Sexual expression should be kept in moderation. After the 12th give more attention to the liver and thighs. Thigh massage will be wonderful. You also respond well to spiritual therapies from the 12th onwards.

Your 11th house of friendship has been strong since the 23rd of last month, and is still strong until November 22. This is a social kind of period and it will be good to be more involved with friends, groups and group activities. It will also be good to expand your technology knowledge and to be more involved online. Children or children figures in your life are having a banner romantic kind of month. They seem popular.

A parent or parent figure is prospering now.

December

Best Days Overall: 1, 2, 3, 10, 11, 19, 20, 29, 30
Most Stressful Days Overall: 8, 9, 14, 15, 21, 22
Best Days for Love: 2, 3, 8, 9, 12, 13, 14, 15, 17, 18, 21, 22, 29
Best Days for Money: 4, 5, 8, 9, 12, 13, 16, 17, 21, 22, 26, 27, 31
Best Days for Career: 2, 3, 12, 13, 21, 22

The planetary power is now at its maximum Eastern position (and this will be the case next month too). You have the power to create your personal happiness now. You have the power (and independence) to change conditions that displease you. This is the time to use it.

A happy month ahead, Capricorn – enjoy! Until the 21st you are in a very spiritual kind of period. This was the case last month too. It is a month for spiritual breakthroughs and spiritual experiences. The dream life is active and prophetic. Synchronicities happen in your life. Extrasensory perception is sharper than ever. One spiritual breakthrough – and you will have more than one – is enough to change your life for ever. The spiritual world is close to you now. Cultivate your connection. The spiritual world is full of benevolent beings who can do anything if you know how to call them and ask.

Until the 21st your growth is interior – unseen and perhaps unnoticed. But on the 21st, as the Sun enters your sign, your growth becomes noticeable. You're in a yearly personal pleasure peak. The appearance shines. There is more sex appeal to the image. You are strong and independent. Venus in your sign until the 7th adds beauty and grace to the image. Mercury in your sign brings happy job opportunities to you – and perhaps opportunities for overtime or second jobs, if you are already employed. This is a month to pamper the body and enjoy the physical delights of life. It is also wonderful for getting the body and image in right shape.

Finances are excellent until the 21st. But Uranus, your financial planet, is still retrograde so be patient with the glitches and delays. Your finances are still under review at the moment. You still need clarity about the financial facts of life. After the 21st finances are more stressful. It's nothing serious, you just need to work harder to attain your goals. Venus's move into your money house on the 7th is helping matters. It shows luck in speculations and the financial favour of bosses, elders, parents and parent figures. The spouse, partner or current love also seems generous after the 21st. The family seems financially cooperative until the 20th as well.

It is good to have things your way, as long as your way isn't destructive. A destructive path will create pain and anguish once the initial pleasure wears off.

Health and energy are excellent now. You can achieve whatever you desire.

Aquarius

THE WATER-BEARER

Birthdays from
20th January to
18th February

Personality Profile

AQUARIUS AT A GLANCE

Element – Air

Ruling Planet – Uranus
   Career Planet – Pluto
   Love Planet – Sun
   Money Planet – Neptune
   Planet of Health and Work – Moon
   Planet of Home and Family Life – Venus
   Planet of Spirituality – Saturn

Colours – electric blue, grey, ultramarine blue

Colours that promote love, romance and social harmony – gold, orange

Colour that promotes earning power – aqua

Gems – black pearl, obsidian, opal, sapphire

Metal – lead

Scents – azalea, gardenia

Quality – fixed (= stability)

Qualities most needed for balance – warmth, feeling and emotion

Strongest virtues – great intellectual power, the ability to communicate and to form and understand abstract concepts, love for the new and avant-garde

Deepest needs – to know and to bring in the new

Characteristics to avoid – coldness, rebelliousness for its own sake, fixed ideas

Signs of greatest overall compatibility – Gemini, Libra

Signs of greatest overall incompatibility – Taurus, Leo, Scorpio

Sign most helpful to career – Scorpio

Sign most helpful for emotional support – Taurus

Sign most helpful financially – Pisces

Sign best for marriage and/or partnerships – Leo

Sign most helpful for creative projects – Gemini

Best Sign to have fun with – Gemini

Signs most helpful in spiritual matters – Libra, Capricorn

Best day of the week – Saturday

Understanding an Aquarius

In the Aquarius-born, intellectual faculties are perhaps the most highly developed of any sign in the zodiac. Aquarians are clear, scientific thinkers. They have the ability to think abstractly and to formulate laws, theories and clear concepts from masses of observed facts. Geminis might be very good at gathering information, but Aquarians take this a step further, excelling at interpreting the information gathered.

Practical people – men and women of the world – mistakenly consider abstract thinking as impractical. It is true that the realm of abstract thought takes us out of the physical world, but the discoveries made in this realm generally end up having tremendous practical consequences. All real scientific inventions and breakthroughs come from this abstract realm.

Aquarians, more so than most, are ideally suited to explore these abstract dimensions. Those who have explored these regions know that there is little feeling or emotion there. In fact, emotions are a hindrance to functioning in these dimensions; thus Aquarians seem – at times – cold and emotionless to others. It is not that Aquarians haven't got feelings and deep emotions, it is just that too much feeling clouds their ability to think and invent. The concept of 'too much feeling' cannot be tolerated or even understood by some of the other signs. Nevertheless, this Aquarian objectivity is ideal for science, communication and friendship.

Aquarians are very friendly people, but they do not make a big show about it. They do the right thing by their friends, even if sometimes they do it without passion or excitement.

Aquarians have a deep passion for clear thinking. Second in importance, but related, is their passion for breaking with the establishment and traditional authority. Aquarians delight in this, because for them rebellion is like a great game or challenge. Very often they will rebel strictly for the fun of rebelling, regardless of whether the authority they defy is right or wrong. Right or wrong has little to do with the rebellious actions of an Aquarian, because to a true Aquarian authority and power must be challenged as a matter of principle.

Where Capricorn or Taurus will err on the side of tradition and the status quo, an Aquarian will err on the side of the new. Without this virtue it is doubtful whether any progress would be made in the world. The conservative-minded would obstruct progress. Originality and invention imply an ability to break barriers; every new discovery represents the toppling of an impediment to thought. Aquarians are very interested in breaking barriers and making walls tumble – scientifically, socially and politically. Other zodiac signs, such as Capricorn, also have scientific talents. But Aquarians are particularly excellent in the social sciences and humanities.

Finance

In financial matters Aquarians tend to be idealistic and humanitarian – to the point of self-sacrifice. They are usually generous contributors to social and political causes. When they contribute it differs from when a Capricorn or Taurus contributes. A Capricorn or Taurus may expect some favour or return for a gift; an Aquarian contributes selflessly.

Aquarians tend to be as cool and rational about money as they are about most things in life. Money is something they need and they set about acquiring it scientifically. No need for fuss; they get on with it in the most rational and scientific ways available.

Money to the Aquarian is especially nice for what it can do, not for the status it may bring (as is the case for other signs). Aquarians are neither big spenders nor penny-pinchers and use their finances in practical ways, for example to facilitate progress for themselves, their families, or even for strangers.

However, if Aquarians want to reach their fullest financial potential they will have to explore their intuitive nature. If they follow only their financial theories – or what they believe to be theoretically correct – they may suffer some losses and disappointments. Instead, Aquarians should call on their intuition, which knows without thinking. For Aquarians, intuition is the short-cut to financial success.

Career and Public Image

Aquarians like to be perceived not only as the breakers of barriers but also as the transformers of society and the world. They long to be seen in this light and to play this role. They also look up to and respect other people in this position and even expect their superiors to act this way.

Aquarians prefer jobs that have a bit of idealism attached to them – careers with a philosophical basis. Aquarians need to be creative at work, to have access to new techniques and methods. They like to keep busy and enjoy getting down to business straightaway, without wasting any time. They are often the quickest workers and usually have suggestions for improvements that will benefit their employers. Aquarians are also very helpful with their co-workers and welcome responsibility, preferring this to having to take orders from others.

If Aquarians want to reach their highest career goals they have to develop more emotional sensitivity, depth of feeling and passion. They need to learn to narrow their focus on the essentials and concentrate more on the job in hand. Aquarians need 'a fire in the belly' – a consuming passion and desire – in order to rise to the very top. Once this passion exists they will succeed easily in whatever they attempt.

Love and Relationships

Aquarians are good at friendships, but a bit weak when it comes to love. Of course they fall in love, but their lovers always get the impression that they are more best friends than paramours.

Like Capricorns, they are cool customers. They are not prone to displays of passion or to outward demonstrations of their affections. In fact, they feel uncomfortable when their other half hugs and touches them too much. This does not mean that they do not love their partners. They do, only they show it in other ways. Curiously enough, in relationships they tend to attract the very things that they feel uncomfortable with. They seem to attract hot, passionate, romantic, demonstrative people. Perhaps they know instinctively that these people have qualities they lack and so seek them out. In any event, these relationships do seem to work, Aquarian coolness calming the more passionate partner while the fires of passion warm the cold-blooded Aquarius.

The qualities Aquarians need to develop in their love life are warmth, generosity, passion and fun. Aquarians love relationships of the mind. Here they excel. If the intellectual factor is missing in a relationship an Aquarian will soon become bored or feel unfulfilled.

Home and Domestic Life

In family and domestic matters Aquarians can have a tendency to be too non-conformist, changeable and unstable. They are as willing to break the barriers of family constraints as they are those of other areas of life.

Even so, Aquarians are very sociable people. They like to have a nice home where they can entertain family and friends. Their house is usually decorated in a modern style and full of state-of-the-art appliances and gadgets – an environment Aquarians find absolutely necessary.

If their home life is to be healthy and fulfilling Aquarians need to inject it with a quality of stability – yes, even some conservatism. They need at least one area of life to be enduring and steady; this area is usually their home and family life.

Venus, the generic planet of love, rules the Aquarian's 4th solar house of home and family, which means that when it comes to the family and child-rearing, theories, cool thinking and intellect are not always enough. Aquarians need to bring love into the equation in order to have a great domestic life.

Horoscope for 2016

Major Trends

The love life sparkled in 2014 and 2015 but this year it is not so prominent. Most likely your love and romantic goals have been achieved and you're moving on to other areas of interest.

When Jupiter enters your 9th house on September 10 there will be more foreign travel in your life. This will also be a wonderful aspect for students at college level or who are about to enter college. There is success in their studies and good news here.

Neptune has been in your money house for some years now and will be there for many more. This shows a reliance on the financial intuition and a deeper exploration of the spiritual laws of affluence. There's more on this later.

Saturn has been in your 11th house since December 2014. This shows the testing of friendships. Those that are not up to par will dissolve. You generally love being involved in groups and group activities. This love is still there, but you're becoming more choosy about it. The focus is more on quality rather than quantity.

Uranus, the ruler of your Horoscope, is still in Aries and your 3rd house. (He has been there for many years.) This shows a strong interest in communication and intellectual activities, in writing, teaching, sales and marketing – areas that you naturally love. This is also a nice position for students (below college level). It suggests interest, and this tends to success.

Jupiter spends most of the year (until September 9) in your 8th house. This shows good fortune in your projects of personal transformation. It also shows good fortune with tax, insurance or estate issues. More on this later.

Pluto in your 12th house for many years now shows that a spiritual detox is going on. Impurities in the spiritual life – in the practice and especially the attitudes – are being purged. This is a long-term project.

Your areas of greatest interest this year are: finance; communication and intellectual interests; personal transformation, occult studies, sex (until September 9); religion, philosophy, higher education and foreign travel (from September 10 onwards); friends, groups and group activities; and spirituality.

Your paths of greatest fulfilment this year are: personal transformation, occult studies, sex; and religion, philosophy, higher education and foreign travel (from September 10 onwards).

Health

(Please note that this is an astrological perspective on health and not a medical one. In days of yore there was no difference, these perspectives were identical. But now there could be quite a difference. For a medical perspective, please consult your doctor or health practitioner.)

When Saturn left Scorpio late in 2014 there was an immediate improvement in health and energy. And this trend continues this year. There are no long-term planets stressing you out. They are either in harmonious aspect to you or leaving you alone. Health will be good. If there are any pre-existing conditions, there is good news about them. They seem much improved. Sure, there will be periods in the year when health and energy are less 'easy' than usual. These periods are caused by the short-term planetary transits. They are temporary and not trends for the year. When they pass the normal good health returns.

Your 6th house of health is empty this year (only short-term planets will move through there), which I read as another positive health signal. You can sort of take good health for granted. You have no need to focus here overly much.

Good though your health is, you can make it even better. Give more attention to the following areas – the vulnerable areas of your chart (the reflexology points are shown in the following diagram):

- The ankles and calves. These are always important for Aquarius and should be regularly massaged. The ankles need more support when exercising.
- The stomach and breasts. These too are particularly important for Aquarius. Right diet is always important for you (not so with many other signs) and this should be checked out with a professional. As our regular readers know – *how* you eat can be just as important as *what* you eat. Meals should be taken in a calm and relaxed way. It is beneficial to have calm, soothing music playing as you eat (sacred music, yoga music, or 'elevator' music – hard rock is not advisable). Grace, in your own words, should be said before and after meals. Food should be blessed. The act of eating should be elevated from mere animal appetite to an act of worship. This raises the energy vibration of the food – and, more importantly, that of the body and digestive system.

The Moon is your health planet. She is the fastest moving of all the planets and every month she moves through your entire Horoscope. Thus there are many short-term health trends that are best discussed

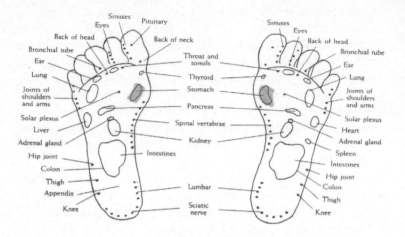

Important foot reflexology points for the year ahead

Try to massage all of the foot on a regular basis – the top of the foot as well as the bottom – but pay extra attention to the points highlighted on the chart. When you massage, be aware of 'sore spots' as these need special attention. It's also a very good idea this year to massage the ankles and the middle of the top of the foot especially.

in the monthly reports. If the Moon is receiving positive aspects, health is super. If she is stressed out (and this is always a short-term issue) you could feel under the weather. Much of what you feel in your body is merely the Moon receiving certain kinds of aspects.

With the Moon as your health planet, good health for you means much more than just 'no symptoms'. It is more than just testing negative on an ultrasound. It means good emotional health. A healthy family and domestic life. If health problems occur (God forbid) examine the family relationship and bring it into harmony as quickly as possible. Keep the moods positive and constructive. Meditation will be a big help here.

Home and Family

Your 4th house of home and family is not prominent this year. (It has not been prominent for some years now.) This tends to a stable kind of year. There is nothing especially against a move or renovation, but there's nothing that supports it either. You have greater freedom in the home and family life, but not that much interest.

Aquarius is not known for being family oriented. You tend to be freedom-loving, unconventional types. Anything that interferes with freedom (and family often does) is looked on with suspicion.

Now that Saturn has left Scorpio, a parent or parent figure seems less of a disciplinarian than usual. Less stern. Less serious. He or she is probably feeling much better as well. He or she has financial challenges these days and needs to reorganize the finances – to shift things around. He or she is not likely to move this year.

The other parent or parent figure could have already moved in recent years and now seems satisfied with the status quo.

If the parents or parent figures are still married, the relationship is much improved these days. There was a severe testing of the marriage in 2013 and 2014. If they are divorced, one of them has good romantic aspects this year.

You seem very devoted to siblings or the sibling figures in your life. They seem more rebellious and difficult to handle. In one sense they are much like you – they need their freedom and space. Romance is likely after September 10, but marriage is not advisable. They have a stable kind of family year. They have excellent job aspects and the health looks good. (They do need to be careful about experimenting with the body, though – this can lead to injury.)

Children or children figures in your life are likely to move this year. It could have happened last year too. The move seems happy. Sometimes people don't 'literally' move, but they make renovations or other investments in the home and the effect is as if they had moved. Children and children figures are more fertile than usual. Their health looks good. However, their marriage or current relationship is getting tested. Grandchildren (if you have them) are having a spiritual kind of year. They are making renovations in the home. On September 10 they enter a multi-year cycle of prosperity.

You seem very involved in the health of a parent or parent figure. His or her job situation seems unstable. He or she benefits from new, cutting-edge therapies and from alternative medicine. The other parent figure has wonderful job opportunities from September 10 onwards. Health looks good for this parent.

If you're beautifying the home – repainting, redecorating, or buying new furniture or art objects – April 19 to May 24 is a good time for this.

Finance and Career

In finance, the trend for many years has been to understand and apply the spiritual laws of prosperity. You already understand much about this, but you're going deeper into it.

Neptune, your financial planet and the most spiritual of the planets, has been in your money house for some years now and will be there for many more. It is 'miracle money' that interests you and not so much 'natural' money. You like the money that comes to you from 'left field' – from unexpected places and ways. Even what we think of as 'natural money' comes from the spirit world – but its origins are more disguised. It is the unexpected kind of money – the miracle money – that has the overt signature of spirit.

Finances are more challenging this year. This doesn't mean poverty or loss, only that you have to work harder (and in a more spiritual kind of way) to attain your goals. Next year will be much better financially.

Neptune as the financial planet has a mundane interpretation. It shows that there is much 'hidden' activity going on in the financial life and in financial dealings. No question that you need to do more homework around important investments or purchases. There can be unpleasant revelations in finance, with the money people in your life, in financial deals, etc. Things are not what they seem. You can't take things at 'face value'.

There are also two eclipses in your money house this year. This will shake things up and force you to make needed changes – changes in thinking and strategy. This is when one usually learns about the 'hidden' things. The changes will ultimately be good.

Jupiter spends most of this year in your 8th house. This shows that the spouse, partner or current love is having a banner financial year.

Things may be more difficult for you, but not for him or her. This person will be more generous with you.

Jupiter in your 8th house often shows inheritance. (He makes very nice aspects to Pluto, the ruler of inheritance.) Hopefully no one has to die. You can be the recipient of a trust fund, or be appointed to some administrative post in an estate. Or, as often happens, you can be named in someone's will. It also shows good fortune in tax or insurance issues. Money will often come from insurance payments or tax refunds.

Since the 8th house rules debt, Jupiter in this house indicates an increase in your line of credit and greater ease in borrowing – if you need to. It also shows an ability to pay down debt. There is good access to outside money this year – either through borrowing or through investors. Creative kinds of financing can be a path to profits.

But the main headline this year is the career. Jupiter is making very nice aspects to your career planet, Pluto, and Saturn has now moved out of your career house. The career is going much better these days. You're not that focused on the career, but success is happening anyway. Next year, 2017, will be an even better career year.

It is good to pursue the career through online activities and through involvement with groups and professional organizations.

Love and Social Life

Romance doesn't seem a big issue this year, as we have mentioned. Four out of the five long-term planets are in the Eastern sector of your chart – the sector of the self and of personal interests. Your 7th house is basically empty, with only short-term planets moving through there this year. So personal interests are more important than relationships.

As we mentioned, the past two years were very powerful love and social years. Many of you married or got involved in serious love relationships. Thus there's no longer a need to focus on romance. You seem content with the status quo. Thus married couples will tend to stay married and singles will tend to stay single.

Romance and social activities might not be prominent, but the sex life seems hyperactive. As in most things, you're experimental in this area.

The Sun is your love planet and he is a fast-moving planet. In any given year he moves through all the signs and houses of your Horoscope. Thus there are many short-term trends in love, depending on where the Sun happens to be and the kind of aspects he receives. These are best dealt with in the monthly reports.

There will be two solar eclipses this year. These will tend to shake up the love life and current relationship. You go through this every year, so it doesn't necessarily mean the end of a relationship. It only shows that dirty laundry is brought out to be washed, to be corrected. Hidden flaws in the relationship make themselves known so that corrections can be made. Solid relationships tend to survive and get even better. It's the shaky ones that are in danger. These solar eclipses are on March 9 and September 1, and we will discuss them more fully in the monthly reports.

The Sun as the love planet shows that you like strength in a lover – someone prominent such as an athlete, celebrity or entertainer. You can be 'star struck' when it comes to love. You like authority figures, and you like to rebel against them. It is almost like some personal romantic dance that you have. Attract the authority figure, and then defy the authority.

The area of friendship also seems less active than usual. We have mentioned this earlier. Your tendency is to attract myriads of friends. But every now and then there is a need to prune them. To separate the real ones from the unreal ones. This is what's going on now. (It started last year.) Better to have fewer friends, but good ones, than hosts of lukewarm friends.

In astrology we have a simple definition of a real friend. This is some-one who wishes for you your 'fondest hopes and wishes' and is willing to assist in the process. This will guide you in the coming year. I have heard another good definition of a friend – but it's not astrological. 'A true friend is someone who rushes in when everyone is rushing out.'*

It is great to be involved in groups and organizations. Networking is one of your natural strengths. But here too some pruning is necessary. You can't be involved in every group. You have to be more discerning. You have to separate the important from the unimportant.

---

* A Facebook post

Self-improvement

Pluto has been in your 12th house of spirituality for many years now, as we have mentioned. This is bringing a purification – a cosmic detox – of the whole spiritual life. Perhaps there is no area of life more confusing, more filled with fantasy and misinformation than this area. I would say that most people need a good detox here, and now it is your turn.

These days, ever since your spiritual planet, Saturn, moved into your 11th house in December 2014, this detox is happening through a disciplined and scientific approach to the spirit. You tend to have this approach naturally, but these days even more so.

This is a time for testing spiritual attitudes, axioms and practices in a scientific way. Many forms of superstition will fall by the wayside with this approach. Does such and such a practice lead to such and such a result? Practise will reveal it. The mystics of old – the ones who instituted many of the practices extant today – understood the science behind spirituality. It's now your job to rediscover this science and apply it.

Spiritual interests are considered 'otherworldly' and 'impractical'. Otherworldly is perhaps correct, but when understood, spiritual practice is extremely pragmatic in any area where it is applied, whether it be finance, health or career. When understood and practised it has the potential to eliminate poverty, disease and even death itself (eventually).

The other positive things about the scientific approach is that it bolsters faith. The Bhakti methods – the exaltation of the feelings and emotions – often bring dramatic results, but with little stability. In a good mood, the person sits at the right hand of the Divine surrounded by choirs of angels. In a bad mood, they can actually become atheists. All the previous experiences are forgotten. It is as if they never happened. But with the scientific approach, one maintains faith (so important in this kind of work) regardless of mood.

Pluto is your career planet. His position in your 12th house gives many messages. Spirituality is high on your priorities. Spirituality – your spiritual practice and understanding – will boost the career. And, in many cases, spirituality *is* the real career, the real mission for the year ahead. Sometimes Pluto in the 12th house shows a spiritual-type career – a career with a non-profit company, or with some spiritual organization. Sometimes people devote themselves to a charity or altruistic cause. But sometimes, the spiritual practice itself is the career. People will go off to a spiritual retreat and just focus on their practice. Many changes in the world are the result of a lone person's spiritual breakthrough – usually in private, unheralded and unsung. The outer changes – in governments or in movements – are just the side effects of this.

Month-by-month Forecasts

January

Best Days Overall: 1, 2, 3, 11, 12, 19, 20, 29, 30
Most Stressful Days Overall: 4, 5, 17, 18, 24, 25, 31
Best Days for Love: 6, 7, 8, 9, 10, 15, 16, 18, 24, 25, 26, 29, 30
Best Days for Money: 4, 5, 9, 10, 13, 14, 17, 18, 21, 22, 23, 26, 27
Best Days for Career: 4, 5, 9, 10, 17, 18, 26, 27

You begin your year on a spiritual note – which is as it should be. In many cultures New Year is a solemn occasion. A time for prayer and reflection. For you this is even more the case. Many of you are having 'personal new years' (birthdays) in the coming month – others next month. So it is good to spend time reflecting on the past year. Good to look at what has been or hasn't been accomplished. Where have you gone off the mark? Where have you hit the target? What mistakes were made and how can they be corrected? Then to look at where you want to go in the coming year. How much money do you want? What are your love and social goals? Career goals? Write them down on a piece of paper and visualize yourself attaining them. When your birthday happens – when your personal new year begins – you can start putting your plans into action.

The planetary power is at its maximum Eastern point during this month and the next, thus you begin your year in a place of maximum personal power and independence. You have the power to change conditions that irk you or are uncomfortable. You have the power to have things your way. Your happiness is as important as the happiness of others. It is time to take personal responsibility for it. Later, when the planets shift to the West, these things will be more difficult to do.

The month ahead is happy and prosperous. On the 20th as the Sun enters your 1st house you begin one of your yearly personal pleasure peaks. You live on a higher level. You're able to enjoy all the pleasures of the senses. The personal appearance shines and you have more self-confidence and self-esteem. The love life seems especially happy then too. Love pursues you. You only need to go about your daily business and it will find you soon enough. Until the 20th love was spiritual and idealistic. After that date it is more material – hands on. The physical pleasures of love are important – not just sex, but the physical expressions of affection. An attractive partner is part of your persona this month, like a fashion accessory. Romance is good all month, but especially on the 13th and 14th.

Health is excellent this month. Your energy tends to be high. There is a sparkle in your eyes and a spring to your step. This is the kind of month where you take good health for granted and have no need to pay special attention to it.

Mars crosses the Mid-heaven and enters your 10th house on the 4th. This indicates a busy and hectic career. You're fending off competitors and need to be more aggressive here.

February

Best Days Overall: 7, 8, 15, 16, 17, 25, 26
Most Stressful Days Overall: 1, 13, 14, 20, 21, 27, 28, 29
Best Days for Love: 5, 6, 7, 8, 13, 14, 17, 20, 21, 25, 27, 28
Best Days for Money: 1, 5, 6, 9, 10, 13, 14, 18, 19, 22, 23, 24, 27, 28
Best Days for Career: 1, 5, 6, 13, 14, 22, 23, 27, 28, 29

This is the best month of the year to start a new business or new venture – much better than spring, the traditional best time. The universal solar cycle has been waxing (growing) since December 21. Your personal solar cycle waxes from your birthday onwards, and 90 per cent of the planets are moving forward. If you were born between January 20 and February 8, you have a great 'starting' energy from the 8th to the 22nd. If you were born after February 8, your best time is from your birthday until February 22.

Mars is still in your 10th house of career this month, showing great career activity. There is much conflict happening there. The demands of the career seem strong. However, this month the planetary power is beginning to shift to the lower half of your Horoscope. So it is time to shift some energy and attention to the home, family and your emotional needs. You won't be able to ignore the career, but you can start to downplay it a bit.

You're still in a happy and prosperous period. You're still having life more or less on your own terms and are still in a period of maximum personal power and independence. The challenge will be what you do with these gift, how you will use them.

Your personal pleasure peak, which began on January 20, gets extended this month. The Sun leaves your 1st house on the 19th, but Mercury, the ruler of your 5th house of fun and creativity, enters on the 14th and stays there for the rest of the month. So there is much fun and personal pleasure happening. Singles have the choice of serious love or 'fun love' this period. Both types pursue you.

On the 19th the Sun enters your money house and you begin a yearly financial peak. Prosperity soars. You have the support of the spouse, partner or current love. He or she seems very helpful. Social connections also seem helpful. There is a very nice payday on the 28th and 29th. The beloved also prospers then. Speculations are favourable from the 5th to the 7th. This is a good financial period for the spouse, partner or current love as well.

The dream life can be overly disturbed from the 1st to the 5th. Don't pay too much attention to it as your spiritual planet Saturn is re-activating an old eclipse point. There can be dramas in the lives of guru figures and shakeups in a spiritual or charitable organization you belong to.

March

Best Days Overall: 6, 7, 14, 15, 23, 24
Most Stressful Days Overall: 12, 13, 18, 19, 26, 27
Best Days for Love: 6, 7, 8, 9, 16, 17, 18, 19, 26, 27, 28, 29
Best Days for Money: 3, 4, 8, 9, 12, 13, 16, 17, 21, 22, 26, 27, 31
Best Days for Career: 3, 4, 12, 13, 21, 22, 26, 27, 31

Things have been going easy for you so far this year, so it's time to have a few challenges to keep you on your toes, and to prevent you from getting too complacent. We have two eclipses this month that shake things up in the world and in your environment.

The solar eclipse of the 9th (in America it happens on the 8th) occurs in your money house and announces important financial changes. Generally these changes happen as a result of some unexpected expense or financial upheaval. You're forced to change your thinking and strategy. The eclipse will show you why your previous thinking was unrealistic.

Every solar eclipse tests love and partnerships and this one is no different. Sometimes these tests happen because of suppressed grievances – dirty laundry – being forced up by the eclipse. Sometimes it is due to some drama in the life of the spouse, partner or current love. If the relationship is fundamentally sound, it will survive and get even better. It's the flawed ones that are in danger. Though the beloved seems more affected than you by the eclipse, it won't hurt for both of you to reduce your schedules over this period.

This solar eclipse impacts on Mars, so it will be a good idea to drive more defensively at this time. There can be communication failures and glitches. Communication equipment will get tested and might need replacement or repair. There are dramas in the lives of siblings, sibling figures and neighbours – and often disruptions in the neighbourhood. Students can change schools or education plans. This eclipse also impacts on Saturn, which shows spiritual changes for you; changes in practice, attitude and perhaps even teachings. There are shake-ups in a spiritual or charitable organization that you belong to, and dramas in the lives of guru figures.

The lunar eclipse of the 23rd occurs in your 9th house. This also indicates educational changes for students. The previous eclipse affected students below college level; this one affects college or post-graduate students. Children and children figures are affected too. They should stay out of harm's way. Communication problems are likely with this eclipse too, as Mercury is affected, and as before it will be a good idea to drive more carefully. Every lunar eclipse tests the current health regime (as the Moon is your health planet), and there will be changes here over the coming months. Job changes could also happen – either within your present company or with another one. There are shake-ups in the place of work.

Career is less of a priority this month but there is success happening from the 12th to the 20th. Friends seem helpful here. Your technology expertise plays a role too.

April

Best Days Overall: 2, 3, 10, 11, 19, 20, 21, 29, 30
Most Stressful Days Overall: 8, 9, 14, 15, 16, 22, 23
Best Days for Love: 6, 7, 14, 15, 16, 25, 26, 27
Best Days for Money: 1, 4, 5, 8, 9, 12, 13, 17, 18, 22, 23, 27, 28
Best Days for Career: 1, 8, 9, 17, 18, 22, 23, 27, 28

Your 3rd house of communication and intellectual interests became very powerful last month, on the 20th, and is still strong in the month ahead. This is a comfortable kind of place for you. It is especially wonderful for students of all ages (Aquarius is an eternal student!). You're generally communicative, but this month you could go overboard if you're not careful.

There is some family drama on the 7th or 8th. Thus it is good that you're focusing more on the home and family this month, at least from the 19th onwards. They need you.

On the 19th the planetary power reaches the lowest point of your Horoscope (the nadir). Planetary power is most distant from the 10th house of career. So career, though very good this year, is in abeyance for now. Most of the planets are below the horizon in the bottom half of your chart; your 4th house of home and family is strong and your 10th house is empty (only the Moon will move through there on the 22nd and 23rd).

This period, from the 19th onwards, is wonderful for those of you in therapy. There will be breakthroughs and new understanding happening. And even if you're not in any formal kind of therapy, the cosmos has its own therapeutic regime for you. You will be more nostalgic. Past memories will spontaneously arise (especially in the love realm). As you review them from your present state and present understanding, history will get reinterpreted. (Note that this is very different from history being rewritten.) Many things that seemed like disasters at the time will be seen as only 'incidents' – and all leading to good.

Health needs some attention from the 19th onwards. Overall, your health is good. This is a short-term situation. The most important thing is to get enough rest. Avoid depression. Keep your mood constructive and positive and do your best to maintain family harmony.

Love looks happy this month. The New Moon of the 7th looks especially good. It can also bring a good work opportunity for job seekers. Love is close to home all month. Until the 19th it is in the neighbourhood and perhaps with neighbours. It happens in educational-type settings – at school, the library, the bookstore or a lecture or seminar. After the 19th love, for singles, comes through the family or family connections. Old flames from the past can come back into the picture. Sometimes it's not the literal old flame but someone who reminds you of him or her – someone who has a similar appearance or personality to the old flame. This too is part of nature's therapy. Old issues will get resolved.

May

Best Days Overall: 7, 8, 17, 18, 27, 28
Most Stressful Days Overall: 6, 12, 13, 19, 20, 21
Best Days for Love: 6, 12, 13, 14, 15, 26, 27
Best Days for Money: 1, 2, 3, 6, 10, 11, 14, 15, 19, 20, 24, 25, 29, 30
Best Days for Career: 6, 14, 15, 19, 20, 21, 24, 25

The planetary power shifts this month. The Western, social sector of your chart is now more powerful than it has been all year. However, at this time the Eastern sector is still very strong too. So, you are neither overly dependent nor overly independent. You walk a fine line over the next few months between self-interest and the interests of others. Between getting things done through personal initiative or through the cooperation of others. Now you go one way, now another. But one thing is sure, you're not as independent as you have been since the beginning of the year. It is much more difficult now to get your own way than it was before. You have to brush up on your social skills now.

Health still needs watching until the 20th. Your overall health is good, but energy is not up to its usual standard. This can make you more susceptible to bugs and disease. If you have any pre-existing conditions they often act up when energy is low. So, do your best to get more rest. Keep energy levels as high as possible. Enhance the health in the ways discussed in the yearly report. Health and energy will improve after the 20th.

The lower half of your chart – and especially your 4th house – is still very powerful. There are many happy career events happening, but your focus should be on the home and family. Review our discussion of this last month.

Your career is expanding. You're being elevated. New and happy opportunities are coming, although most probably with a delayed reaction. Pluto, your career planet, is in retrograde motion all month. New opportunities need more research; don't just jump in. It is also doubtful that you will accept anything that violates your emotional harmony.

Love is close to home this month, like last month. Love is a matter of mood these days. In one mood you're in love, in another you're not. Probably the spouse, partner or current love is also like this. This is a period where love is shown by emotional support. This is how you give love, this is how you feel loved. Emotional intimacy is important these days – perhaps more important than physical intimacy. On the 20th, however, everything changes. Love becomes about having a good time, about having fun. You gravitate to the person who shows you a good time. The problem with this is the 'honeymoon syndrome' – love has to be a constant honeymoon. When the tough times come, you or the partner want out. Still, it's a fun period for you after the 20th.

June

Best Days Overall: 4, 5, 13, 14, 23, 24
Most Stressful Days Overall: 2, 3, 8, 9, 15, 16, 17, 29, 30
Best Days for Love: 4, 5, 8, 9, 13, 14, 25, 26
Best Days for Money: 2, 3, 6, 7, 10, 11, 15, 16, 20, 21, 25, 26, 29, 30
Best Days for Career: 2, 3, 10, 11, 15, 16, 17, 20, 21, 29, 30

The Sun has one of its solstices this month. Mars had one last month – from May 7th to the 14th. Mars paused and then changed direction. This is what was happening with your writing and intellectual interests – a pause and then a new direction.

You will feel this phenomenon in your love life this month. Until the Summer Solstice love is all about fun and games, nothing too serious about it. But afterwards love becomes more practical. Emotional intimacy is still important, but love is about service to the beloved. This is how you show it, this is how you feel loved. The person who serves your interests is the one you're attracted to.

Venus will have one of her solstices this month – pretty much when the Sun is having his – from the 19th to the 23rd. There is a pause in the family life and family situation and then a change of direction. Students at the college level will also feel this with their studies.

The love planet, the Sun, will re-activate old eclipse points this month. On the 8th and 9th both the Sun and Venus activate an eclipse point. So there are dramas in love and with the family. Short-term dramas. Be more patient with the beloved and with the family on those days. The Sun will activate another eclipse point from the 20th to the 24th. Again more patience is needed.

In general love is happier before the 21st than after. After the 21st you'll have to work harder at your relationship. You and the beloved are not in synch.

Finances are challenging until the 20th. Neptune, your financial planet, is being stressed and goes into retrograde motion on the 13th. He will be retrograde for many months to come. Financial confidence is not up to its usual standard. The financial intuition, which has been super all year, needs verification. Finances improve after the 21st, but earnings come with more delays and glitches. Until November, when Neptune starts to move forward, strive for mental clarity about finances – both your personal finances and in your environment. Review things. See where improvements can be made, and when Neptune starts to go forward again, you'll be able to put your plans into operation. Until then you're more or less 'treading water'. Handle the needs of the hour, but avoid major purchases or financial decisions.

Your 6th house of health and work hasn't been strong all year. Only the Moon has occasionally passed through there. But this month, on the 21st, it becomes powerful. This is excellent news for job seekers and for those needing to catch up on the dull, humdrum tasks of life – like filing and book-keeping. It is also a good period to initiate health regimes and diets.

July

Best Days Overall: 1, 2, 10, 11, 12, 20, 21, 29, 30
Most Stressful Days Overall: 6, 7, 13, 14, 27, 28
Best Days for Love: 3, 4, 6, 7, 13, 14, 15, 24, 25
Best Days for Money: 3, 4, 8, 9, 13, 14, 18, 19, 22, 23, 27, 28, 31
Best Days for Career: 8, 9, 13, 14, 18, 19, 27, 28

The planetary power – the short-term planets – are now in their maximum Western position this month. But the Eastern sector is also strong. On the 22nd you enter a yearly love and social peak. Your challenge is to be popular without being totally self-effacing and without losing personal independence. This was your challenge last month, and even more so now. With the 7th house of love strong peer pressure is felt more keenly. You have to judge when to go along with it and when not to. Self-will and personal independence – which is still strong in you right now – is not always helpful in relationships. Yet, you seem able to handle these challenges from the 22nd onwards. Love seems very happy. If you are in a relationship there is greater harmony with the beloved. If you are unattached, you're meeting good prospects and dating more.

Your financial planet is still retrograde all month. But finances are still good – especially until the 22nd. Things happen with more delays and glitches, but they do happen eventually. Review our discussion of this last month. More care in the handling of financial transactions will minimize delays and glitches. Neptune will spend the month on the Moon's South Node. This can produce a feeling of lack or deficiency that might not be real. You feel it, but the actual reality is different. The cure is a meditation on the affluence of God.

Health needs more attention from the 22nd onwards. Your focus on health early in the month (and last month) will stand you in good stead now. You've most likely built up resistance and strength to deal with the short-term lack of energy. This is the issue right now. Overall health is basically good. But your energy is not up to its usual standard. Thus, things you did without thinking when energy levels were high can't be done so easily now. The solution is to get more rest than usual. Your body will tell you – if you listen – when you need it. Enhance the health in the ways mentioned in the yearly report.

The spouse, partner or current love has been prospering all year. Now he or she enters a period of even greater prosperity – with a few bumps on the road. There is a financial drama on the 1st or 2nd. There are important financial changes on the 10th and 11th. These, it seems to me, are needed for greater prosperity to happen next month.

August

Best Days Overall: 7, 8, 16, 17, 18, 25, 26
Most Stressful Days Overall: 2, 3, 9, 10, 23, 24, 29, 30
Best Days for Love: 2, 3, 12, 13, 14, 15, 23, 24, 29, 30, 31
Best Days for Money: 1, 4, 5, 9, 10, 14, 15, 19, 20, 23, 24, 27, 28, 31
Best Days for Career: 4, 5, 9, 10, 14, 15, 23, 24, 31

Last month on the 22nd the planetary power shifted from the lower to the upper half of your Horoscope. Mars spent last month in your 10th house of career. So career was important and hectic. Things ease up a bit this month as Mars leaves your 10th house on the 2nd, but the focus is still on the career and the outer goals. Love is still the main interest until the 22nd, but afterwards there is much career success happening.

Your career planet, Pluto, has been retrograde since April. He will remain in retrograde motion for the whole of August too. So, the challenge is to gain mental clarity on your career goals. You need a good sense of direction here. Happy opportunities are coming to you after the 22nd, but they need more study.

Personal earnings are stressful. You have to work harder to achieve your goals. Earnings happen but more slowly. The good news is that the spouse, partner or current love is prospering; he or she is in a yearly financial peak and is picking up the slack. This is the kind of period where the financial interests of others are more important than your own. As you support others, as you help them to attain their financial goals, your own supply will happen naturally – albeit with some delays.

Aquarians are independent thinkers. It is normal for them to think 'outside the box' in unconventional ways. This month, though, you're doing this even more so than usual. Mars, the ruler of your 3rd house, goes 'out of bounds' from the 9th to the 31st. Siblings and sibling figures are also spending more time outside their normal sphere.

Avoid travel if possible on the 20th and 21st. The 26th to the 28th is much better for this; a happy travel opportunity comes during this latter period. For students (college level or college bound) there is success in their studies. Good news arrives.

Children or children figures in your life should stay out of harm's way on the 14th and 15th. There's no need for them to undertake any high stress kinds of activities. If they are of appropriate age there is romance from the 26th to the 28th. Even younger children will make new friends at that time.

Health still needs some attention until the 22nd. Review our discussion of this last month. Health improves from the 22nd onwards.

September

Best Days Overall: 3, 4, 13, 14, 21, 22, 30
Most Stressful Days Overall: 5, 6, 7, 19, 20, 25, 26, 27
Best Days for Love: 1, 2, 3, 4, 11, 12, 13, 14, 20, 23, 25, 26, 27, 30
Best Days for Money: 1, 2, 5, 6, 12, 13, 15, 16, 21, 23, 24
Best Days for Career: 1, 2, 5, 6, 7, 10, 11, 12, 19, 20, 28, 29

Your 8th house of transformation became powerful last month, and remains so until the 22nd. This is a turbulent kind of house. Often we deal with 'do or die' kinds of situations when it is strong. Two eclipses this month just add to the turbulence.

The solar eclipse of the 1st occurs in your 8th house. Often there are encounters with death – reminders from the Dark Angel that he is around and is a force to be reckoned with. Life here on earth is short (especially by cosmic standards), and so you need to be about the business that you were born to do. There are shake-ups in the financial life of the spouse, partner and current love. Important changes will have to be made. He or she is not only dealing with financial changes but personal kinds of dramas as well. These could test your current relationship.

The lunar eclipse of the 16th occurs in your money house and brings personal financial changes to you too. Often events happen that show you the flaws in your thinking, planning and approach. You have to change these things. Every lunar eclipse brings job changes or disturbances at work and this one is no different. Job changes can happen in your present company or with another one. If you hire others there is instability with employees and most likely higher than normal employee turnover. Sometimes there is a health scare, but your overall health is good this year and it probably won't be anything more than a scare. However, over the coming months you'll be making major changes to your health regime.

Jupiter makes a major move this month on the 10th. He moves from Virgo, your 8th house, where he's been all year, into Libra, your 9th house of religion, travel and ideas. This is a very nice transit for you. It indicates more travelling in the year ahead (and next year too), more self-esteem and self-confidence, and is excellent for prosperity. The Sun also enters your 9th house, on the 22nd. From the 25th to the 27th he will journey with Jupiter. This brings travel too. It brings success for college-level or college-bound students. It brings religious and philosophical breakthroughs for those who want them and in general a greater interest and joy in theology and philosophy. It also brings happy love and romantic experiences.

Mars has one of his solstices from the 19th to the 28th. He pauses in the heavens and then changes direction. This is what is happening in your intellectual life. A pause and then a change of direction. Your interests will change.

October

Best Days Overall: 1, 2, 10, 11, 19, 27, 28, 29
Most Stressful Days Overall: 3, 4, 17, 23, 24, 30, 31
Best Days for Love: 1, 2, 3, 4, 10, 11, 12, 13, 20, 23, 24, 30
Best Days for Money: 1, 3, 4, 10, 12, 13, 18, 19, 21, 22, 27, 28, 30, 31
Best Days for Career: 3, 4, 8, 9, 17, 25, 26, 30, 31

An interesting and successful month ahead, Aquarius. Pluto, your career planet, began to move forward last month, after many, many months of retrograde motion. Finally there is clear career direction now! Venus has been in your 10th house since September 23 and will be there until the 18th. This shows the success of family members. The family as a whole is raised in status. You have good family support for your career goals. On the 23rd the Sun enters your 10th house and you begin a yearly career peak. A lot of behind-the-scenes developments now become more overt. You are successful, elevated and promoted. You have the support of the spouse, partner or current love (who also seems successful during this period). Mercury enters your 10th house on the 25th, indicating the success of children and children figures in your life. It also shows that you're enjoying your career path. There's fun involved. It's not just work, work, work.

Until the 23rd your 9th house is very strong. This is a happy period. There are travel and educational opportunities, and it is still a very good period for college-level or college-bound students. There is success in their studies and efforts. Children or children figures will most likely not marry, but there is romance this month – the 11th and 12th look especially good.

A strong 9th house brings pleasure in higher learning. If you study the charts of important religious or academic figures, their 9th house is always strong. This is the kind of month where a hot date is at a sermon or lecture of a visiting minister or guru. It is not at the night spots. Until the 23rd the love life is centred on the 9th house. Thus you're attracted to professors, ministers, mentors and highly educated people. Often, under this aspect, one falls in love with the minister or professor. You're drawn to those who can teach you things, who can expand your mind and your horizons. Often there is an attraction to foreigners. This allure has education at its root. The best way to learn about a foreign culture (or to learn a foreign language) is to get into a relationship with someone of that culture.

On the 23rd, as your love planet, the Sun, enters your 10th house, your love needs change. Now you're drawn to power, position and status. Love can seem like 'just another career move' under this aspect. Often there is romance with bosses or other superiors. You like the person who can help you in your career.

Health needs watching from the 23rd onwards. Enhance the health in the ways mentioned in the yearly report.

November

Best Days Overall: 6, 7, 8, 15, 16, 24, 25
Most Stressful Days Overall: 1, 13, 14, 19, 20, 26, 27, 28
Best Days for Love: 2, 3, 9, 10, 13, 18, 19, 20, 21, 22, 29
Best Days for Money: 6, 7, 9, 10, 15, 16, 17, 18, 24, 25, 26, 27
Best Days for Career: 1, 4, 5, 13, 14, 21, 22, 23, 26, 27, 28

Continue to watch the health until the 22nd. The main problem is lack of energy. It is not up to its usual standard. When this happens a person becomes more susceptible to all kinds of things. Often, if there are pre-existing conditions, they tend to act up under these aspects. A good night's sleep will most likely do more good than a visit to the doctor.

Mars moves into your sign on the 9th. From a health perspective this is a mixed blessing. On the one hand, Mars gives energy, which you need, but on the other, he can cause you to overdo things – to push the body beyond its limits. Also Mars tends to impatience and rush – and this can lead to accidents. Temper is another problem with Mars in the 1st house. This can lead to arguments and sometimes even violence.

The good news is that you're more independent and dynamic in this period. Fearless. You get things done in a hurry. You excel in sports and exercise regimes. A sibling, sibling figure or neighbour seems more devoted to you these days.

There will be a big improvement in health and energy from the 22nd onwards.

Along with Mars in your sign, the planetary power has also begun to shift to the independent East. This means that the planetary power is moving towards you rather than away from you. Day by day it gets closer to you. Day by day your personal power and independence increase. You are more able to have your way in life and with people. You have more power to change conditions to your liking.

Career is still very active and successful this month. Like last month you seem to be enjoying it too. You mix with influential people these days and they are helpful in your career. The spouse, partner or current love is also being helpful.

This is an excellent month for love. The love planet near the Mid-heaven shows that love is high on your agenda. For many of you, love is the mission for the month ahead. It is very high on your priorities. This tends to success. Singles still have the aspects for the office romance this month. The attraction is still to power and prestige. This will change on the 22nd as the Sun moves into your 11th house. Now you will want friendship with the beloved, not just passion or status. You will want a relationship of peers and equals. Singles should get involved with groups and organizations – this is where love is this month. Online activities also bring romantic opportunities.

December

Best Days Overall: 4, 5, 12, 13, 21, 22, 31
Most Stressful Days Overall: 10, 11, 16, 17, 24, 25
Best Days for Love: 2, 3, 8, 9, 12, 13, 16, 17, 21, 22, 26, 27
Best Days for Money: 4, 5, 6, 7, 12, 13, 14, 15, 21, 22, 23, 24, 31
Best Days for Career: 1, 2, 10, 11, 19, 20, 24, 25, 29, 30

Your 11th house became powerful on November 22. It is still powerful this month until the 21st, so the month ahead is happy. The 11th house is your favourite house – your natural place of comfort and ability. So you're at home. You're doing what you love – you're involved with friends, groups, group activities and organizations. Your already strong networking abilities are even stronger now. Your technology skills are also stronger.

Love still awaits singles in the online world and as they get involved with groups and group activities. Someone who was 'just a friend' can become much more than that this month. Friends like to play match-maker too.

Health is much improved this month and you can enhance it further in the ways mentioned in the yearly report. Mars is still in your own house until the 20th, so review our discussion of this last month. If someone annoys you, take a few deep breaths before answering. Avoid arguments and confrontations as much as possible. You can be expressing yourself more forcefully than you realize.

On the 7th Venus enters your sign. This is a help. She will tone down some of Mars's aggressiveness. She will enhance the physical appear-ance of women and bring young women into the life of men. Venus in your sign brings travel and the support of family. It is a good aspect for the college-level or college-bound student. There is more interest in study.

Finances have been turbulent for the past two months. Many shake-ups and changes have been happening. Neptune, your financial planet, was camped out on an old eclipse point. But now things seem quieter. Neptune has been moving forward since November 20, and he is receiving good aspects from the 21st onwards. So earnings are getting stabilized now. You have mental clarity and direction. This is a pros-perous month – from the 21st onwards.

On the 21st the love planet moves into your 12th house of spiritual-ity. Again this changes your love needs. Now you want someone more spiritual. You want someone who shares your spiritual ideals. Singles find love opportunities in spiritual settings – at spiritual lectures, semi-nars or charity events.

You end your year as you began it – on a spiritual note. This is a time for prayer and reflection. A time to review the past year, make correc-tions and set goals for the future. Your own personal new year is not far off.

Pisces

THE FISH

Birthdays from
19th February to
20th March

Personality Profile

PISCES AT A GLANCE

Element – Water

Ruling Planet – Neptune
  Career Planet – Jupiter
  Love Planet – Mercury
  Money Planet – Mars
  Planet of Health and Work – Sun
  Planet of Home and Family Life – Mercury
  Planet of Love Affairs, Creativity and Children – Moon

Colours – aqua, blue-green

Colours that promote love, romance and social harmony – earth tones,
  yellow, yellow-orange

Colours that promote earning power – red, scarlet

Gem – white diamond

Metal – tin

Scent – lotus

Quality – mutable (= flexibility)

Qualities most needed for balance – structure and the ability to handle form

Strongest virtues – psychic power, sensitivity, self-sacrifice, altruism

Deepest needs – spiritual illumination, liberation

Characteristics to avoid – escapism, keeping bad company, negative moods

Signs of greatest overall compatibility – Cancer, Scorpio

Signs of greatest overall incompatibility – Gemini, Virgo, Sagittarius

Sign most helpful to career – Sagittarius

Sign most helpful for emotional support – Gemini

Sign most helpful financially – Aries

Sign best for marriage and/or partnerships – Virgo

Sign most helpful for creative projects – Cancer

Best Sign to have fun with – Cancer

Signs most helpful in spiritual matters – Scorpio, Aquarius

Best day of the week – Thursday

Understanding a Pisces

If Pisces have one outstanding quality it is their belief in the invisible, spiritual and psychic side of things. This side of things is as real to them as the hard earth beneath their feet – so real, in fact, that they will often ignore the visible, tangible aspects of reality in order to focus on the invisible and so-called intangible ones.

Of all the signs of the zodiac, the intuitive and emotional faculties of the Pisces are the most highly developed. They are committed to living by their intuition and this can at times be infuriating to other people – especially those who are materially, scientifically or technically orientated. If you think that money, status and worldly success are the only goals in life, then you will never understand a Pisces.

Pisces have intellect, but to them intellect is only a means by which they can rationalize what they know intuitively. To an Aquarius or a Gemini the intellect is a tool with which to gain knowledge. To a well-developed Pisces it is a tool by which to express knowledge.

Pisces feel like fish in an infinite ocean of thought and feeling. This ocean has many depths, currents and undercurrents. They long for purer waters where the denizens are good, true and beautiful, but they are sometimes pulled to the lower, murkier depths. Pisces know that they do not generate thoughts but only tune in to thoughts that already exist; this is why they seek the purer waters. This ability to tune in to higher thoughts inspires them artistically and musically.

Since Pisces is so spiritually orientated – though many Pisces in the corporate world may hide this fact – we will deal with this aspect in greater detail, for otherwise it is difficult to understand the true Pisces personality.

There are four basic attitudes of the spirit. One is outright scepticism – the attitude of secular humanists. The second is an intellectual or emotional belief, where one worships a far-distant God-figure – the attitude of most modern church-going people. The third is not only belief but direct personal spiritual experience – this is the attitude of some 'born-again' religious people. The fourth is actual unity with the divinity, an intermingling with the spiritual world – this is the attitude of yoga. This fourth attitude is the deepest urge of a

Pisces, and a Pisces is uniquely qualified to pursue and perform this work.

Consciously or unconsciously, Pisces seek this union with the spiritual world. The belief in a greater reality makes Pisces very tolerant and understanding of others – perhaps even too tolerant. There are instances in their lives when they should say 'enough is enough' and be ready to defend their position and put up a fight. However, because of their qualities it takes a good deal to get them into that frame of mind.

Pisces basically want and aspire to be 'saints'. They do so in their own way and according to their own rules. Others should not try to impose their concept of saintliness on a Pisces, because he or she always tries to find it for him- or herself.

Finance

Money is generally not that important to Pisces. Of course they need it as much as anyone else, and many of them attain great wealth. But money is not generally a primary objective. Doing good, feeling good about oneself, peace of mind, the relief of pain and suffering – these are the things that matter most to a Pisces.

Pisces earn money intuitively and instinctively. They follow their hunches rather than their logic. They tend to be generous and perhaps overly charitable. Almost any kind of misfortune is enough to move a Pisces to give. Although this is one of their greatest virtues, Pisces should be more careful with their finances. They should try to be more choosy about the people to whom they lend money, so that they are not being taken advantage of. If they give money to charities they should follow it up to see that their contributions are put to good use. Even when Pisces are not rich, they still like to spend money on helping others. In this case they should really be careful, however: they must learn to say no sometimes and help themselves first.

Perhaps the biggest financial stumbling block for the Pisces is general passivity – a *laissez faire* attitude. In general Pisces like to go with the flow of events. When it comes to financial matters, especially, they need to be more aggressive. They need to make things happen, to create their own wealth. A passive attitude will only cause loss and missed opportunity. Worrying about financial security will not provide that security. Pisces need to go after what they want tenaciously.

Career and Public Image

Pisces like to be perceived by the public as people of spiritual or material wealth, of generosity and philanthropy. They look up to big-hearted, philanthropic types. They admire people engaged in large-scale undertakings and eventually would like to head up these big enterprises themselves. In short, they like to be connected with big organizations that are doing things in a big way.

If Pisces are to realize their full career and professional potential they need to travel more, educate themselves more and learn more about the actual world. In other words, they need some of the unflagging optimism of Sagittarius in order to reach the top.

Because of all their caring and generous characteristics, Pisces often choose professions through which they can help and touch the lives of other people. That is why many Pisces become doctors, nurses, social workers or teachers. Sometimes it takes a while before Pisces realize what they really want to do in their professional lives, but once they find a career that lets them manifest their interests and virtues they will excel at it.

Love and Relationships

It is not surprising that someone as 'otherworldly' as the Pisces would like a partner who is practical and down to earth. Pisces prefer a partner who is on top of all the details of life, because they dislike details. Pisces seek this quality in both their romantic and professional partners. More than anything else this gives Pisces a feeling of being grounded, of being in touch with reality.

As expected, these kinds of relationships – though necessary – are sure to have many ups and downs. Misunderstandings will take place because the two attitudes are poles apart. If you are in love with a Pisces you will experience these fluctuations and will need a lot of patience to see things stabilize. Pisces are moody, intuitive, affectionate and difficult to get to know. Only time and the right attitude will yield Pisces' deepest secrets. However, when in love with a Pisces you will find that riding the waves is worth it because they are good, sensitive people who need and like to give love and affection.

When in love, Pisces like to fantasize. For them fantasy is 90 per cent of the fun of a relationship. They tend to idealize their partner, which can be good and bad at the same time. It is bad in that it is difficult for anyone to live up to the high ideals their Pisces lover sets.

Home and Domestic Life

In their family and domestic life Pisces have to resist the tendency to relate only by feelings and moods. It is unrealistic to expect that your partner and other family members will be as intuitive as you are. There is a need for more verbal communication between a Pisces and his or her family. A cool, unemotional exchange of ideas and opinions will benefit everyone.

Some Pisces tend to like mobility and moving around. For them too much stability feels like a restriction on their freedom. They hate to be locked in one location for ever.

The sign of Gemini sits on the cusp of Pisces' 4th solar house of home and family. This shows that Pisces likes and needs a home environment that promotes intellectual and mental interests. They tend to treat their neighbours as family – or extended family. Some Pisceans can have a dual attitude towards the home and family – on the one hand they like the emotional support of the family, but on the other they dislike the obligations, restrictions and duties involved with it. For Pisces, finding a balance is the key to a happy family life.

Horoscope for 2016

Major Trends

For singles, the major headline in 2016 is the love life. You entered a beautiful love cycle in August of last year, and the trend continues in the year ahead. Romance is happening. More on this later.

For those already in relationships, the headline is the career. You're working hard, and earning your success, and success is happening. Again, more details on this later.

Neptune has been in your sign for some years now. Your already strong extrasensory perception and psychic powers are even stronger than normal. The body and image are being refined and spiritualized. Diet has become more important for you too.

Two eclipses will occur in your sign this year. One, a solar eclipse on March 9, the second a lunar eclipse on September 16. These will mean a redefinition of the image and personality. You will be projecting a 'new look' to the world.

Uranus has been in your money house for several years, meaning that the financial life is very exciting, with wild highs and equally wild lows – a real roller-coaster ride. Your challenge is to smooth out your earnings and to learn to deal with financial instability. There are more details below.

Jupiter will move into your 8th house of transformation on September 10. Thus you will be in a sexually active kind of period. Sometimes this transit brings an inheritance. Sometimes it brings good fortune with tax and insurance issues.

Pluto has been in your 11th house of friends for some years now and will be there for many more years to come. This is a long-term trend. Friendships are getting detoxed. Some will 'die'. Some will get 'reborn'. This whole area will eventually become 'ideal' – but the process is not always pleasant.

Jupiter makes nice aspects to Pluto until September 9. This is good news for students at college level, or who are entering college. There is success in the studies and in education plans.

Your areas of greatest interest this year are: the body, image and personal pleasure; finance; love and social activities (until September 9); personal transformation, occult studies, sex, taxes and estates (from September 10); career; and friends, groups and group activities.

Your paths of greatest fulfilment this year are love and romance; and personal transformation, occult studies, sex, taxes and estates (from September 10 onwards).

Health

(Please note that this is an astrological perspective on health and not a medical one. In days of yore there was no difference, these perspectives were identical. But now there could be quite a difference. For a medical perspective, please consult your doctor or health practitioner.)

Health needs more attention this year. Two long-term planets are in stressful alignment with you. Things will improve after September 10, though, as Jupiter moves out of his stressful aspect and leaves you alone.

By themselves the stressful aspects of two long-term planets are not enough to cause serious health problems. However, when the short-term planets temporarily join the party, your vulnerability increases. This year the most vulnerable periods are from May 21 to June 20, August 23 to September 22 and November 22 to December 21. The first two are more serious than the last. Be sure to rest and relax more during those periods. Do your best to maintain high energy levels. This is always the first line of defence against sickness.

Your 6th house of health is not strong this year. Thus there is a tendency to be lax over health matters and this can be a problem. You need to be more zealous here – even when you don't feel like it. Health problems can be caused by this neglect.

Aside from maintaining good energy levels, your health can be enhanced by giving more attention to the following areas:

- The heart. This is always important for a Pisces; the Sun, which rules the heart, is your health planet. The reflexology point for the heart is shown on the following chart. In addition, avoid worry and anxiety, the two emotions that are the root causes of heart problems. Replace worry with faith.
- The feet. These are also always important for a Pisces. You respond beautifully to foot massages, foot baths and foot whirlpools. There are all kinds of gadgets in the market that do these things, and if you don't have one, it might be a good investment. Shoes should fit correctly, and shouldn't squeeze the toes or unbalance you. Comfort is to be preferred over fashion (although sometimes you *can* have both). Keep the feet warm in the winter.

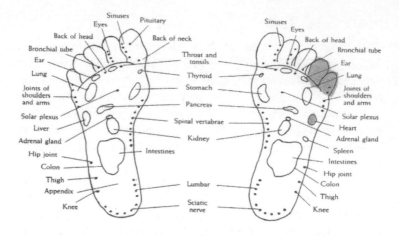

Important foot reflexology points for the year ahead
Try to massage all of the foot on a regular basis – the top of the foot as well as
the bottom – but pay extra attention to the points highlighted on the chart.
When you massage, be aware of 'sore spots' as these need special attention.
It's also a good idea to massage the ankles and below them.

Neptune is in your 1st house, as we mentioned. This indicates that the body is much more sensitive than usual. Thus it is good to avoid alcohol and drugs, as you could overreact to these things.

Neptune in your 1st house gives glamour to the image. It gives the ability to shape and mould the body according to your will. Your body becomes like clay in the hands of the potter.

Your health planet, the Sun, is a fast-moving planet and during the year he will move through all the signs and houses of your chart. Thus there are many short-term trends in health that are best discussed in the monthly reports.

Home and Family

Your 4th house of home and family is not prominent this year – it is not a house of power. Basically it is empty. Only short-term planets will move through there. Generally this tends to the status quo. There is nothing against a move or house renovation, but nothing that especially supports it either. You have more freedom here – but not that much interest.

You seem in disagreement with a parent or parent figure. He or she seems over-bearing and over-controlling. His or her motives are probably good, but it doesn't make it any more pleasant. More compromise is necessary. The problem eases up after September 10, but is not completely solved.

The other parent or parent figure could have moved last year and, if not, it can happen in the year ahead. You're getting on better with this parent figure than with the one mentioned above. Siblings and sibling figures in your life could have moved in 2014 or 2015. They seem content with the status quo this year.

Children and children figures in your life are likely to move or renovate their homes from September 10 onwards. This can happen next year too. They seem more fertile than usual. Grandchildren (if you have them) are not likely to move this year.

The parent figure with whom you're having problems prospers this year, but seems cold and aloof. Perhaps too business-like and lacking in warmth. Their health looks OK, though. The other parent figure has a stable financial year, but has very good job opportunities. Health needs watching.

Children and children figures can enhance their health by paying more attention to liver, thighs, small intestine, kidneys, hips, spine, knees, teeth, bones, skin and overall skeletal alignment. They need to take on a disciplined daily health regime. They seem to be working hard – perhaps they're over-working.

Siblings and sibling figures have wonderful job opportunities after September 10. Health looks OK.

If you're redecorating, buying art objects, furniture or otherwise beautifying the home, May 20 to June 21 is a good time for this.

Finance and Career

Many of you have landed dream jobs in the past two years and you seem satisfied. Two solar eclipses in the year ahead can bring job changes or changes in the conditions of work – these happen on March

9 and September 1. We'll discuss them more fully in the monthly reports.

As we have mentioned, finances have been a roller-coaster for some years now. Uranus has been in the money house and this shows many dramatic changes in the financial life – in your strategy, plans, investments and earnings. Earnings can happen at any time and from any place. You just don't know exactly how or when.

Mars, your financial planet, is a bit erratic this year and this adds to the feeling of instability. First, he will make one of his rare retrogrades, from April 17 to June 29. This doesn't stop earnings, but does create glitches and delays. The financial judgement is not what it should be. It is a time for a financial review. Best to avoid major purchases or investments during that period. This is a time to attain mental clarity in finances. Things are not what they seem, and you need more facts.

Mars will also spend a lot of time 'out of bounds' – from August 9 to October 30. This shows a need to 'think outside the box' in your finances, to abandon 'conventional wisdom' and try other methods. With Uranus in the money house conventional wisdom is out the window anyway, but especially during the Mars 'out of bounds' period. You're likely to venture into new areas – areas outside your normal financial sphere.

Uranus in your money house shows a good affinity with the world of technology. Investors are attracted to high tech and media companies. Your technological expertise is important in finance. It also favours online companies or earning from online activities.

With earnings being so erratic, it is good to set aside money from the good periods to cover you in the low periods. 'Feasts' will not last forever, but will tend to alternate with the 'famines'. Both will be extreme. You shouldn't be overly elated with the good periods, or overly depressed with the lows. It's just the natural action of Uranus.

For some years now the old rule books of finance have been thrown out the window. You're learning, through trial, error and experimentation, the ways that work for you. Finance is the grandest of adventures these days. And, without risk, there is no adventure.

Uranus is also your spiritual planet. Thus you're going deeper into the spiritual laws of wealth. You already know much, but there's always more to learn. This understanding will help you deal with the volatility that is going on.

Mars, your financial planet, is a relatively fast-moving planet. This year he will move through five signs and houses of your chart (sometimes more than once). Thus there are short-term trends in finance that are best discussed in the monthly reports.

Career is challenging this year, but ultimately successful. It is true that you're involved with many influential people socially – and social connections are opening doors for you. But Saturn in your 10th house shows that you have to perform as well. Social connections or no social connections, you simply have to be the best at what you do. You're in a period of 'earned' success. High tech and online activities seem important in the career too, and it will be advantageous to keep up to date with the latest developments.

A boss can be overly exacting and strict with you. The best way to deal with this is to go the extra mile – exceed their expectations.

Your career planet Jupiter is in the 7th house of love most of the year. And the ruler of the 11th house of friendship, Saturn, is in your house of career. Whatever your actual career is, your real mission this year is to be there for your friends and the beloved.

Love and Social Life

This year, as we mentioned, is a banner love and social year, with Jupiter spending most of the year in your 7th house.

All of you will have a more active and expanded social life. Singles will have romance and perhaps even marriage (or a relationship that is like a marriage). For some of you it may have already happened – Jupiter has been in here since last August. But if not, it is still likely in the year ahead.

Your love planet, Mercury, will go retrograde four times this year – usually it only happens three times. There will also be a solar eclipse in your 7th house on September 1. These things will test your relationship, but if it is good it will survive and thrive.

What I like here is the quality of the love life. You're mixing with influential people – people of high status and position. I doubt whether 'average' would even interest you. You like older, more settled people.

People who can help you career-wise. People who can enhance your status.

Love and social opportunities happen at the usual places – at weddings, parties and gatherings. But they also happen as your pursue your career goals – at business gatherings and functions – and with people involved in your career. This is a year where you can fall in love with a boss or superior. An office romance wouldn't be a surprise.

Wealth is another attraction in love.

The love and romance aspects are wonderful whether you're working towards your first, second or third marriage. Those aiming for marriage number four have a stable, static kind of year.

The area of friendships also seems active and prominent this year. Friends are important to you, and you go the extra mile to maintain these friendships (they too are very helpful in your career).

Mercury is a very fast-moving planet. In any given year he will move through all the signs and houses of your Horoscope. Thus there are many short-term trends in love that are best discussed in the monthly reports.

Self-improvement

Neptune has been in your own sign for some years now. Thus many of the trends mentioned in previous years still apply in the year ahead. The body is much more sensitive. Thus, as we mentioned, diet is now more important – as is the need to avoid alcohol and drugs (especially in excess). The other important thing is that the psychic faculties are much stronger than usual. Psychic vibrations – positive or negative – are experienced right in the body, as physical sensations. If this isn't understood, it can lead to all kinds of heartache. For example, perhaps you're sitting in a restaurant enjoying a meal and the person at the next table has a heart condition. You would feel that condition as if it were your own. Perhaps there would be chest pains, or tightness in the heart area. Or, someone you're close to is having heart problems. The person can even be in another country (space and time have no bearing on psychic vibrations). You would experience the same kind of phenomena even if there was nothing physically wrong with your heart. Often, because of things of this nature, people check themselves into a hospital and go through all kinds of needless tests or procedures when there was never a problem in the first place – only a negative psychic rapport. This kind of thing goes on more than anyone realizes.

So, try to be more objective with the body. Look at it as a 'measuring instrument'. Note the sensations that happen, but don't identify with them. This will enable you to detect the source.

If the sensations are overpowering, you might need medical help. But if they're not, work to break the psychic rapport. A hot bath often helps. Sunshine helps. Prayer and meditation are powerful. Detune from the sensation and put the attention elsewhere. If it is a rapport, the unpleasant sensations will leave.

With the ruler of your Horoscope, Neptune, in your 1st house you have great ability to mould your body as you will – as we have mentioned. The body has no will of its own. It is totally subservient to the mind. So, with will and determination, imagine how you want the body to be. Hold fast to it. Eventually the body will start to take on the image you desire. This will be an internal process. The appetites will change. Some foods you won't crave, some you will. If you need a vitamin or supplement, it will come to you. If you need some exercise regime (it might not be necessary, but sometimes it is) this too will come. The end result will be what you imagine the body to be. It takes perseverance, but it can be done.

Uranus in your money house makes the financial life like a rollercoaster and tends to much instability. With Mars as your financial planet, the spiritual agenda here is to develop financial courage. And these days, the need for courage is even greater. More important than financial gain or loss is the ability to meet situations with courage. By now it is happening.

Month-by-month Forecasts

January

Best Days Overall: 4, 5, 13, 14, 21, 22, 23, 31
Most Stressful Days Overall: 6, 7, 19, 20, 26, 27
Best Days for Love: 6, 7, 8, 10, 15, 16, 17, 18, 26, 27
Best Days for Money: 2, 3, 4, 9, 10, 13, 15, 16, 17, 18, 21, 22, 26, 27
Best Days for Career: 6, 7, 9, 10, 17, 18, 26, 27

You begin your year with most of the planets in the independent, Eastern sector of the Horoscope. The planetary power flows towards you rather than towards others. It is time to take care of number one. Time to focus on the things that make you happy (so long as they are not destructive to others). Time to use your enhanced personal power to create conditions that please you. Other people are very important this year – especially in regard to your career – and they should be treated with respect. But your personal happiness is up to you and they have nothing to say about it.

The upper half of the Horoscope is dominant as the year begins. Thus you are in a strong career period. Focus on the career. Home and family issues need time to resolve themselves – Mercury, your family planet, is retrograde from the 5th to the 25th. So you may as well focus on your outer goals.

Career is successful this month but complicated. You're meeting people socially who open career doors for you, but Saturn in your 10th house shows that you're earning your success by sheer merit. Social contacts open doors, but ultimately you have to deliver the goods – and you seem to be doing that. You might be trying too hard, though. Your work ethic is noticed by your superiors on the 13th and 14th and a happy job opportunity can come too. Your career planet Jupiter goes into retrograde motion on the 9th. This suggests a methodical step-by-step career growth – slow and steady. For the next few months while Jupiter continues to travel backwards, you need to get some clear ideas on your career direction. Sometimes we have to go backwards in order to go forward.

Prosperity seems good this month too. On the 4th Mars enters Scorpio and makes beautiful aspects to Neptune, the ruler of your Horoscope. You are in tune with money and with the money people in your life. The money people are supportive. Money is earned in comfortable ways. Mars in Scorpio suggests a need to get rid of inessential possessions – to get rid of waste or redundancy in the financial life.

The love life is happy but also complicated. Jupiter has been in your 7th house for many months now and he is bringing love and new friendships into your life. But many personal compromises are necessary. Romance can work if you're able to bridge your differences. There are romantic opportunities with people of high status and position. They like having their own way.

February

Best Days Overall: 1, 9, 10, 18, 19, 27, 28, 29
Most Stressful Days Overall: 2, 3, 4, 15, 16, 17, 22, 23, 24
Best Days for Love: 5, 6, 13, 14, 15, 16, 22, 23, 24, 25, 26
Best Days for Money: 1, 5, 6, 9, 10, 11, 12, 13, 14, 18, 19, 22, 23, 24, 28, 29
Best Days for Career: 2, 3, 4, 5, 6, 13, 14, 22, 23, 24

The planetary momentum is overwhelmingly forward this month. Ninety per cent of the planets are moving forward. Thus, with the exception of your career, there is fast progress towards your goals.

Prosperity is still strong this month and basically happy. Mars, your financial planet, is still in Scorpio and still making nice aspects to Neptune. Review our discussion of this from last month. Foreigners, foreign companies and foreign investments seem important this month. Prosperity will be even greater after the 19th, when the Sun enters your sign and starts to make nice aspects to Mars. Happy job opportunities are coming to you from the 19th onwards.

Health was good last month and is good in the month ahead. Until the 19th (and this was the case last month) you respond beautifully to spiritual-type therapies. Health is enhanced through ankle and calf massage. After the 19th enhance the health through foot massage.

Spiritual therapies are powerful after the 19th as well. When the Sun enters your sign there will be more of a focus on health. You discover that good health has cosmetic advantages – better than any cream or lotion. Your state of health determines your physical appearance.

Career is still successful, but you're working harder – overcoming more obstacles – this month, especially after the 19th. Like last month there is slow, steady, methodical progress. The tortoise, not the hare, wins the race in the end.

Love is still a balancing act this month. Your interest and the interest of the spouse, partner or current love seem diametrically opposed. You want your way; the beloved wants his or her way. Compromise will be essential. There are happy romantic opportunities from the 5th to the 7th and from the 9th to the 11th.

Computers and high tech gadgetry seem temperamental, unstable, from the 1st to the 5th. Some of it might need replacing. There can be dramas in the lives of friends during that period too. Be more patient with them.

Your 12th house of spirituality has been powerful since January 20. You're in a very spiritual period until the 19th and even afterwards. Your challenge will be to keep both feet on the ground and not drift off into nirvana.

March

Best Days Overall: 8, 9, 16, 17, 26, 27
Most Stressful Days Overall: 1, 2, 14, 15, 21, 22, 28, 29
Best Days for Love: 6, 7, 8, 16, 17, 21, 22, 26, 27, 28, 29
Best Days for Money: 3, 4, 10, 11, 12, 13, 18, 19, 21, 22, 28, 29, 31
Best Days for Career: 1, 2, 3, 4, 12, 13, 21, 22, 28, 29, 31

A bittersweet kind of month. On the one hand, there are many planets in your sign and you're in the midst of a personal pleasure peak. On the other hand we have two eclipses that shake things up – both personally and in the world at large. It is a happy but eventful kind of month.

The solar eclipse of the 9th (in America it happens on the 8th) occurs in your own sign, thus it affects you strongly. It shows a need to redefine yourself – your personality, your image and your self-concept. Generally this happens because others are slandering or misrepresenting you. If you don't define yourself, they will. Thus over the next six months you'll adopt a new look – a new image. The career is affected by this eclipse too as Jupiter, your career planet, is impacted by it. Thus there are career changes and shake-ups in your company or industry. The rules of the game change. There are likely to be dramas in the lives of bosses, parents and parent figures.

This eclipse also impacts on Saturn, bringing dramas in the lives of friends, the testing of friendships and the testing of computers and high tech equipment. (Such equipment is likely to be erratic and temperamental over this period, and even before the eclipse actually happens.) It would be a good idea to have your important files backed up. Every solar eclipse brings job changes and changes in the health regime, because the Sun is your health and work planet. Sometimes the job changes are within your present company, but sometimes it is with a new one. Often there are health scares with a solar eclipse and these will probably cause the changes in your health regime. However, overall health is good this month (but take it easy during the eclipse period).

The lunar eclipse of the 23rd is more benign for you, but it won't hurt to take it easy during that period too. This eclipse occurs in your 8th house, indicating that the spouse, partner or current love is making dramatic financial changes. Events happen that show that the current strategy and thinking is not realistic. The 8th house is the house of death. This doesn't mean literal death (at least most of the time it doesn't) but encounters with death – close calls. Sometimes someone close to you dies or has a near-death kind of experience. Sometimes people have dreams of death. This is all educational rather than punitive. There is a need for better understanding of this issue. When death is understood, life is better understood. Every lunar eclipse affects children and children figures in your life. Best to keep them out of harm's way during this period. They are likely to be more temperamental, so be more patient with them. They are redefining themselves too.

April

Best Days Overall: 4, 5, 12, 13, 22, 23
Most Stressful Days Overall: 10, 11, 17, 18, 24, 25, 26
Best Days for Love: 6, 8, 9, 14, 15, 17, 18, 25, 26, 27, 28
Best Days for Money: 1, 6, 7, 8, 9, 14, 15, 17, 18, 24, 25, 27, 28
Best Days for Career: 1, 8, 9, 17, 18, 24, 25, 26, 27, 28

You entered a yearly financial peak on March 20 and it is still going on until the 19th of this month. Prosperity is happening. The financial intuition, always good, is even better during this period. There are job opportunities happening too. If you're already employed, there are opportunities for extra work or overtime. The family seems supportive of this until the 6th. On the 5th Venus enters your money house. This suggests earnings from trading, buying and selling – from sales, marketing and PR. Mars, your financial planet, spends the month in your 10th house of career. This shows that money is high on your priorities and that you're focused here. This transit also tends to prosperity and shows that you have the financial favour of bosses, parents and parent figures – they seem supportive. Pay rises are happening – either monetary ones or 'in kind'. Your good professional reputation boosts earnings. On the 17th Mars starts to make one of his rare retrograde moves (they only happen every two years), so earnings come with more delays and glitches attached – but they do still come. From the 17th onwards, your job is to gain mental clarity on your financial situation. Your plans or thinking might not be realistic. Avoid major purchases or important financial decisions after the 17th.

Last month the planetary power shifted to the bottom half of your Horoscope. Night is falling in your year. It is time to be involved in the activities of night. Time to be more focused on the home, family and your emotional well-being. You won't be able to ignore the career – your 10th house is very strong all month – but you can shift some energy to the family.

Health is good all month. If you want to enhance it further you can give more attention to the head, face and scalp until the 19th. Face and scalp massages are wonderful if you feel under the weather. After the

19th pay more attention to the neck and throat. These areas should be massaged regularly.

Love is happy this month, but complicated. Mercury, your love planet, goes retrograde on the 28th. Love is close to home, in the neighbourhood. There are still romantic opportunities with influential kinds of people – especially on the 15th and 16th. There are also opportunities in educational-type settings at schools, lectures, bookstores, libraries – these kinds of places. But the main issue, as it has been all year, is to bridge the differences with the beloved – you have diametrically opposite perspectives.

Retrograde activity is very strong this month. From the 18th onwards 40 per cent of the planets are retrograde, and after the 28th half the planets are. Patience, patience, patience. When delays happen you will understand why and they will be easier to handle.

May

Best Days Overall: 1, 2, 3, 10, 11, 19, 20, 21, 29, 30
Most Stressful Days Overall: 7, 8, 14, 15, 22, 23
Best Days for Love: 6, 14, 15, 24, 25, 26, 27
Best Days for Money: 4, 5, 6, 12, 14, 15, 21, 22, 24, 25, 30, 31
Best Days for Career: 6, 14, 15, 22, 23, 24, 25

With half the planets still in retrograde motion until the 9th, the keyword is patience. Nor is there any need to make matters worse by being sloppy in what we do. The cosmos wants perfection in all the little details of life (especially in finance, career, love and family life). Doing things perfectly will lessen the risk of delays. It might be slower initially, but will save time in the long run.

Happily retrograde activity will lessen as the month progresses. Jupiter, your career planet, moves forward on the 9th and Mercury moves forward on the 22nd. We end the month with 30 per cent of the planets retrograde – a reasonable percentage.

The planetary power approaches its nadir (lowest point) in your chart this month (and this will be the case next month too). Your 4th house of home and family is strong from the 20th onwards, but your 10th house of career is also strong. You are in the situation of having to balance a successful career with a successful home and family life. There are no rules to this. Sometimes you shift one way, sometimes another. Finding your point of emotional harmony is not that easy when career duties call. But you can do it. Symbolically speaking your situation is equivalent to someone who keeps getting awakened in the middle of a sound sleep by some emergency at the office. The natural benefits of a good night's sleep are not happening.

Health is more stressed from the 20th onwards. You have many planets in stressful alignment with you this month – at least 60 per cent of them and sometimes more. So pay more attention to health. You seem involved in some major project – something very big – and these are always complicated and stressful. Maximize energy by concentrating on the essentials and letting go of trivial things. Try to schedule massages during lunch breaks or after work. Enhance the health with neck and throat massages until the 20th and with arm and shoulder massages afterwards. Breathing exercises are helpful after the 20th too.

Your financial planet is still retrograde this month. Earnings will happen but with more delays and glitches. Mars also has his solstice from the 7th to the 14th. He will pause in the heavens – he will occupy the same degree and minute of latitude – and then change direction. This is happening in your financial life too. There is a pause and then a change of direction. This will all be good. This is all natural.

The love life seems happy this month. Mercury, the love planet, makes nice aspects with Neptune and Jupiter. There is harmony with the beloved. When Mercury goes forward on the 20th, the love life will get better. The 22nd to the 25th seems especially happy.

June

    Best Days Overall: 6, 7, 15, 16, 17, 25, 26

    Most Stressful Days Overall: 4, 5, 10, 11, 12, 18, 19

    Best Days for Love: 2, 3, 4, 5, 10, 11, 12, 13, 14, 23, 24, 25, 26

    Best Days for Money: 1, 2, 3, 7, 10, 11, 16, 17, 20, 21, 25, 26, 27, 28, 29, 30

    Best Days for Career: 2, 3, 10, 11, 18, 19, 20, 21, 29, 30

Mars retrograded out of your 10th house on May 27. The demands of career are still there but are less urgent than last month. You can afford to spend more time with the family and handle affairs in the home.

The tension between home and career will have some therapeutic value this month. It will force up old memories and old patterns that need cleansing. Issues involving the parents will also come up – old traumas. You will have opportunities to resolve these things.

Health still needs watching as many planets are still in stressful alignment with you. This can make you vulnerable to all kinds of germs and bugs. With normal energy levels they wouldn't stand a chance, but now it is easier for them to get in. So rest more. Make sure you get enough sleep. If you feel tired during the day, take a short nap. Enhance the health by giving more attention to the arms and shoulders until the 21st and to the stomach afterwards. (Women should give more attention to the breasts too after the 21st.) Right eating is important after the 21st. Moods and emotions need to be kept positive and constructive. Health will improve after the 21st, but still needs some attention. The Sun will re-activate eclipse points twice this month. These are like 'mini-eclipses'. They will force some changes in the health regime and indicate some instability at the job. These 'mini-eclipses' happen on the 8th and 9th and again on the 23rd and 24th.

Love is happy until the 13th but becomes challenging after that date. Love is still found close to home – in the neighbourhood and perhaps with neighbours – until the 13th. Good communications and mental compatibility are important in love. You gravitate to people who are easy to talk to. Like last month, social and romantic opportunities are to be found in educational settings – at school or school functions, lectures, the library or bookshop. This will be true after the 13th as well, but after the 13th the family seems more involved. Family members play cupid. You like good communication but now you also like emotional intimacy. You gravitate to those who know how to give emotional support. There is a nostalgic feeling in love during this time. It is as if you're trying to recapture happy romantic experiences from the past. While this is understandable, this tendency can make you lose the joy of the 'now'. Now is always the best time for love. The past is over with.

Mars is still retrograde this month. Continue to gain clarity on your financial situation. See where improvements can be made, and when

Mars goes forward again next month, you'll be able to put your plans into action.

July

Best Days Overall: 3, 4, 13, 14, 22, 23, 31
Most Stressful Days Overall: 1, 2, 8, 9, 15, 16, 29, 30
Best Days for Love: 3, 4, 8, 9, 14, 15, 24, 25
Best Days for Money: 3, 4, 8, 9, 13, 14, 18, 19, 22, 23, 24, 25, 27, 28, 31
Best Days for Career: 8, 9, 15, 16, 18, 19, 27, 28

Last month on the 13th the Western, social sector of your chart became more powerful than the Eastern sector. Thus the planetary power is moving away from you and becoming ever more distant. It flows towards others – and so should you. Personal independence is lessened now. It is not absent but it is not as strong as it has been since the beginning of the year. There is more of a need to attain goals through consensus and cooperation rather than through unilateral direct action. The Eastern sector of your chart is still strong, so we get the feeling of someone who is working to balance self-interest with the interests of others. Someone who wants popularity but also some independence. It is still possible to create conditions to your liking, but it is now more difficult than it has been.

On June 21, the Summer Solstice, you entered a yearly personal pleasure peak. This is a time to enjoy your life, to indulge in leisure activities, to do the things that you most love to do. It is a period of great personal creativity as well. Party time. This goes on until the 22nd.

There has been a rare Grand Trine in Water – your own element – since June 18. This continues until the 22nd. This is an era of good feeling. People are more sensitive to the feeling level of life. People are kinder and more compassionate. You are very comfortable in this situation and it is very positive for health. Health is much improved this month. You can enhance it further through right diet, emotional harmony and paying more attention to the stomach – until the 22nd. Joy itself is a healing force. If you feel under the weather a night out on the town might be just the ticket. Do something that's fun. After the 22nd give more attention to the heart (this is always important for you, Pisces, and even more so now). A creative hobby is therapeutic these days.

The month ahead is prosperous, especially until the 22nd. Earnings come easily. Financial goals are attained with little fuss. Foreigners, foreign companies and investments in foreign lands seem important. Mars is now moving forward and you have sound financial judgement and good direction. The financial planet in your 9th house shows increased earnings.

Love is happy but with a few bumps on the road. The love planet, Mercury, re-activates an old eclipse point on the 1st and 2nd. He also squares Pluto on the 7th and Uranus on the 10th and 11th. These events indicate some shake-ups and dramas in love, but it will probably just add more spice to the love life. Love is about fun and games until the 14th. Afterwards it becomes more serious and service oriented. Love in the second half of the month is about serving the beloved's interests.

August

Best Days Overall: 1, 9, 10, 19, 20, 27, 28
Most Stressful Days Overall: 4, 5, 12, 13, 25, 26, 31
Best Days for Love: 3, 4, 5, 14, 15, 23, 24, 31
Best Days for Money: 1, 2, 4, 5, 12, 14, 15, 21, 22, 23, 24, 29, 30, 31
Best Days for Career: 4, 5, 12, 13, 14, 15, 23, 24, 31

Love is still happy this month. The love and social life has been important all year and becomes even more important in the month ahead. On the 22nd you enter a yearly love and social peak, and in many cases this will be a lifetime peak (much depends on your age). Your 7th house is filled with beneficent planets from the 22nd onwards. It's as if there is a cosmic conspiracy to get you to the church. Wedding bells or an engagement wouldn't be a surprise. But it need not happen in this exact way. There can be relationships that are 'like' marriages instead.

Many planets in your 7th house from the 22nd onwards shows that you get along with many different kinds of people. Your social sphere is broad and inclusive. There are intellectuals, influential people, healers, health professionals and artistic types. The 20th to the 24th and the 26th to the 28th seem especially good.

Your challenge in love – as it has been all year – is to balance your interests with the interests of the beloved; to be able to love and cooperate in spite of opposite perspectives.

Career looks successful and active this month. On the 2nd Mars crosses your Mid-heaven and enters your 10th house, indicating activity – aggressiveness – in the career. You're active in a physical kind of way. On the 22nd, the planetary power shifts to the upper half of your chart – again fostering the career and outer objectives. Jupiter, your career planet, receives much stimulation this month – positive stimulation – especially from the 20th to the 24th and the 26th to the 28th. These are successful career periods. You are working hard for all this good, to be sure – but the opportunities are happening.

Health, however, is a major concern from the 22nd onwards. Yes, the month ahead is active and there are many obligations. But it is better to take voluntary rests than to be forced into rest because of a health problem. You can handle the social and career whirl if you pace yourself and let go of the trivial things in your life. A good night's sleep will cure many a problem. Enhance the health though more attention to the heart until the 22nd. After the 22nd pay more attention to the diet and the small intestine. Discords in love or with friends should be avoided as they affect your physical health. Should a problem occur (God forbid), restore harmony as quickly as possible.

September

Best Days Overall: 5, 6, 7, 15, 16, 23, 24
Most Stressful Days Overall: 1, 2, 8, 9, 21, 22, 28, 29
Best Days for Love: 1, 2, 3, 4, 10, 11, 12, 13, 14, 19, 20, 23, 28, 29
Best Days for Money: 1, 2, 8, 9, 12, 13, 17, 18, 21, 27, 28
Best Days for Career: 1, 2, 8, 9, 12, 13, 21

A hectic kind of month, Pisces. Health still needs attention until the 22nd, so keep in mind our discussion of this last month. Health is further stressed by two eclipses this month, which both have a strong effect on you, so take it nice and easy this September. Schedule more massages and rest periods into your days. Enhance the health through right diet and by paying more attention to the small intestine until the 22nd and to the hips and kidneys afterwards. Hip massage will be very beneficial if you feel under the weather. A herbal kidney cleanse might be just the ticket too.

The solar eclipse of the 1st occurs in your own sign and you're personally very affected by it. There can be a detox of the body if you haven't been careful in dietary matters. There is a need to redefine yourself now (basically a healthy thing), a need to gain clarity on your personality and image that you project to others. These will all change in the coming months. Things that didn't get changed in March will get changed now. This solar eclipse impacts on Mars and Saturn. Thus there are financial dramas and a need to make important financial changes. Events will show that your thinking and approach haven't been realistic. The impact on Saturn brings dramas in the lives of friends and will test friendships. There are probably shake-ups in professional organizations you belong to. High tech equipment will get tested and often will need replacement. Keep your anti-hacking software up to date and back up your important files.

The lunar eclipse of the 16th, which occurs in your 7th house of love, also has a great impact on you. You've made many new friends in the past year and in the past few months. Now they get tested. Your current relationship will also get tested. Often such an eclipse shows long-buried grievances coming up for cleansing, but sometimes it shows a drama in the life of the beloved. Good relationships survive, flawed ones are in danger. Every lunar eclipse impacts on children or the children figures in your life and this one is no different. They should take it easy during this period. Big changes are happening in their lives now. Some could move, some could have babies, some are redefining themselves – changing the self-image and self-concept. This will go on for the next six months. Every lunar eclipse impacts on your creative life. Pisceans are creative people. So, your creativity will now take a new turn. Important changes are happening here.

Your financial planet will have one of his solstices from the 19th to the 28th. Mars will pause in the heavens during that period and then, after the 28th, will change direction (in latitude). This happens in your financial life too. There is a pause in your financial pursuits and then a change of direction – a good change.

October

Best Days Overall: 3, 4, 12, 13, 21, 22, 30, 31
Most Stressful Days Overall: 5, 6, 7, 19, 25, 26
Best Days for Love: 3, 4, 10, 12, 13, 19, 20, 23, 24, 25, 26, 30
Best Days for Money: 1, 8, 9, 10, 14, 15, 17, 18, 19, 25, 26, 27, 28
Best Days for Career: 1, 5, 6, 7, 10, 18, 19, 27, 28

Last month, on the 10th, Jupiter, your career planet, changed signs. He moved out of Virgo and into Libra, your 8th house of transformation. This brings changes in your career direction. The social dimension, which has been strong all year, is still important. Your ability to get on with others is still just as important as your actual skills. But now other skills seem important – the ability to cut costs, cut waste, cut the needless and effete, becomes important. Superiors will be impressed by this. This transit also shows a few 'near death' career experiences in the year ahead. You're getting on better with bosses and superiors, though they still seem demanding.

Health is much improved this month. Jupiter, Mars and other short-term planets have moved away from their stressful aspect to you. If you got through last month with your health and sanity intact, give yourself a pat on the back. You did very well. Detox regimes are very effective this month if you feel under the weather – a kidney detox especially. After the 23rd pay more attention to the colon, bladder and sexual organs.

Short-term social goals seem to have been more or less achieved. Now it is time to provide more practical help for the beloved – helping him or her achieve financial goals. The spouse, partner or current love is in a yearly financial peak this month. There is prosperity for him or her well into next year.

Your personal finances are basically good but you're going way out of your natural sphere to attain your goals. Mars is 'out of bounds' all month. There is a boost in earnings from the 18th to the 20th and a disturbance in them, which requires you to make some changes, from the 27th to the 29th.

Neptune, the ruler of your Horoscope, is camped out on an eclipse point all month. Your health is OK, but there is no need for any daredevil type stunts. Avoid confrontations and arguments whenever possible.

On the 23rd your 9th house of religion, philosophy and foreign travel becomes powerful. This is a time for religious or philosophical breakthroughs. Travel opportunities are happening. College students seem successful.

On the 18th Venus crosses your Mid-heaven and enters your 10th house of career. This is another good financial signal for the spouse, partner or current love. He or she seems willing to invest in your career. Career is fostered by social means and through good communication skills.

November

Best Days Overall: 1, 9, 10, 17, 18, 26, 27, 28
Most Stressful Days Overall: 2, 3, 15, 16, 21, 22, 23, 29, 30
Best Days for Love: 1, 2, 3, 10, 13, 19, 20, 21, 22, 23, 29, 30
Best Days for Money: 4, 5, 6, 7, 11, 12, 15, 16, 24, 25
Best Days for Career: 2, 3, 6, 7, 15, 16, 24, 25, 29, 30

Neptune is still camping on an eclipse point in November (opposite the solar eclipse of September 1), as was the case last month too. The ruler of your Horoscope is a very slow-moving planet and this is why. Stay out of harm's way as much as possible. Drive more carefully and avoid confrontations. This is good advice all month, but especially after the 22nd when health and energy become more delicate. As always the important thing is to get enough rest. You're very ambitious this month - perhaps even a workaholic - but when the gas tank is empty, don't try to drive the car. You can enhance health by attending to the colon, bladder and sexual organs until the 22nd (safe sex and sexual moderation are important). After the 22nd give more attention to the liver and thighs. Thigh massage will be helpful and if you feel under the weather a herbal liver cleanse might be just what the doctor ordered. Try to stay focused on the really important things and let go of trivialities. This will maximize energy.

Career is the main headline this month. You're in one of your strongest career periods of the year from the 22nd onwards. You're succeeding too – but you're earning every bit of it. Saturn in the 10th house (he has been there all year) shows success by sheer merit. The Sun shows a good work ethic. You just work harder than your competitors. Mercury, your love planet, enters the 10th house on the 12th. This indicates that social connections are playing a role too. Likeability is a big factor in your success, and this has been the case all year. Venus in your 10th house (until the 12th) shows the importance of good communication and marketing. Even the family is supporting the career. There's no tension between family obligations and your career – they're in synch. The family as a whole is raised in status this month (from the 12th onwards). Your career path is difficult, but there is great satisfaction this month.

The love life seems happy too. Until the 12th there is harmony in your current relationships. Singles will meet harmonious kinds of people – perhaps foreigners, perhaps people at university or your place of worship. Sexual magnetism seems very important, but no less important is philosophical compatibility. Good sex won't cover up philosophical differences for too long (although it may do so for a little while). Philosophical compatibility is important after the 12th too, but now you also want someone of influence and position, someone who can further your career, someone you can look up to. But after the 12th Mercury makes stressful aspects to Neptune. You and the beloved will have to work harder to keep things going. You seem in conflict.

December

> Best Days Overall: 6, 7, 14, 15, 24, 25
> Most Stressful Days Overall: 12, 13, 19, 20, 26, 27
> Best Days for Love: 2, 3, 10, 11, 12, 13, 19, 20, 21, 22, 29, 30
> Best Days for Money: 4, 5, 8, 9, 12, 13, 21, 22, 24, 31
> Best Days for Career: 4, 5, 12, 13, 21, 22, 26, 27, 31

Your love planet Mercury has been 'out of bounds' since November 19 and is this way until the 17th. This suggests that your love interests are carrying you far outside your normal sphere. You're taking risks here and going outside your comfort zone. Perhaps it is the spouse, partner or current love who is pulling you out here. Or perhaps it is your search for love. You also seem involved with people who are far above you in status, and sometimes this can be uncomfortable. It just means more work and effort is needed in your relationship. The good news is that you're willing to put in the work and this tends to success (love is high on your agenda until the 3rd).

Career is still going strong. You're very serious about it and are putting in the effort required. Advancement and success are happening now, and no one can argue about it. You have earned it.

Finances are good this month. Your financial planet Mars is in your spiritual 12th house until the 20th. This shows that you are exploring the spiritual realms of wealth, the spiritual rather than the natural causes of wealth. It shows a fabulous financial intuition. It shows more generosity and charitable giving as well. Being involved in charities is not only good for its own sake but will help your bottom line. Financial guidance will come in dreams, from psychics, astrologers, spiritual channels and ministers. On the 20th Mars crosses your Ascendant and enters your 1st house, bringing you financial windfalls. You spend on yourself. You don the image of wealth. Others see you as prosperous and this opens all kinds of doors. Financial opportunity seeks you out and there's not much you need to do – it will find you. The money people in your life are favourably disposed to you. The 31st is an especially good financial day. Your intuition is very sharp.

Health and energy are much improved after the 21st. There is only one long-term planet in stressful aspect to you – Saturn. The short-term planets are either in harmonious aspect or are leaving you alone. Mars in your own sign also increases your energy level. You get things done fast. You have a more dynamic kind of personality. You excel in sports and exercise regimes. However, the downside is rush, impatience and temper, and these can lead to arguments or accidents. When Mars is in your 1st house you can come over as being aggressive even when you don't mean to. It just comes out that way. Soften the speech.

Last month the planetary power began to shift from the West to the East: Mars is in your sign from the 20th onwards. You're back in independence mode. Personal power is growing day by day. It is time to make the changes that need to be made. Time to take responsibility for your own happiness. Others have nothing to do with it right now. It's up to you.